A Basic History of the United States
Volume

THE BEGINNING
OF
THE REPUBLIC
1775-1825

by
Clarence B. Carson

Beth A. Hoffman
Editorial Consultant

American Textbook Committee
www.americantextbookcommittee.org

email Byron_Mallory@hotmail.com

Cover painting *Washington at Yorktown* courtesy of Library of Congress.

ISBN 1-931789-10-X

Contents

Chapter 1
Introduction

Independence is the main theme of this 50-year period of American history. It begins with the year in which an increasing number of Americans were seriously considering the desirability of independence, and ends shortly after the proclaiming of the Monroe Doctrine. In between lie the declaring of independence, the War for Independence, the recognition of the independence of the states by the British, the acknowledgement of American independence by foreign nations, the continuing struggle during the French Revolution and the Napoleonic wars of the United States to steer clear of European disputes, the acquiring of vast new territories by which the United States increased the surrounding area free from foreign control, and the War of 1812, which has been called by some historians the Second War for Independence. While there were many other momentous events and developments during these years, independence provides a unitary theme for the period.

The independence theme, however, involved more than national independence from European powers. There was the question also of the independence of the states. First, there was the struggle of the states to establish their independence from Britain. During and after that came the effort of the states to retain a portion or all of their independence from the government of the United States. This led to two major efforts at constitution making. The first was the Articles of Confederation, in which the states retained their independence by joining in a league or, as they styled it, a confederation. The government of the confederation was almost entirely dependent on the states. The second effort produced the Constitution of 1787—our Constitution—, in which the states yielded up a portion of their governmental jurisdiction to the government of the union. That is not to say that the question of the relationship between the states and the United States was finally settled in 1787 or 1789—when the Constitution went into effect. On the contrary, it remained a vital issue throughout this 50-year period and continues to enliven American politics down to the present. At any rate, the independence of the states was a part of the theme of independence over the years under consideration.

There is a sense, too, in which individual and family independence constitutes a part of the theme of independence during these formative years. Certainly, the disestablishment of the churches was a measure favoring individual and family independence. The removal of government controls over the disposal of land also enhanced individual independence. Where slaves were freed, as in northeastern states, or where slavery was prohibited, as in the Northwest Territory, individual and family independence was expanded. More broadly, the limiting and restraining of governments, a characteristic activity of this period, worked to provide breadth for individual independence.

But individual independence should not be stretched to make it appear identical with individual liberty, and it is much more important that national independence not be confused with individual liberty. It sometimes happens that a colonial revolt will result in both national independence and increased protections of individual liberty. It happened in America in the 1770s and 1780s. But it hardly follows that one will lead to the other. In the 20th century there have been colonial revolutions in many lands. Often, they have been promoted and defended under the banner of freedom. In fact, 20th century revolutions have usually resulted in one party rule, dictatorship, and tyranny, even those that did achieve national independence. However desirable national independence may be, it is something quite different and separable from freedom.

However, the founding of the American republic is closely tied to individual liberty. That was so not only because the leaders proclaimed that British oppressive acts endangered liberty and it was made the cause of the revolt, but also when they gained the opportunity they restrained their governments in order to establish liberty. Thus, the quest for and establishment of liberty is one of the themes of this period. Indeed, the story of the revolt by the American colonists from England and the establishment of their own governments is one of the major epochs in the advance of human liberty. Although Americans were not the first to conceive of the idea of limiting government, they went further in erecting safeguards against government oppression than had been done before. They had both the opportunity to establish their own governments and a much clearer than usual understanding of the dangers of government to liberty.

It is not going too far to assert that there is an epic quality to the years of the founding and the early beginnings of the American republic. They are the centerpiece of American history. What went before is prologue; what came after is more than epilogue, but it has been conditioned and may well be judged by what the Founders wrought. The political foundations of these United States were laid during these years and the future course of America charted. Strip the years 1775-1825 from American history and what went before and came after loses much of its meaning. It is well, then, to think of these years as the American epic.

Strictly speaking, of course, these years do not quite comprise a classic epic. An epic, essentially, is a "poetic composition in which a series of heroic achievements or events, usually of a hero, is dealt with at length as a continuous narrative in elevated style." The models for the epic in Western Civilization are the *Iliad* and *Odyssey*, the great narrative poems attributed to Homer. Epics frequently have as their subject the founding of a city, a nation, or the coming together under a single rule of a people. Most often, they have to do with legends and myths, with early accounts of a people that go back before any precise historical record, accounts that were often passed along from one generation to another by word of mouth.

But this serves mainly to point up the differences between the founding of the United States and most countries which had preceded it in history. The origins of most of the European nations are available to us mainly in myths and legends, leavened by a few chronicles and other references. Little enough is known, for example, of the coming of the Anglo-Saxon peoples to what then became England, much less about their forebears on the continent. The establishment of English monarchy is, for us, a tangled web of chronicle, legend, lore, and historical glimpses of such shadowy figures as Ethelred the Redeless. Even more so was this the case with Rome and Greece, and it is only somewhat less so with France and Spain.

These United States, by contrast, came into being in what are for us modern times, with the abundant paraphernalia of literary records, events substantiated from many independent sources, minutes of meetings, court records, and printed books. There is not the slightest doubt that the familiar names associated with the founding of the United States belonged to actual persons, and even the legends about some of them have been subjected to minute inquiries in later times. All this makes for rough going for epic poets, of course. Prosaic factual materials are not the readiest grist for the mills of poets. Heroes have great difficulty surviving the probing of their lives by modern biographical techniques. Elegant language requires an informing vision which has not fared well since the onset of the naturalistic outlook in the 19th century. The prose of professional historians has replaced epic poetry; irreducible facts which will stand careful scrutiny have tended to supplant elegantly worded narrative. We have, however, gained from that exact knowledge often at the expense of impoverishment of the spirit.

Even so, there are the makings of an epic in the men, events, documents, and developments of these years. The rudiments of the stuff of epics can be found in the bold statements, heroic pronouncements, and measured declarations of this period: "Give me liberty or give me death"; the midnight ride of Paul Revere, warning that "The Redcoats are coming"; "Taxation without representation is tyranny"; Nathan Hale's "I regret that I have but one life to give for my country"; the Declaration of Independence's resounding "We hold these Truths to be self evident...."; "We have not yet begun to fight"; George Washington's farewell, "Interwoven as is the love of liberty with every ligament of your hearts, no recommendation of mine is necessary to fortify or confirm the attachment." Thomas Jefferson's ringing description of the sum of good government in his First Inaugural Address: "Still one thing more fellow-citizens—a wise and frugal Government, which shall restrain men from injuring one another, shall leave them otherwise free to regulate their own pursuits of industry and improvement, and shall not take from the mouth of labor the bread it has earned." The language was often measured prose, but the breadth of the vision provided the poetic gloss.

An unusual crop of men peopled this era, among them both major and minor characters who would fit well amidst the elegant language of an epic: James Otis, Patrick Henry, Samuel Adams, John Dickinson, Benjamin Franklin, George Washington, John Hancock, Thomas Paine, Thomas Jefferson, Gouverneur Morris, Horatio Gates, Baron von Steuben, Marquis de Lafayette, James Madison, John Adams, Alexander Hamilton, John Marshall, and many, many others who have well been called Founding Fathers.

Many of the events and documents of this period have a symbolic ring to them, too, symbolic of the coming into being and growth of the United States. Among the events are Lexington and Concord, the meeting of the Second Continental Congress, the declaring of independence, the Battle of Saratoga, the Franco-American Alliance, the Battle of Yorktown, the Treaty of Paris, the Constitutional Convention, the XYZ Affair, the Purchase of Louisiana, the Battle of New Orleans, the Acquisition of Florida, and the Monroe Doctrine. The period is studded with momentous documents: the *Novanglus Letters*, the Olive Branch Petition, *Summary View of the Rights of British America, Common Sense,* the Declaration of Independence, *The Crisis,* the Articles of Confederation, the Virginia Bill of Religious Liberty, the Constitution, the *Federalist,* the Bill of Rights, Hamilton's Report on Manufactures, Washington's Farewell Address, the Virginia and Kentucky resolutions, and others.

What gives dramatic character to any series of episodes which make up an epic is conflict. Of conflicts, there were more than enough during these years: Parliament versus colonial assemblies, King against American congresses, the opposition of loyalists to patriots, Redcoats against Continentals, Federalists versus anti-Federalists, the partisan conflict between Federalists and Jeffersonian Republicans, the republican principle versus monarchy, nationalists versus state's-righters, and European domination versus self-determination in the New World.

What takes these men, events, documents, developments, and conflicts out of the ordinary and raises them to epic proportions are the great ideas which informed and enlivened them. Professor Clinton Rossiter has noted the habit the people of this time had "of 'recurring to first principles,' of appealing to basic doctrines....Few men were willing to argue about a specific issue...without first calling upon rules of justice that were considered to apply to all men everywhere." The following are some of these ideas: natural law, natural rights, balance of power, separation of powers, limited government, freedom of conscience, free trade, federalism, and republican forms of government. As Rossiter says, "The great political philosophy of the Western world enjoyed one of its proudest seasons in this time of resistance and revolution."[1] To which should be added, it had its finest season in the laying of the political foundations during the constitution-making years.

Perhaps the greatest wonder of all during these years is what these Americans wrought out of revolution. The modern era has had revolutions aplenty, and then some. All too often they have followed what is by now a familiar pattern, that is, great proclamations of liberty and fraternity, the casting off of the old rules and restrictions, the subsequent loosening of authority, the disintegration of society, and the turning to a dictator to impose a more confining order. Though some have tried to tell the story of early America along such lines, the interpretations are not only strained, but also do not explain the American achievements. Many things help to explain this, but one thing is essential to any explanation. Americans did not cut themselves off from their past experience, from ideas and practices of long standing, or from older traditions and institutions as so many revolutionists have done. In their reconstruction they relied extensively upon ancient and modern history and that which had come down to them through the ages. What separates their accomplishment from so many abortive revolutions is that these men brought to a fertile junction their heritage— which contained several great streams, especially the Classical, Christian, and English—, their experience, and contemporary ideas. The Founders stood on the shoulders of giants, and their own determination and ingenuity raised them to even greater heights.

Chapter 2

Independence

...In this state of extreme danger, we have no alternative left but an abject submission to the will of those overbearing tyrants, or a total separation from the Crown and Government of Great Britain, *uniting and exerting the strength of all* America *for defence, and forming alliances with foreign Powers for commerce and aid in war:—Wherefore, appealing to the Searcher of hearts for the sincerity of former declarations expressing our desire to preserve the connection with that nation, and that we are driven from that inclination by their wicked councils, and the eternal law of self-preservation.*

—*Preamble of the Virginia Convention, May 15, 1776.*

Resolved, *That these United Colonies are, and of right ought to be, free and independent States, that they are absolved from all allegiance to the British Crown, and that all political connection between them and the state of Great Britain is, and ought to be, totally dissolved.*

—*Resolution by Richard Henry Lee, introduced in the Continental Congress, June 7, 1776.*

Chronology

September 1774—Suffolk Resolves of First Continental Congress.

October 1774—Formation of Continental Association.

March 1775—New England Restraining Act.

April 1775—Battles of Lexington and Concord.

May 1775—Second Continental Congress Convenes.

June 1775—Battle of Bunker Hill.

July 1775—Olive Branch Petition to George III.

January 1776—Publication of *Common Sense.*

July 1776—Declaration of Independence.

September 1776—Congress appoints Ministers to France.

December 1776—Washington's Victory at Trenton.

November 1777—Congress approves Articles of Confederation.

The colonies did not move quickly to declare their independence from Britain. They did not take that step until more than a dozen years after the first provocation. It was more than a year after the first battles of the war before they acted decisively. Many months elapsed between the time of George Washington's appointment as commander-in-chief, after armies were encamped against one another, and even after the colonists launched expeditions against British forces that the fateful move was made. In fact, Washington and his officers still toasted George III and professed their allegiance to him during the winter of 1775-1776 when they were in camp against his army. There is much evidence that many colonists clung to the British connection as long as they could honorably do so.

On its face, this was strange behavior. It is easy enough to understand why the colonists did not assert their independence until 1774. After all, until the passage of the Coercive Acts by Parliament in 1774 the British had made concessions in the face of colonial resistance. In practice, they had backed down from the hard line they had taken in theory about their power to tax the colonies. Moreover, there were well-placed Englishmen, especially in the House of Commons, who took the colonial side each time, up to the very time when independence had been declared. Thus, there was reason to hope that the British might move once again to compose the differences.

There was more to the delay than that, however. There were a few people who would have favored independence before 1774. Certainly by 1775 the number was increasing, but only events and a shift in opinion would provide the backing for a revolt. That is not to question the sincerity of colonial professions of attachment for Britain. Both interest and sentiment were engaged in the connection. All real property in America traced its ownership origins to grants made by the monarch. Break the attachment, and the security of property would be open to question. The British roots of most colonists was a telling argument against a precipitate break. Moreover, if the revolt failed, those involved in it would be rebels, and the leaders might well be put to death. In any case, prudence required that they move with care, and personal safety necessitated avowing allegiance to the end.

The Move toward Independence

Even so, the colonists moved inexorably toward independence from 1774 to 1776. The British did not make concessions or back down; they determined to use the measure of intimidation and force necessary to make the colonies comply with their decrees and laws. The colonies, on the other hand, began to prepare to take united action and were less and less open to the idea that Parliament could lay down rules for governing them.

The Coercive Acts were aimed mainly at Boston and Massachusetts. They might have succeeded in isolating Massachusetts from the other colonies. But there were groups and organizations in most of the colonies determined to prevent that from happening. Thus, shortly after the passage of the acts, first Providence (Rhode Island), then Philadelphia, then New York City called for a general congress. In Massachusetts, where the initial intention had been to resist on their own, the House of Representatives welcomed the idea of united action by sending out a call for a congress itself. The First Continental Congress met in September, 1774, in Philadelphia. Twelve colonies sent 56 delegates. Only Georgia was not represented and, in view of its remote location, small population, and history of dependence on Britain, that is not surprising.

Even before the congress assembled, however, two important new publications appeared which attempted to shift colonial opinion even further from the British view than it already was. In July 1774 Thomas Jefferson published *A Summary View of the Rights of British America* and James Wilson *Considerations on...the Legislative Authority of... Parliament.* Both writers leaned toward the position that the colonies had their own legislatures and that, therefore, Parliament had no authority over the colonies. Jefferson did not state it that bluntly, but that was the tendency of his argument. For example, his comment on the action of Parliament in suspending the New York legislature was, "One free and independent legislature takes upon itself to suspend the powers of another, free and independent as itself...."[2] In conclusion, Jefferson said, "Let no act be passed by any one legislature which may infringe on the rights and liberties of another."[3] Up to this point, the colonists had generally accepted British regulation of their trade, as they had accepted the desirability of government regulation of trade. Rather, they had objected to taxing regulations for the purpose of raising revenue. Jefferson now went well beyond this position. Not only did he question the authority of Parliament over the colonies, but also the desirability of the regulation of trade in general. He made these observations about it, "That the exercise of a free trade with all parts of the world as of natural right..., was next the object of unjust encroachment...." Their "rights of free commerce fell once more the victim of arbitrary power....A view of these acts of Parliament for regulation...of the American trade...would...[evidence] the truth of this observation."[4] In short, the colonies did not need parliamentary regulation of their trade, but should rather see it as a violation of their rights and an instrument of tyranny.

Thomas Jefferson
(1743-1826)—

In an age of talented and versatile men, Jefferson stood head and shoulders above most of his contemporaries in the range of his accomplishments. He was a Virginia planter, lawyer, writer, phrasemaker, political thinker, diplomat, statesman, architect, inventor, scholar, and farmer. He was born in Virginia, graduated from William and Mary College, studied and practiced law, authored the Declaration of Independence in the Continental Congress, served as governor of Virginia during a portion of the War for Independence, minister to France, first United States Secretary of State, second Vice President, and third President. He also founded the Republican party, supported the Louisiana Purchase, and both founded and designed the early buildings of the University of Virginia. He died on July 4, the 50th anniversary of the signing of the Declaration of Independence.

James Wilson of Pennsylvania argued in his pamphlet that Parliament had no authority over the colonies. Instead, their connection with England was with the king from first to last.[5] After all, the colonies were not represented in Parliament, and they could hardly be expected to submit to its authority. Wilson was moving toward what has since been called the dominion theory of empire. Later in the year, John Adams stated the case for this view more directly and in greater detail in the *Novanglus Letters*.[6] But before these appeared, the First Continental Congress had already met and adjourned.

The Congress, which met only for a short time in September and October of 1774, dealt with four main problems: (1) instructions to Massachusetts on resistance to the Coercive Acts, (2) the statement of a policy position toward recent British acts, (3) consideration of a plan of union, and (4) what concerted action to take.

Instructions to Massachusetts were contained in the Suffolk Resolves. The Suffolk Resolves declared that the Coercive Acts were unconstitutional, advised Massachusetts to form its own government until such time as the acts were repealed, recommended that the people of the colony arm themselves and form a militia, and called upon them to adopt economic sanctions against Britain. In effect, they advised Massachusetts to defy the British.

A plan of union was proposed by Joseph Galloway of Pennsylvania. It called for a general government for the colonies in America within the British empire. The plan was defeated, but there is little reason to suppose that the British would have accepted it had it been approved.

Congress stated its position toward Britain in a set of Declaration and Resolves. This declared the rights of the colonies, described the colonial understanding of the limits of parliamentary authority, and listed the British abuses of recent years. A debate occurred as to whether the colonists should trace their rights from natural law or from British grants. If they traced their rights from natural law, they would be establishing a basis for the break from England. Actually, they traced them from both, as can be seen in this quotation from the preamble of the document:

> That the inhabitants of the English colonies in North America, by the immutable laws of nature, the principles of the English Constitution, and the several charters or compacts, have the following rights:
>
> That they are entitled to life, liberty, and property, and they have never ceded to any sovereign power whatever, a right to dispose of either without their consent.
>
> That our ancestors, who first settled these colonies, were at the time of their emigration from the mother country, entitled to all the rights, liberties, and immunities of free and natural born subjects within the realm of England.
>
> That by such emigration they by no means forfeited, surrendered, or lost any of those rights....[7]

The Congress established a Continental Association to impose economic restrictions on trade with Britain in an effort to get that country to alter its policies. The restrictions consisted of agreements of the colonists neither to import, consume, nor export goods from, of, and to Britain. Since the colonists reckoned they would be harmed most by stopping exports to Britain, they scheduled non-exportation to go into effect last. Local committees were charged with enforcement, and a major effort was made to get people to agree not to consume British goods.

None of these statements or actions had much discernible effect on British policy. Parliament refused to allow colonial agents to present petitions, and declarations and resolutions from the colonies were rejected out of hand. When William Pitt, now in the House of Lords as the Earl of Chatham, introduced a resolution for the withdrawal of British troops from America, it was defeated by the lords temporal and spiritual, 68-18. On February 2, 1775, Lord North, the king's chief minister, declared that some of the colonies were in a state of rebellion and that more troops should be sent to America. A few days later, Parliament made it official that Massachusetts was in a state of rebellion.

Lord Frederick North, Earl of Guilford (1732-1792)—

North was born in England, entered politics at the age of 22, and made a career of it. He was a Tory, and began to rise at a time when the king was bent on displacing the Whigs from power. Lord North (a courtesy title) became Prime Minister in 1770, and occupied that position until 1782, following the British defeat at Yorktown. His years of leadership were much taken up with events in America, first the attempt to quell the mounting resistance to British acts, then to conduct a war to end the revolt. In both efforts, he failed. First and last, or at least until 1782, North was the king's man, doing the bidding of his monarch, and accepting the blame for the failure of the policies.

The British were no longer in a mood to make significant concessions. Parliament did approve a plan whereby the colonies could levy the taxes and turn the revenue over to the British, but Americans were hardly in a mood to be swayed by such an empty gesture. A last ditch effort to persuade Parliament to alter its course was made by Edmund Burke, who saw merit in the colonial position, on March 22, 1775. Parliament was unmoved.

The mood in America was shifting away from conciliation as well. As Britain prepared to put down the rebellion, some, at least, were ready to have done with the efforts at peace. At the forefront of these was Patrick Henry, who addressed his fellow Virginians in March in words to this effect:

> Gentlemen may cry peace, peace—but there is no peace. The war is actually begun! The next gale that sweeps from the North

will bring to our ears the clash of resounding arms! Our brethren are already in the field! Why stand we here idle? What is it that gentlemen wish? What would they have? Is life so dear or peace so sweet as to be purchased at the price of slavery? Forbid it, Almighty God—I know not what course others may take; but as for me, give me liberty or give me death!

The Struggle on Concord Bridge

No more were Lord North and the king determined upon peace. On March 30, Parliament passed the New England Restraining Act, which barred the North Atlantic fisheries to New Englanders and prohibited any trade between these colonies and anyone else except Britain and the British West Indies. The next month these provisions were extended to several of the colonies south of New England. On April 14, General Thomas Gage, British military commander in America, got orders to use force to break up the rebellion in New England. He acted with dispatch by sending troops to Concord on April 19, 1775, under orders to seize a munitions depot there. These troops were met by militia at Lexington; someone fired ("the shot heard round the world," Thomas Paine said), and a battle took place. It was enlarged during the course of the day, as riflemen gathered from all sides and threatened to destroy the British forces at one point. Reinforcements arrived, however, and the British managed to return to their haven in Boston. Seventy-three British troops were killed during the day; fighting on a war-like scale had taken place. The resolution of the British and Americans would now be tried by arms.

Edmund Burke (1729-1797)

Burke was born in Ireland—Dublin, it is supposed—but he spent much of his life in British politics. But however important the political issues that occupied him or how well he conducted himself, he might have gone down as a minor character had it not been for his writings. For it was these that gave him title to be called the father of conservatism, and, if sociology had developed along different lines, he might well be denominated as founder of it as well. His most famous and influential work was *Reflections on the French Revolution*. In it, he made a lasting case against revolutionary change and for building upon the inherited order of things. He is remembered, too, as a friend of America for his opposition to British policies of provoking colonial resistance and trying to suppress the revolt by an untimely application of force.

Less than a month after Lexington and Concord, a Second Continental Congress assembled at Philadelphia (May 10). The first congress had voted its own dissolution but provided that a new one should meet if the disputes had not been resolved. In the meanwhile, of course, the situation had become much more explosive. So it was that a second congress met. This was the congress which would direct the continental forces for the next half-dozen years. It had no constitution and no authority except such as the states gave it. Among the members of the Second Continental Congress were some of the most talented men ever to grace the American scene, men whose names will live as long as the founding of the Republic is remembered. From Massachusetts came John and Samuel Adams along with John Hancock, who was chosen to preside over the congress; from Pennsylvania came Benjamin Franklin, Robert Morris and James Wilson, among others; from Connecticut came Roger Sherman and Oliver Wolcott; from Virginia came George Washington, Richard Henry Lee, and Thomas Jefferson, and so on through the roll call of the signers of the Declaration of Independence, as well as some who had left the Congress by that time. Of necessity, some, such as Washington, Franklin, and John Adams, were called to more exacting work during the war, but at its inception the Congress contained a goodly portion of the leading men in America.

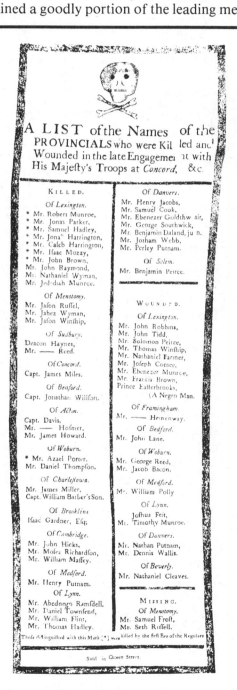

A LIST of the Names of the PROVINCIALS who were Killed and Wounded in the late Engagement with His Majesty's Troops at *Concord*, &c.

KILLED.

Of *Lexington*.

* Mr. Robert Munroe,
* Mr. Jonas Parker,
* Mr. Samuel Hadley,
* Mr. Jona" Harrington,
* Mr. Caleb Harrington,
* Mr. Isaac Muzzy,
* Mr. John Brown,
Mr. John Raymond,
Mr. Nathaniel Wyman,
Mr. Jedediah Munroe.

Of *Menotomy*.

Mr. Jason Ruffel,
Mr. Jabez Wyman,
Mr. Jason Winship,

Of *Sudbury*.

Deacon Haynes,
Mr. —— Reed.

Of *Concord*.

Capt. James Miles.

Of *Bedford*.

Capt. Jonathan Willson.

Of *Acton*.

Capt. Davis,
Mr. —— Hosmer,
Mr. James Howard.

Of *Woburn*.

* Mr. Azael Porter,
Mr. Daniel Thompson.

Of *Charlestown*.

Mr. James Miller,
Capt. William Barber's Son.

Of *Brookline*

Isaac Gardner, Esq;

Of *Cambridge*.

Mr. John Hicks,
Mr. Moses Richardson,
Mr. William Massey.

Of *Medford*.

Mr. Henry Putnam.

Of *Lynn*.

Mr. Abednego Ramsdell,
Mr. Daniel Townsend,
Mr. William Flint,
Mr. Thomas Hadley.

Of *Danvers*.

Mr. Henry Jacobs,
Mr. Samuel Cook,
Mr. Ebenezer Goldthwait,
Mr. George Southwick,
Mr. Benjamin Daland, jun.
Mr. Jotham Webb,
Mr. Perley Putnam.

Of *Salem*.

Mr. Benjamin Peirce.

WOUNDED.

Of *Lexington*.

Mr. John Robbins,
Mr. John Tidd,
Mr. Solomon Peirce,
Mr. Thomas Winship,
Mr. Nathaniel Farmer,
Mr. Joseph Comee,
Mr. Ebenezer Munroe,
Mr. Francis Brown,
Prince Easterbrooks,
(A Negro Man.

Of *Framingham*.

Mr. —— Hemenway.

Of *Bedford*.

Mr. John Lane.

Of *Woburn*.

Mr. George Reed,
Mr. Jacob Bacon.

Of *Medford*.

Mr. William Polly

Of *Lynn*.

Joshua Felt,
Mr. Timothy Munroe.

Of *Danvers*.

Mr. Nathan Putnam,
Mr. Dennis Wallis.

Of *Beverly*.

Mr. Nathaniel Cleaves.

MISSING.

Of *Menotomy*.

Mr. Samuel Frost,
Mr. Seth Russell.

Those distinguished with this Mark [*] were killed by the first fire of the Regulars

Sold in Queen Street.

John Hancock (1737-1793)

Hancock was a prominent Boston merchant and shipper, and one of the leaders in Massachusetts opposed to the taxing policies of the British. He served as president of the Second Continental Congress, was the first to sign the Declaration of Independence, and is famed for penning the largest signature on the document. He served as the first elected governor of Massachusetts, and was reelected several times to that post. In the 1780s, well after the ratification of the Articles of Confederation, once again he became president of the Congress. His last great public service was to preside over the Massachusetts convention which ratified the Constitution.

Congress was confronted with the task of what to do about the budding war from the moment it met. New England had already taken matters in hand to the extent that Ethan Allen and Benedict Arnold led a force of colonials in taking Fort Ticonderoga on Lake Champlain on the same day that Congress met in Philadelphia. And on June 17 the Battle of Bunker Hill took place as a result of a British decision to drive the Americans from a redoubt on Breed's Hill. This battle pitted a British army against a colonial army, and though the British drove the Americans from their positions they did so at the expense of heavy casualties.

Before the Battle of Bunker Hill, however, Congress had made the first steps toward taking over the conduct of the war. George Washington was appointed commander-in-chief of the armed forces. He left straight-away to take charge in Massachusetts, which he accomplished on July 3. George Washington had gained considerable military experience in the French and Indian War, and was already emerging as a leader to whom others were drawn for advice and counsel. Washington was a man of great feeling and strong sentiment, but it was above all his firmness and steadfastness that made him invaluable to the American cause. A very important consideration at the time of his selection, of course, was that he was from Virginia, the most populous of the colonies; and the New Englanders especially could see that it was essential to bring the other colonies to their support. The choice of Washington was unanimous and, through all the difficult years and much wrangling between Washington and Congress, that body never really faltered in its support of him. No more did Washington falter in his determination to serve the Congress by winning the war. Washington took no salary for his military contribution; rather, he required only that his expenses be paid.

Though feeling was running high in America against Britain, there were those in Congress who believed that they would be remiss in their duty if they did not make yet another appeal for reconciliation. John Dickinson took the leadership in drawing up and getting through Congress the Olive Branch Petition on July 5, 1775. The members assembled declared themselves "Attached to your Majesty's [King George III] person, family, and government, with all devotion that principle and affection can inspire...." This being the case, "We, therefore, beseech your Majesty, that your royal authority and influence may be graciously interposed to procure us relief from our afflicting fears and jealousies...."[8] Congress did not blink the fact, however, that armed conflict was going on already, and the next day they declared their reasons for taking that course.

Congress adjourned on August 2 to await developments. These were not long in coming. George III declared the colonies to be in open rebellion on August 23. Benedict Arnold led an expedition to Canada in the fall, with the permission of General Washington. (There was hope at the time that if British forces in Canada could be overcome, Canada would join with the other colonies.) Congress authorized a

Richard Henry Lee
(1732-1794)—

Lee was born in Virginia, a descendant of early settlers of the colony, and a brother to Arthur Lee, who was a diplomat to France for the Continental Congress. He was educated in England, but he emerged early as an opponent of British misrule and in favor of independence. He was a member of the Virginia Committee of Correspondence, a delegate to the First and Second Continental Congress, and introduced the resolution for independence which was adopted by Congress on July 2, 1776. Although he did not approve the extent to which the Constitution of 1787 threatened the powers of the states, he was one of the first Senators from Virginia, and in that position he proposed the 10th Amendment, which set limits to the jurisdiction of the Federal government.

navy, and a further move was made toward independence by opening up correspondence with foreign nations in November. In the same month, the colonies received word that the king had refused to receive the Olive Branch Petition. The House of Commons then defeated a motion to make the Petition the basis of reconciliation, defeated it by a vote of 83 to 33. Late in 1775 a royal proclamation was issued closing the colonies to all commerce after March 1, 1776.

That all these things had occurred and that the colonists still could not bring themselves to declare for independence indicates how reluctantly they took that step. But as 1775 gave way to 1776, the colonists were in their winter of decision. In that winter they were divided into three camps: those for independence, those undecided, and those who opposed it. However alluring the prospect of independence, it was difficult for many to resolve actually to take the step. To do so, they would have to forswear ancient allegiances, must commit the most heinous of crimes (or so they had been taught) by becoming traitors in the eyes of their British rulers, must hazard their lives and fortunes upon the uncertain outcome of a war, must almost certainly divide the country, and might well let loose domestic disorder on a large scale. Arguments were made in public for and against independence even as men wrestled inwardly with the difficult question. Those who took the public step for independence would be called Patriots; those who finally persisted in opposing it were Loyalists.

A little book, *Common Sense*, written by Thomas Paine in January of 1776 went far toward galvanizing American opinion in favor of independence. Within three months, 120,000 copies of it were in circulation. George Washington said that it "worked a powerful change in the minds of many men," and the testimony of other contemporaries as well as later historians confirms this judgment.

That this little pamphlet should have had such currency and impact must surely be attributed to the fact that it raised up an idea whose time had come rather than to the character of its author. Few would have predicted before 1776 that Thomas Paine would have the niche in history he gained. He had hardly distinguished himself in England before coming to America, and he was far too much a revolutionary to be welcome in any land for long. However, his striking way of writing caught Benjamin Franklin's eye, and he encouraged Paine to come to America, which he did in 1774. Somehow he grasped the tendency of the current in his new land and was able to fortify it in flashy language which moved his newly acquired fellow countrymen.

Paine took as his main task in *Common Sense* the convincing of Americans that the time had come for independence. The British, not they, had broken the ties of consanguinity. All that was left was for the

Americans to grasp the nettle. Indeed, as he pictured the matter, their only choice was tyranny or independence. The colonists had moved to the point where they were ready to dispense with Parliament. Thus, Paine focused his attention on the one tie that would remain, that to the king. Of the institution of monarchy, Paine said:

> Government by kings was first introduced into the world by the heathens, from whom the children of Israel copied the custom. It was the most prosperous invention the devil ever set on foot for the promotion of idolatry. The heathens paid divine honors to their deceased kings, and the Christian world had improved on the plan by doing the same to their living ones. How impious is the title of sacred majesty applied to a worm, who in the midst of his splendor is crumbling into dust![9]

As for George III, Paine disposed of him as "the royal brute of Britain," a descendant of a long line of monarchs hardly worthy of mention. In sum, his view of monarchy was that "Of more worth is one honest man to society, and in the sight of God, than all the crowned ruffians that ever lived."[10] Many Americans, who had never seen or been in the vicinity of a monarch, in any case, undoubtedly nodded their assent.

Thomas Paine (1737-1809)

Paine was born in England, tried his hand at several occupations, but such success and fame as he ever achieved was as a supporter of revolutions and writer. He lived in America from 1774-1787, returned to Europe and became very much involved in the French Revolution, then returned to America to live out his days in relative obscurity. Paine's little book, *Common Sense*, propelled Americans toward independence, and another series, *The American Crisis*, fortified their patriotism during the dark days of the War for Independence. The French Revolution turned out to be not so fortunate an undertaking, and, though Paine wrote a book in defense of it, titled *The Rights of Man*, he was later imprisoned in France and had to have American help to secure his release.

Another difficult point for the Americans, or so Paine thought, was the idea of severing the ties with the mother country. In the first place, Paine alleged, with some exaggeration, Europe, not England, was the homeland of Americans. But, in any case, Britain did not mother America; the inhabitants of the New World were driven from her shores and, in contrast even with the behavior of brutes to their young, she was now making war on them. Besides, there is no reason in an island attempting to govern a continent. That is unnatural, or so he argued.

Above all, Paine held out a vision of what an independent America could become. In a passage which belongs more to oratory than the written word, he declaimed:

O ye that love mankind! Ye that dare oppose not only the tyranny but the tyrant, stand forth! Every spot of the Old World is overrun with oppression. Freedom has been hunted round the globe. Asia and Africa have long expelled her. Europe regards her like a stranger, and England has given her warning to depart. O! receive the fugitive, and prepare in time an asylum for mankind.[11]

His admonition was a prophecy as well, as matters turned out.

It took little more to tip the scales for independence. In May of 1776 Congress learned that the king had succeeded in hiring German (generally referred to as Hessian) troops to send against them. On June 7, Richard Henry Lee introduced a resolution to Congress to the effect that the colonies were independent of Britain. On June 11, Congress appointed a committee to draw up a declaration. The painful decision was all but made.

The Declaration of Independence

How the Declaration of Independence came to be drawn up and adopted is a simple enough story. Richard Henry Lee's resolution, introduced into Congress in early June, was not immediately adopted. Instead, Congress decided to delay action until July 1, to enable those delegates who had not received instructions from their legislatures on independence time to contact them. Meanwhile, Congress appointed a committee composed of Benjamin Franklin, John Adams, Robert R. Livingston, Thomas Jefferson, and Roger Sherman for the purpose of preparing a declaration. Lee's simple and straightforward resolution would have been adequate if all that were wanted was to state that the colonies were independent of Britain. Actually, something more was wanted. The colonists suspected that they would need aid, recognition, and assistance from foreign nations if their revolt was to succeed.

Thomas Paine had suggested the idea of a general manifesto in order to get foreign friends for the American cause. He said, "Were a manifesto to be published and dispatched to foreign courts, setting forth the miseries we have endured and the peaceable methods which we have ineffectually used for redress; declaring at the same time that...we had been driven to the necessity of breaking off all connections...—such a memorial would produce more good effects to this continent than if a ship were freighted with petitions to Britain."[12] It was just such a manifesto that Congress wanted.

Thomas Jefferson was assigned the task of producing a draft of the proposed declaration. If John Dickinson had been favorably disposed toward independence, he would have been the logical candidate for the job. But since he had been maneuvering for the past several months to delay, if not prevent, independence, he was assigned instead to a committee to draw up articles of confederation. In any case, the choice of Jefferson to do the writing turned out to be one of the happiest decisions ever made by a committee. His draft was accepted by the committee after some minor changes had been made by Franklin and Adams. Congress also made a few alterations. But the finished work was substantially what Jefferson had presented to the committee. Much of the honor which has come to the Declaration should be credited to Jefferson's felicity of style, graceful turns of phrase, and the evocative power of words appropriately juxtaposed.

Congress acted quickly once the Lee resolution came before it again on July 1. Those favoring independence had succeeded in swaying most state legislatures and conventions to instruct their delegates to vote for independence. The resolution was approved unanimously by 12 colonies, with New York abstaining. And then—on the July 4 date which was to be celebrated by posterity—Congress approved the Declaration of Independence.

It is not so simple a matter, however, to deal with the document itself. The Declaration of Independence occupies a unique place in the history of the United States. It is well that it should, no doubt, for it both signifies the beginning of American independence and the birth of the United States. Yet the Declaration itself might not have been used as the symbol of those things. John Adams thought that it would be appropriate to celebrate the second day of July, since it was on that day that the resolution for independence (Lee's) was adopted. Moreover, he later declared of the Declaration that "There is not an idea in it, but what had been hackneyed in Congress for two years before."[13] Be that as it may, it was the Declaration drawn by Jefferson that was raised above any other document in American history, except for the Constitution itself. It has been generally revered by the American people, provided texts for orations, and even books, has been the source of slogans, has been quoted by Supreme Court justices, and the first two paragraphs have often been memorized by school children.

The difficulty is this. As an object of veneration the ideas in it are not considered within their context. Moreover, phrases have even been wrenched from the sentences of which they are a part and used contrary to their meaning. Prevailing ideas have shifted since that time, and the Declaration does not even make sense in terms of some of these later ideas.

The first thing to do, then, is to place the Declaration in its context as precisely as can be done. For purposes of consideration, it can be divided into three parts. The first two paragraphs contain the general justification for forming new governments and being independent of England. There is a succinct statement of the natural law-natural rights doctrine of the origin and purpose of government within the framework of God as Creator and maker of the laws. It was entirely logical that they should appeal beyond the British Constitution for a justification, since they were breaking from it. Hence, the Declaration appeals to a higher law, "the Laws of Nature and of Nature's God."

The second part of the Declaration consists of a listing of the British abuses which impelled the Americans to the separation. This is by far the longest part of the document. It should be noted, too, that the abuses are all laid at the door of the king. Each charge begins with the word, "He," by which is meant King George III. Two purposes were served by this way of listing of abuses. One, of course, was to show to the world that the rights of the colonists had been violated. The other was to focus upon the monarch the blame for the abuses. Theretofore, all the blame in documents had been ascribed to Parliament and agents of the king. But, according to the British Constitution, the monarch is ultimately responsible for the acts of the government. Even acts of Parliament are acts of the Crown-in-Parliament.

The third part of the Declaration consists of a paragraph which states the independence of the former colonies. The central point is contained in these words: "That these United Colonies are, and of Right ought to be Free and Independent States, that they are Absolved from all Allegiance to the British Crown, and that all political connection between them and the State of Great Britain, is and ought to be totally dissolved...." In short, the document proclaimed both the fact of independence and asserted the rightness of it.

The broad purpose of the Declaration of Independence was to get other nations to recognize the United States. As such, it was an appeal to the "laws of nations," as they were once called, that is, not to the laws of any particular nation, but to universal laws, i.e., natural laws.

In CONGRESS, July 4, 1776.

The unanimous Declaration of the thirteen united States of America,

Since the states were, in effect, going to war against Britain, there was underlying hope, no doubt, that the British would observe the rules and conventions of warfare in dealing with them. Otherwise, it should be stated, the Declaration had, and has, no standing at law. It is not a preamble to the Constitution; it is not a legislative enactment whose rules apply to persons.

Some of the phrases and ideas in the Declaration may need some further amplification and explanation. Among these are "self-evident" truths, "unalienable Rights"—"Life, Liberty and the pursuit of

Happiness", and "all men are created equal". It is, said Jefferson, a "self-evident" truth "that all men are created equal." Self-evident is often used nowadays as if it were a synonym of obvious, apparent, something true on the face of it. Yet few things are less obvious than that all men are created equal. On the contrary, they differ from one another in height, in weight, in strength, in native intelligence, in up-bringing, in inclinations, and in almost every other way that comes to mind. Indeed, these very differences make up one of our most prized possessions, our individuality. Nor in our differences are we all equal. Some have talents for doing all sorts of things; others can learn to do anything only with great difficulty. It follows, therefore, that if the statement is to be taken seriously, its meaning is hardly obvious.

In his original draft, Jefferson had used the phrase, "sacred and un-deniable truths." Benjamin Franklin suggested the change to "self-evident truths".[14] Thus, he shifted the emphasis away from the quality of the truths toward how we come to know them. We come to know them by reference to the "Laws of Nature and of Nature's God," not by attending to the evidence brought to us by our senses. To put it an-other way, witnesses in a courtroom could not attest to the equality of men; their testimony could only be used to prove the contrary. In legal terms, then, the proposition is self-evident. It is based on the most fundamental understanding of the nature of man and of God.

On the sacred side, Russell Kirk explains equality this way. "In Chris-tian teaching," he says, "as in Jewish, there exists moral equality among all men: that is, God judges men not according to their station in life, but according to their deserts as persons; Dives and Lazarus are punished or rewarded in the divine knowledge of how well or badly they have obeyed God's commandments, not with regard to their worldly success. Some are weighed in the balance, and found wanting, but not because of their rank below. To this doctrine..., the members of the Continental Congress assented: it was a pillar of the Laws of Nature's God."[15]

All men are created equal, too, in that they come into this world with wants to be fulfilled and with the faculties (normally) of mind and body to provide for themselves.

There are three kinds of equality which can be deduced from the con-text of the Declaration and the general beliefs of those who subscribed to it. In the context, the Declaration affirms, by indirection, that *Amer-icans are equals of Englishmen*. And, since they are, they are entitled to the same rights as these or any other peoples anywhere. It is in this sense particularly that the acts alleged against the king are held to be abuses of power.

Second, the Declaration affirms that all men are entitled to certain unalienable rights, "that among these are Life, Liberty and the pursuit of Happiness." This was a reiteration of the natural rights doctrine. It was, however, a variation on the usual way of stating the doctrine, which was, that men have a natural right to life, liberty and *property*. Jefferson substituted "pursuit of happiness" for property. The usual way of saying it is more logical, even if there are no substantial differences in meaning. The right to life means, most basically, that no one has a right to take a life. The right to liberty means, most basically, the right to the exercise of one's faculties (mind and limbs) without restraint by others. The right to property means the right to the fruits of one's labors. (These rights were understood to be conditioned, of course, by respect for the equal rights of others. For example, one may forfeit his right to life by taking the life of another.) The right to the "pursuit of happiness," on the other hand, tends to fuse liberty and property. It means something like this: the right to use one's own faculties for one's own ends or purposes. Happiness, it should be noted, did not then refer to some sort of subjective state of bliss, as we might nowadays suppose. It meant rather that satisfaction that arises from developing one's abilities and receiving the rewards from doing so.

One other point needs to be made about the Declaration of Independence. It does set forth what might be, and has been, called the right of revolution in general. But there are three qualifications to this right, either explicit or implicit, in the Declaration. First, the people have no right to revolt against "light and transient causes...." Instead, there must be "a long train of abuses and usurpations..." evincing "a design to reduce them under absolute Despotism...." Second—and this is implicit—, there must be no peaceful means available by which the course of the government may reasonably be altered. To put it another way, the people must exhaust all efforts to change the course of the government, which is what the Declaration asserts the Americans had done. Third, the right to revolt belongs to the people generally, not to some small portion of them. The right to revolt is a majority right, ideally, a right of a consensus of the people. There is no such thing as the right of a minority to revolt. Not only would it be unlikely to succeed, but, if it did, it also could only do so by imposing its will on the majority. The corollary of the majority right to revolt is the right of a minority to migrate. This was at one time well enough understood by many Americans, for America had been peopled largely by minorities who migrated.

Of course, no government may grant a right of revolution. To do so would be to proclaim its own dissolution. Governments can acknowledge the right of migration, but they are not the source of it, or so Jefferson held. He called it the "right of expatriation," and in a letter, written in 1817, he both declares it to be a natural right and illuminates the early passages of the Declaration of Independence. "The evidence of this natural right," Jefferson said,

> like that of our right to life, liberty, the use of our faculties, the pursuit of happiness, is not left to the feeble and sophistical investigations of reason, but is impressed on the sense of every man. We do not claim these under the charters of kings or legislators, but under the King of kings. If he has made it a law in the nature of man to pursue his own happiness, he has left him free in the choice of place as well as mode, and we may safely call on the whole body of English jurists to produce the map on which Nature has traced, for each individual, the geographical line which she forbids him to cross in pursuit of happiness.[16]

The Articles of Confederation

The bent to have a written constitution ran strongly in the American blood. So strong was their commitment that they would as soon have a government without a constitution as a man appear in public without his clothes. This bent, or tradition, can be traced to many sources. Americans were, above all, a people of the book—the written word—, the Bible. There was the Puritan idea, too, of the Covenant, an agreement between man and man and between man and God. There was the British tradition of written affirmations of rights and of restraints upon the government: the Magna Carta, the Petition of Right, and the Bill of Rights. There was the social contract theory, already a part of the Western tradition. Colonists had drawn their own political agreements, such as the Mayflower Compact and the Fundamental Orders of Connecticut. There was the inheritance of the Middle Ages of having corporate charters for towns. Then, there were the numerous charters by which plantations and colonies had been settled.

So it was that even as the Continental Congress was contemplating independence it appointed a committee to draw up a constitution for a government for their prospective union. John Dickinson headed the committee, and the first draft of the Articles of Confederation, the name given to the constitution, is often attributed to him. This draft was presented to Congress July 12, 1776, a little more than a week after the adoption of the Declaration of Independence. Congress did not, however, finally approve a version of the Articles and send it out for ratification by the states until November 1777. The major objections to the Articles, as originally drawn, were that they granted too much power to the confederation, thus taking away from the independence and authority of the states.

Once the colonies had broken away from England, the only historical allegiances that remained were to the states and localities. It was very much a part of the American experience, too, that what now became states were the defenders of their rights and liberties. Colonial experience had taught them to fear any government, especially one remote from them. Thus, they were loath to grant the powers with which the states were clothed to any general government. In 1775 Samuel Adams declared that each state "is and ought to be the sovereign and uncontrollable power within its own limits or territory." Another New Englander, a citizen of Salem, Massachusetts, asserted that his "affections still flow in what you will deem their natural order—towards Salem,—from Massachusetts,—New England,—the Union at large."[17]

The states existed prior to the United States. They existed as colonies before they were states, but they were organizing and acting independently of Britain even before independence had been declared. The United States was brought into being by the states, or, to be absolutely precise, by representatives of the states. (This question should not be confused with the drawing, adoption, and ratification of the Constitution of 1787—the present United States Constitution. The United States has had a continuous existence going back well before that momentous event.) It was representatives of the states in Congress assembled who declared the independence of the United States, who drew up and ratified the Articles of Confederation, who conducted the War for Independence, and who achieved recognition of the United States by other nations. Thus, it was brought into being, and there should be no question that the United States is a creature of the states.

At any rate, there should be no doubt that the government of the United States under the Articles of Confederation was brought into being by the states. Each of them is listed by name in the opening sentence. Moreover, the continued independence of the states is vigorously affirmed in these words: "Each State retains its sovereignty, freedom and independence, and every power, jurisdiction and right, which is not by this confederation expressly delegated to the United States, in Congress assembled." The character of the union is described in the Articles as a "confederacy" and a "league of friendship". Actually, it was nearer to what we might think of as a league of nations than a union of states. The word, "state," has taken on a much altered meaning in American speech since that time than it had then in America or elsewhere. It meant approximately the same thing as an independent nation. And a confederation was ordinarily a league of more or less independent nations. However, the Americans wished to present a united front to the rest of the world, so they went considerably further than an alliance or most leagues.

Congress was empowered by the Articles to make war and peace, treaties and alliances, conduct alliances, have an army and navy, to borrow money, to coin money, to establish uniform weights and measures, to settle disputes among the states, and the like. Moreover, the Articles contain various restraints upon the states, such as prohibiting them to declare war, to enter into alliances with one another, and others of a similar character. However, the Congress was made entirely dependent upon the states. The members of Congress were chosen as state legislatures might direct. They were to be paid by the states. Each state had one vote, though it might have several delegates in the Congress. Congress had no power to tax, nor to act directly upon individuals. It could make requisitions upon the states for troops or money, but it had no power to enforce them, except, possibly, by making war upon them. The Confederation had no separate executive nor courts of its own.

All the states except Maryland had ratified the Articles of Confederation in the course of 1778 and 1779. The major objection raised by Maryland was to the extensive claims of some of the states to western lands. Some states, by their charters, could advance claims at least as far as to the Mississippi River. Maryland held out until these states generally made clear that they would give up their claims beyond the Appalachians. Finally, in 1781, Maryland ratified the document and the Articles could go into effect.

The Continental Congress, then, exercised many of the powers of government for five years after the declaring of independence before it had a fully ratified constitution. It did so largely in terms of the Articles, which were expected to be ratified. No great changes occurred with the ratification, but it was undoubtedly much more satisfactory to Americans to have the constitutionality of their government fully established.

Chapter 3

The War for Independence

These are the times that try men's souls. The summer soldier and the sunshine patriot will, in this crisis, shrink from the service of their country, but he that stands it now deserves the love and thanks of man and woman. Tyranny, like hell, is not easily conquered; yet we have this consolation with us that, the harder the conflict, the more glorious the triumph.

—Thomas Paine, 1776.

I am firmly of the opinion...that there never was a paper pound, a paper dollar, or a paper promise of any kind, that ever yet obtained a general currency but by force or fraud.... That the army has been grossly cheated...in consequence of our disgraceful depreciated paper currency.

—Josiah Quincy in a letter to George Washington.

Mr. President: The great events on which my resignation depended having at length taken place; I have now the honor of offering my sincere Congratulations to Congress and of presenting myself before them to surrender into their hands the trust committed to me, and to claim the indulgence of retiring them from the service of my country.

—George Washington, December 23, 1783.

Chronology

December 1775—Battle for Quebec.

March 1776—British evacuate Boston.

September 1776—British occupy New York City.

January 1777—American victory at Princeton.

June 1777—Congress approves Stars and Stripes for U.S. flag.

September 1777—British occupy Philadelphia.

October 1777—Battle of Saratoga.

Winter 1777-1778—Washington at Valley Forge.

February 1778—Franco-American Alliance.

1779—Naval battle of the *Bonhomme Richard* and *Serapis*.

1780—British take Charleston.

March 1781—Ratification of Articles of Confederation.

October 1781—British surrender at Yorktown.

November-December 1783—British evacuate New York.

It is well to keep in mind, even as this chapter focuses upon war, upon the doings of states and nations, of the thrust of former colonies for independence, on strategies of war, armies, navies, and battle, that much of life goes on as before. However much the lives of some may be disrupted by war, there are still fields to be plowed, forges to be run, livings to be made, and personal and family problems to be handled. Babies are born; people marry and give in marriage; there are deaths and funerals as at all other times. It is especially the case in war that people are often torn between pursuing their own particular interests and contributing to broader causes. There are heroes and villains, patriots and slackers, those who suffer great deprivation and those who use the occasion of hardship of others to find ways to prosper. So it was then; so it ever is, with variations, of course.

It is especially important to keep these things in mind as the backdrop for the American War for Independence. It serves both to highlight the tenacity with which some persevered all the way to attaining national independence and to underline the struggles and difficulties involved. It was one thing to declare independence; it was another to achieve it. It was one thing to rebel against British rule; it was another to bring off a successful revolution. It was one thing to make war against a long-established country; it was another to win it. It was one thing to deny the old authority; it was another to establish a new rule. The pledge that closes the Declaration of Independence was one to be taken seriously; those who signed it committed their "Lives," their "Fortunes," and their "sacred Honor." True, there was some bravado in the midst of the signing, as there is apt to be in such circumstances. John Hancock scrawled his name large enough that the king could read it without his "specs," as he said. When Charles Carroll of Maryland stepped forward to sign he was chided by others with the fact that there were so many people by that name in his state that he would be safe. So, with a flourish, he added "of Carrollton" to his signature, noting that there was only one of those.

Amidst all the difficulties the Americans confronted there were two so broad that attention needs to be called to them at the outset. One was the fiercely independent and individualistic character of the people.

This was both a major source of strength and a great hazard in prosecuting a war. Americans were not a people that would be easily regimented. They were not overly fond of political authority, did not relish being taxed much, and preferred managing their own lives to being commanded by others. They would not have resisted British actions so sturdily if they had. They were a people who would have to be led, not driven. The best military leaders understood this about their troops. Even the commander-in-chief was sometimes at the front of his army and would shame those who fled under fire by standing fast himself. But it was quite difficult to muster the strength of America for the long and arduous war.

The other difficulty is one that inheres in revolutions—revolts against the established authority. John Adams encountered the seeds of this difficulty when he made his way home from the Continental Congress on one occasion. A fellow New Englander said: "Oh! Mr. Adams, what great things have you and your colleagues done for us! We can never be grateful enough to you. There are no courts of justice now in this province, and I hope there never will be another."[18] Studied as he was in ancient and modern history, Adams was aware of the peril of such sentiments. The tendency of revolutions is to unravel the bonds of community, both political and social.

It is not difficult to understand why revolutions often have this disintegrative impact, especially when they are undertaken for some noble cause such as liberty. What such notions often bring forth is that all the old restraints will be cast off and a fresh start can be taken. After all, what man is there who would not like to be free of his old debts, who would not like to be relieved of the tangle of duties and obligations in which he finds himself, who would not relish the opportunity to start over? Revolution appears to offer such a prospect, at least for those who have not studied and reflected upon the outcome of such illusions.

The usual course of revolutions is for a breakdown of authority to follow in the wake of the repudiation of the old authority. When this happens, there follows an often brutal contest for power, won more often than not by a strong man who imposes his will upon the people. American leaders were especially aware of the dangers of military rule by the most successful general. Oliver Cromwell had emerged as such a man during the British Civil War. One successful Roman general after another had imposed his rule over Rome many times in ancient history. Americans were especially fearful of professional standing armies, and the leaders wished to avert this course for their revolt.

British and American Power to Make War

Wars were quite different undertakings in the 18th century than they had become by the 20th. The state of communication and transportation generally, plus American geography and the primitive conditions of most roads, contributed much to differences in the War for Independence. There were no mechanical means of communication. Travel by land for soldiers was usually on foot, and supplies were hauled in wagons. Cannons were drawn by horses or pushed by soldiers. Bridges over wide streams were rare, and armies must either have boats or go inland to cross them. Battles were brief, though wars might be long. Rarely did a major battle last for longer than a few daylight hours. One army usually overcame the other in that span of time. The musket was the main weapon of combat, though the long rifle was in use. The rifle was more accurate at a greater distance, but it took so long to load at the muzzle that soldiers much preferred the musket. Most of the weapons could only do damage at close range, so that most fighting was what has come to be called hand to hand. To be effective in battle, armies had to be moved close to one another and the troops needed to be massed in ranks. Once the ranks were broken communication was lost, and the army was likely to stampede, as it were. That helps to explain the brevity of most battles. Sieges were sometimes carried on for longer periods, but they were more effective in cutting off supplies or reinforcement than doing damage.

Navies had to operate at fairly close range to do damage as well. While ships could carry fairly large cannons, they could not fire for effect at long distance. Moreover, a ship was best taken by coming abreast of her and boarding. Yet this involved maneuvers which were difficult to accomplish with sailing vessels, which navy ships were. A contrary wind or storm could delay or avert a naval battle. In general, then, warfare in the 18th century was beset with transportation and communication difficulties which tended to make movement slow, battles brief, and military undertakings especially open to disruption by wind, weather, and panic. The supplying of military forces was far from being a science, even if the state of transportation had been more dependable. Both sides tried to conduct war much as it was done in Europe, yet the great distances in America, the fact that so much of the country was forested, and the rudimentary condition of the roads and absence of bridges made this difficult.

The British had both advantages and disadvantages in contrast with the Americans. Among their advantages were an established government and credit, a focus of loyalty and authority in the monarch, probably the most powerful navy in the world, a small but disciplined army, and extensive wealth. (This last was counterbalanced by a large government debt and British resistance to increased taxation.) The small British military force was considerably increased by the hiring of Hessian troops. On the other hand, the British had to conquer the Americans by transporting troops and supplies from Europe to America. Moreover, British leaders were divided over the wisdom of attempting to conquer America. After all, if so many Americans were opposed to British rule, how would they be ruled even if they were conquered in battle? Moreover, the British could look for little help from European countries and might well have expected that their enemies, with which they were well supplied from earlier wars, might take full advantage of their difficulties, as some did.

Among the American advantages that were most obvious were: they were fighting on their own soil; potentially, at least, they could have supplied most of their needs at home, without having to cross oceans. They did not have to conquer Britain, only to drive the forces from the continent. America had much greater prospects of gaining foreign allies than did Britain. The Americans had a cause, too, which much outranked that of the enemy. They were fighting for liberty and independence, and the British had to appeal mainly to past allegiances and such protections as they provided for the established order in America.

The Americans suffered from many disadvantages during the course of the war. Not only did they not have an established central government, but the Continental Congress was hardly a government at all. It had no powers to tax or to enforce its will upon the people. It was dependent upon the states for funds, for troops, and support for all its measures. Even its control over the Continental Army was compromised by the fact that it could only appoint field officers. Officers of lower rank were appointed by the states. Congress had no navy at the outset, and never managed to get more than a few ships out to sea. The Continental Army frequently lacked most of the things that make an army effective: uniforms, discipline, effective officers for the smaller units, adequate shot and powder and other supplies. The initial enlistments were for six months or a year, and even when Congress authorized longer periods there were few takers.

But the American cause was not simply the cause of a government nor the Continental Army nor the United States Navy. If it had been it would certainly have failed, for all these were certainly inadequate to the tasks that lay before them. The American cause was much more than and different from that. It was the cause of resolute and determined leaders, on the one hand, and a considerable portion of the American people. Both these played a crucial role in the American victory.

There were a goodly number of outstanding leaders, of course. John Adams comes to mind as one who devoted himself singlemindedly to the cause over the years, as one who labored to gain support for independence, who served in the Congress, and then devoted several arduous years of his life seeking funds and alliances in Europe. Benjamin Franklin, already advanced in years, provided services only possible for a man of his world eminence, in obtaining a French alliance. Robert Morris came close to working miracles in financing. Of military leaders who stood out, there were Henry Knox, Anthony Wayne, Nathanael Greene, Daniel Morgan, and, until he betrayed the cause, Benedict Arnold. Although John Paul Jones stood above any others as a naval leader, there was also Nicholas Biddle, John Barry, and a goodly number of commanders of privateers. There were foreign volunteers to the American cause who performed valuable leadership service as well. Among these were the young, dashing, and charming Marquis de Lafayette, Baron von Steuben, and Baron de Kalb.

But one man emerged to rise above all others as a leader in the War for Independence. That man was the commander-in-chief himself,

George Washington (1732-1799)

Washington was born at Bridges Creek, Virginia, the first child of the second marriage of Augustine Washington. His father had several plantations, but the family lived modestly, and George was not schooled beyond the elementary level. He was a tall man for his day, over 6 feet, and was heavyset. George learned the trade of surveying and also emerged as a military leader, serving under General Braddock, during the prelude to the French and Indian War. He inherited the plantation at Mount Vernon from his brother Lawrence and married a wealthy widow, Martha Custis. In the years before the War for Independence, Washington served in the Virginia House of Burgesses as well as leading the life of a Virginia gentleman and planter. As a planter, he kept careful accounts, grew a variety of crops, and treated those who worked for him well. He belonged to the Episcopal church and served as a vestryman in the local congregation. He lived only two years after his retirement from the presidency, dying as a result of contracting pneumonia.

George Washington. Whether he was a great tactician or not is a question that can be left to military historians. But there should be no doubt that he had that peculiar combination of qualities which made him an invaluable asset to the American cause as well as a great leader. He was dignified, tenacious, farsighted, disciplined, correct, and a gentleman. His personal bravery was of the sort that is called fearless among soldiers and sometimes foolhardy for a general. More than once he rallied his troops by exposing himself to enemy bullets. A lesser man than he would have committed and lost several armies, if he could have assembled that many. Washington was sorely tempted to risk his army to redeem his reputation and build morale. He needed victories very badly, especially in the first year or so of the war. Yet he resisted the temptation to commit his army to battle when the chances of losing it were too great. After being driven from Long Island, he stated: "We should on all occasions avoid a general action, or put anything to risk, unless compelled by a necessity into which we ought never to be drawn."[19] He understood both the importance of the Continental Army as a reality and as a symbol or rallying point of the American cause. And to the task of doing this he devoted his energies and, above all, he persevered. The sunshine soldiers melted away after discouraging withdrawals and unpleasant defeats. Washington persevered, holding together a remnant until a larger army could again be assembled.

The American cause had not only leaders but also many who joined in at crucial times from among the American populace. Of course, there were those who served in the Continental Army. But beyond that each state had a militia. In theory, every able-bodied male who was old enough was a member of the militia, if he was not in the continental service. While those who served in it at one time or another fell short of all that would fall in that classification, a large number did so serve. It was an occasional army, called out for emergencies, when the enemy approached, or to undertake some particular military task.

The militia were not trained and seasoned soldiers. They were simply farmers, woodsmen, and townspeople who drilled from time to time and answered local calls to arms. Most Americans were at home with guns, prided themselves upon their marksmanship, and had their own weapons. How they would perform in battle was always a question. If they were outnumbered, the militiamen might remove themselves from the scene of the battle as quickly as possible. If they were enraged, they could be ferocious; when they outnumbered the enemy they could help to carry the day in the battle. Several major battles were won with major aid from the militia. It must have had an unfavorable psychological impact on the British, too, to have much of the countryside rise

Henry Knox (1750-1806)

Knox was an American general and one of Washington's most trusted advisers during the War for Independence. He was born in Boston of Scots-Irish lineage. In addition to his activities in the Boston militia, he ran a bookstore until the war, when he joined the army. Knox fought at Bunker Hill and at Trenton, where his service was so outstanding that Washington made him chief of artillery. He fought in most of the major battles of the war, and, after the victory at Yorktown, he was promoted to the rank of major general. After the war, he was one of the movers in founding a society of American and French officers who had fought in the war under the title the Order of Cincinnati. Washington called on him to serve as the first Secretary of War under the Constitution.

up against them at crucial junctures of the war. It is probably true, as Washington and others believed, that the war might have been won more quickly with a larger, better trained army with longer enlistments. But the war was fought in a way that was in keeping with the fiercely independent American temperament.

There was one other major difficulty, and disadvantage in contrast with the British, for the American cause. The country was divided between Patriots—who favored independence—and Loyalists—who favored continuing the connection with Britain. Some Loyalists not only were loyal to Britain but aided the British cause when they could and actually took up arms against other Americans. Thus, the Patriots were sometimes faced with civil war conditions at home as well as the conflict with Britain.

How many Loyalists there were was in doubt at the time and has remained so ever since. Those prosecuting the war in Britain wanted to believe that Americans in general retained their loyalty, especially that the sober and substantial inhabitants did. Therefore, they were favorably disposed to exaggerated accounts of their numbers. Such a view made sense of the idea of subduing the "rebels," for after such a conquest Britain still might rule America if a substantial portion of the population was loyal. Moreover, British armies were continually being encouraged to come to this or that part of America on the grounds that Loyalists would turn out to support them in great number.

The extent of loyalism has been revived as an important historical question in the 20th century. It is grist for the mills of those attempting to make a Marxist or class struggle interpretation of the origins of the United States. These historians have resurrected what was once the British view for reasons quite different from those that would have interested George III. According to this class struggle interpretation, men of wealth and position in America were usually Loyalists, and the thrust for revolt came from the lower classes. This view is not substantiated by the facts. A recent historian describes the social status of the Loyalists this way: "Some came from quasi-aristocratic families, like the Fenwicks of South Carolina, and others were the humblest folks. They were rich, like Joseph Galloway of Pennsylvania, and they were poor; they were large landowners, and they were middling and small men of property; they stood behind counters, and they possessed hands unwrinkled by trade or toil....Truth to tell the Loyalists were of every station and every occupation."[20] Of course, Anglican clergymen and others dependent upon Britain for appointments and livelihood were likely to remain loyal. There were, as already noted, people of conspicuous wealth among the Loyalists, but there were prosperous men among the Patriots as well.

Estimates of how many Loyalists there were vary widely. Undoubtedly, there were those who wavered back and forth and some who never took much of a stand one way or the other. In any case, no census was ever taken, and such evidence as there is is indirect. The best evidence may be who turned out to fight when the occasion arose. Judging by that, Loyalists were in a decided minority in most places. Loyalists were able to achieve military success only in conjunction with British armies. They could not even hold territory gained by the British. Once the main army moved on, they were usually easily overcome by Patriot militia. The following estimate of Loyalist strength may be very near the mark: "In New England they may have been scarcely a tenth of the population; in the South a quarter or a third; but in the Middle colonies including New York perhaps nearly a half."[21] The estimate for the Middle colonies, however, needs to be read in the light of two important facts. One, British forces were ordinarily present in large numbers only in the Middle colonies. Two, the number of pacifists among Quakers and other religious sects was large in these colonies, and they were unlikely to fight on either side.

The British had another advantage of sorts, too, over the Patriots. They were in better position to form alliances with the Indians beyond the Appalachians. After all, they could claim that they were defending the Indians from the intrusion of the states into their territory. At any rate, the British did form some Indian alliances.

Strategy of the War

Neither side had a consistent grand strategy for winning which was followed throughout the war. Yet the elements of a strategy are there in British military and naval activity, and the very word "Continental" bespeaks the main outlines of a Patriot strategy.

The first prong of the British strategy was to isolate the continent from the rest of the world. They attempted to do this by a blockade which was imposed throughout the war. The British intended to interdict and stop American trade and intercourse with other countries. At one time or another they controlled the major American seaports. Second, they sought to divide and conquer their former colonies. During the first year of the war, they focused on New England in the belief that the center of resistance was there. Following that, a major military effort was made to cut off New England from New York by land or inland waterways. Before that effort had failed, however, major forces had shifted to the Middle States which, if they had been completely occupied, would have cut off both New England and the South. In the later stages of the war, the main conflict shifted to the South, but that too failed.

As it turned out, British successes were closely tied to naval support. Any British armies that ventured far beyond naval support were likely to be cut off from supplies and support and were subject to being overwhelmed by militia.

The Continental strategy was just that: to hold or gain the continent east of the Mississippi, including Canada. In short, the Patriots sought to exclude the British from North America. To that end, they invaded Canada, preyed on British shipping with privateers, constructed a navy of sorts, sought foreign allies, kept a Continental Army in the field, and tried to muster the resources of the continent. There could be no grand strategy except to harry British force wherever it appeared and outlast any British determination to conquer them.

Battle for Canada

Hostilities broke out in Massachusetts—Lexington and Concord—in April of 1775, more than a year before the declaring of independence. For the remainder of that year and a good part of the next, the bulk of the British force was concentrated around Boston. This force was under siege and cut off on land by Patriots.

The first major battle of the war took place June 17, 1775. It has gone down in history as the Battle of Bunker Hill, though, in fact, it was a battle over Breed's Hill. The Americans, some 1,200 strong, built a redoubt on Breed's Hill, which the British attacked with 2,200 men against a slightly reinforced American force. The British took the hill, but at a cost of 1,000 casualties, two and one-half times the losses of the Patriots. The British General Gage observed that he could ill afford another victory like that. Shortly afterward, Washington assumed command of the Patriot forces, and a stalemate ensued for the next several months.

The scene of action shifted elsewhere. For some time, Benedict Arnold, and others, had been promoting the idea of an expedition into Canada. They hoped to defeat the British forces there, bring the Canadians in on the side of the states, remove Canada as a land base for British armies, and demonstrate to the British the quality of the American determination. The idea was doubly attractive because Canada was lightly defended. Congress was reluctant to authorize the expedition because there was still hope of reconciliation with the British, but finally it gave its approval.

Two armies were launched into Canada in late 1775. The main army, which set out by way of Lake Champlain, was under the command of General Philip Schuyler at first, but he fell ill and was replaced by the much more energetic Richard Montgomery. This army met with a series of successes, taking Forts Chambly and St. John's as well as the town of Montreal. The path was then open to Quebec, which was the major port and fortress on the St. Lawrence, control of which was the key to the domination of Canada.

Meanwhile, the second army, under the command of Benedict Arnold, was making its way toward Quebec by a more easterly route. Arnold set out by way of the Kennebec River to go through Maine. Neither he nor anyone else knew what hazards and difficulties lay before them. They braved rapids, unsuspected waterfalls, long overland journeys with boats and supplies on their backs, and some of the harshest weather ever recorded to reach their destination. The hardships and perils were so great that 350 of the men and officers turned back. Others were lost or died on the way. At the end of a month the 600 scarecrows of men who persevered and survived reached Canada.

On December 2, 1775, Montgomery's army joined forces with Arnold's outside Quebec. Although they were superior in number to the British force, they were unable to take advantage of that. Unlike Montcalm during the French and Indian War, the British commander Sir Guy Carleton chose to defend the city from behind its walls rather than to come out into the open. It was left to the Americans to attack the fortress. The assault, which was made on December 31, failed. General Montgomery was able to get a small force within the walls, but he was killed, and Arnold's men, who were supposed to make a rendezvous with Montgomery's were turned back after Arnold, who was wounded, relinquished the command. For several months after that, Americans continued to lay siege to Quebec. When superior British forces arrived, the Americans were driven out of Canada in 1776. The failure of this mission doomed the hopes of bringing Canada into the United States.

Struggle for the Middle States

The Middle States consisted of New York, New Jersey, Pennsylvania, and Delaware. They contained the two largest cities—Philadelphia and New York—in America and were major seaports. Also, as already noted, Loyalists were most numerous in these states; thus, British armies might expect to be less harassed there than elsewhere. It is not surprising, then, that most of the British force in America was concentrated in the Middle States from 1776-1780, and that several major battles occurred there.

In early 1776, Washington placed cannons on Dorchester Heights overlooking the British position around Boston. Sir William Howe, now in command of the British army, judged his position to be too exposed, and in March the British abandoned Boston. Howe withdrew by sea to Halifax to await reinforcements. Meanwhile, Washington moved his army to New York in the expectation of a British attack there. It came in August. Howe drove Washington's army from Long Island, from Manhattan, and then from White Plains. It then became a near rout as the British under the field command of Cornwallis followed Washington in a retreat through New Jersey. Washington managed to halt the British advance at the Delaware River in early December. He had gathered all the boats in the vicinity to transport his army across the river, once he had the boats on the other side, he kept them there. Consequently, Cornwallis had no transport to get across the river and continue the pursuit.

In any case, General Howe did not follow up his earlier advantage. He went into winter quarters in New York City, leaving much of his army spread out over New Jersey. For the Continentals, it had been a year of defeats and withdrawals, except for the British evacuation of Boston. On the heels of the withdrawal from Canada had come the ousting of Washington's army from New York. The British were now only a few miles from the capital at Philadelphia. (Since the capital in those days was portable, so to speak, it did not greatly matter where it was located.)

Howe could retire to the comforts of New York; he had victories enough to sustain him through the winter. No such pleasant option was open to Washington; his army was dissolving as enlistment periods were running out, and recent defeats hindered the attraction of new enlistees. He had to do something to bolster the morale of the remnant of an army and gain some victories if he could. Under the cover of darkness on Christmas night he crossed the Delaware with his army to make a dawn attack on the Hessian army at Trenton. The Germans were caught by surprise and quickly surrendered. A few days later, Washington gained another victory at Princeton. From his base at Morristown, Washington continued to drive the British from their positions. The extent and impact of this campaign is spelled out by Samuel Eliot Morison: "In a campaign lasting only three weeks, at a time of year when gentlemen were not supposed to fight, the military genius of America's greatest gentleman, and the fortitude of some five thousand of his men, had undone everything Howe accomplished, recovered the Jersies, and saved the American cause."[22]

Sir William Howe (1729-1814)

Howe succeeded Thomas Gage in command of the British forces in America, drove the Patriots out of New York and took Philadelphia. William and his brother, Richard, an admiral, were in command of land and naval forces in America during a crucial part of the war. William Howe entered the army in 1746, fought in America in the French and Indian War, and had some sympathy with the American cause. Whether that affected his prosecution of the war has been an open question from that day to this, but he resigned his command on the grounds that the home government did not provide sufficient support for the conquest of America.

In 1777 the British launched their great offensive aimed at dividing America and destroying the Patriot ability to resist. At the beginning of the year, the massive force of British arms was centered in New York City under General Howe. Another large army was in Canada under the tactical command of General John Burgoyne. The strategy called for the army in Canada to attack southward and be joined by an army moving northward through New York state. If the plan succeeded in a conquest along the line of Lake Champlain, Lake George, and the Hudson, New England would be cut off by land from the other states. However, General Howe went to sea with the major portion of his army with the object of taking Philadelphia as the army in Canada began its move to the South. He did leave behind an army, of sorts, under Sir Henry Clinton, but it was too small to perform both the task of occupation of the city and conducting a major offensive campaign.

For a good portion of the summer of 1777, Washington was uncertain about Howe's destination. The fleet was delayed first by an extended calm and then by contrary winds. Upon hearing that the fleet had been sighted to the south, Washington took the main body of his army to the vicinity of Philadelphia, leaving Burgoyne to the mercy of the New England militia, as he said. Washington tried to block Howe's advance toward the capital with a smaller army at Brandywine Creek in early September, but was defeated and driven off. Howe moved on to the occupation of Philadelphia, which Congress had lately abandoned in haste. He attacked the main British force at Germantown, outside Philadelphia, in October, but failed to overcome it. Washington withdrew to Valley Forge after this defeat.

At about the same time, momentous military events were taking place to the north. Burgoyne marched into New York State with about 8,000 men (not including the wondrous assortment of camp followers in his wake), including Loyalists and Indians. Baron St. Leger was dispatched through the Mohawk Valley from Oswego toward Albany. This detachment was dispersed by troops under Benedict Arnold. Burgoyne proceeded southward at a leisurely pace, one not entirely of his choosing, since the path of his army was frequently blocked by trees newly felled by Patriots. Meanwhile, militia began to assemble around a core of Continentals whose task was to stop Burgoyne. Eventually, so many militia had gathered to augment the Continentals under the command of General Horatio Gates that Burgoyne was outnumbered two to one. His supply route was cut by Patriots. Burgoyne's hope of being relieved from New York City did not materialize; Clinton only made a foray up the river, stopping well short of Albany. Burgoyne's army was surrounded by much larger American forces, and they failed in such efforts as they made to break through. Burgoyne surrendered his whole army at Saratoga on October 17, 1777. Gates was credited with the victory, but John Stark, Daniel Morgan, and Benedict Arnold led the aggressive actions which bottled up Burgoyne.

Saratoga was the first great American victory. Trenton and Princeton had been important battles for keeping up morale, but they had been won at the expense of contingents of British forces. Burgoyne surrendered one of the major armies in America at Saratoga. Burgoyne's defeat showed what could well happen to any British general who committed his forces beyond naval support. Far from finding numerous Loyalists in the back country, Burgoyne found a countryside alive with Patriot militia waiting to demonstrate the marksmanship of the backwoods. Nor would the continent succumb to the capture of this or that eastern port city, even if one was the capital. America had no central city; it was a land of farmers mainly who knew not the dependence, common in Europe, on a single city. There was no Rome to fall in America. The victory at Saratoga also influenced the French to recognize America and provide extensive aid.

Surprisingly, however, the success at Saratoga did not improve conditions for the Continental Army. The militia assembled for battle, mainly from New England, but once the battle was won they returned to their communities. The winter of 1777-1778 was one of the low points for the Continentals. It was the winter which Washington and his army spent at Valley Forge. The men had only such shelter as they could build—log huts, and the like. They worked against time and the

Benedict Arnold (1741-1801)—

Arnold is often remembered as the turncoat who joined the British toward the end of the war. However, he was an important and valuable officer from the taking of Fort Ticonderoga until his appointment to command forces at Philadelphia in 1778. Arnold braved the wilds of Maine to lead an expedition to Quebec and contributed to the victory at Saratoga. He was born in Connecticut to an old American family, and, except for a youthful adventure, engaged in trade with the West Indies until the war. Two things may have influenced him to defect to the British side. One was his court martial. Though he was not found guilty of most of the charges, Arnold was sentenced to be reprimanded. The other was his marriage to the daughter of a Philadelphia Loyalist in 1779. In 1780 when his plot to surrender West Point to the British failed, he joined the British army. In 1781 he went to England where he lived out his days, most of them in despondency.

onset of winter to erect these. It was the middle of January before all the men had such shelter. Many men did not have sufficient clothing to work outdoors. Large numbers of them had no bed covers, and often they could find no straw to cover the bare floors. Often, all they had to eat was bread cooked on their own fires. Early in 1778 the commissary announced that it would issue no more provisions because it had none. "A prospect now opens," Washington wrote on February 17, 1778, "of absolute want such as will make it impossible to keep the Army much longer from dissolution...."[23] Indeed, the Continental Army was already dissolving. Over 2,000 men went home in December, and during the difficult time several hundred officers resigned their commissions.

It might be supposed that Americans in general were suffering privations during the war. But that was by no means the case. For example, at the very time when the army was in desperate straits, such things as this were going on: "at a ball in Lancaster, Pennsylvania [not so far from Valley Forge], in January, 1778, over one hundred ladies and gentlemen gathered in all their finery to enjoy a 'cold collation with wine, punch, sweet cakes..., music, dancing, singing...,' which lasted until four o'clock in the morning."[24]

The Ravages of Inflation

Indeed, Americans had the means to supply the wants of the army. True, the British blockade sometimes kept foreign goods or made them difficult to obtain. But Americans could and did produce enough food, clothing, bed coverings, and the like to prevent the army from suffering. The reason the army did not have enough to meet its minimal needs lay elsewhere; it lay in the failure or inability of governments to muster these goods.

More specifically, the deprivation of the army can be ascribed to the inadequate methods of financing the war. The most common means of financing government is by taxation. Beyond that, governments may, if they can, resort to borrowing from willing lenders to meet military and other requirements. Very little of the cost of the War for Independence was paid for by direct taxes during the conflict. There were two main reasons for this. First, Congress had no power to levy taxes. The most it could do was to make requests for money from the states. This it did, of course. For example, in 1777 Congress admonished the states to "raise by taxation in the course of the ensuing year, and remit to the treasury such sums of money as they think will be most proper in the present situation of the inhabitants...."[25] Such pleas availed little, which was the second reason taxes did not help much in paying for the war.

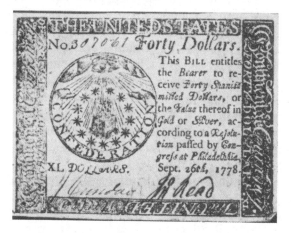

Continental Currency.
This is a $40 bill, issued in 1778. Like most of the Continental currency it was small—only three inches by four inches. The Continental Congress issued more than $240 million in paper money between 1775 and 1779.

Congress couldn't levy taxes, and the states wouldn't levy them heavily. "Before 1780 most of the states shrank from collecting taxes for any purpose. Massachusetts did not vote any levy in 1776, and in 1778 resorted to a lottery to raise $2,000,000. Virginia waited until 1781 before making a serious attempt to obtain revenue from taxes. The performances of the other states were not much better."[26] One reason for the reluctance of the states to impose taxes was that their hold on the inhabitants was not yet well established. Heavy taxes might drive more into the arms of the British, in addition to further alienating those who were already Loyalist in sympathy. But the main reason was that Americans were not accustomed to paying high taxes. Taxes had generally been light by colonial governments. The break from England had been provoked by the British determination to tax them, among other things. True, colonists did not object to the amount, but to taxation without representation. Even so, it is clear that Americans were in no mood to pay much by way of taxation. "In Pennsylvania, for example, from 1778 to 1781, less than half the taxes assessed were collected; it was not uncommon for citizens to slam the door in the tax collector's face—and get away with it."[27] Moreover, it was not good politics to raise taxes. One historian noted that "governors of the States could not urge taxation and zeal upon the legislatures without a painful and unpopular contest. The members of a legislature who laid taxes must expect to return to their constituents to face grumbling and dissatisfaction."[28] Thus, the states did not raise much of the money needed for the conduct of the war.

There was some borrowing, too. Both the Congress and the states borrowed to finance the war and other undertakings. They borrowed from foreign countries and from domestic lenders.

However, the main device for financing was the issuance of paper money. Congress issued what is known as Continental currency. The notes (paper money) did not bear interest, as such currency sometimes does, but they were supposed to be redeemed by the states at a later date. (They never were.) Just how much was issued from the first issue in 1775 until an entirely new currency was issued in 1780 is in doubt. The estimates range from over $190 million to just under $250 million. Even if an exact figure could be agreed upon, however, we would still not know how much of the currency actually circulated, for it was extensively counterfeited. There were domestic counterfeiters, and the British government, as a matter of policy, attempted to destroy the currency by counterfeiting it.

There is general agreement, though, that Congress issued more and more of the currency over the years through 1779. A recent estimate of the sums issued by years is as follows:[29]

1775	$6,000,000
1776	19,000,000
1777	13,000,000
1778	63,500,000
1779	90,052,380

This process of issuing more and more set in early. The initial issue was to have been for $2 million, but before the printing had been done Congress authorized another $1 million. Before the end of the year an additional $3,000,000 was issued. This despite the fact that Congress had intended only one issue at the beginning. And, there were those who attempted to prevent the increase. Benjamin Franklin said: "After the first emission I proposed that we should stop, strike no more, but borrow on interest those we had issued. This was not then approved of, and more bills were issued."[30]

Instead of taxing to retire the Continental currency, the states issued large amounts of paper money themselves. "The emission of all the states exceeded $200,000,000. Virginia led the way, followed by North Carolina. Then came South Carolina. Georgia, Delaware, and New Jersey exercised the most restraint."[31]

The Continental currency as well as that of the states was *fiat* money. Fiat money is money because government has proclaimed it to be so. Actually, however, governments cannot bring money into being by simply announcing that it is money. It would not be accepted for what it would be said to be worth, if it would be accepted at all. The invention of the printing press opened up the possibility of printing notes in whatever quantity desired. Inexpensive paper made it possible to produce them at nominal cost. There are two rather large problems, even for government, in trying to produce money this way. First, there is the problem of getting it accepted as money. Second, there is the problem that the more of it that is put into circulation the less it will bring in other goods. To put it another way, prices of goods will rise generally to offset the increase in the money supply. (This effect is often referred to as inflation. It would be much more accurate and helpful to refer to the cause—the increase of the money supply—as inflation.)

Congress tried to get the Continental notes accepted as currency in two ways mainly. First, they promised that the states would redeem them at some indefinite time in the future, redeem them in precious metals of gold and silver, most likely. For such promises to work effectively, however, the paper money must be immediately redeemable. A vague, future promise of redemption will not do. Even a specific promise of redemption that would occur sometime in the future would result in the discounting (giving less) of the paper money in terms of the value of the goods for which it would exchange in the future. The Continental currency declined from the beginning in relation to silver and gold. Thus, there was an effort to make Continental paper *legal tender*. This is an attempt by government to force people to accept its fiat or reduced value money at face value.

The specific actions to make Continental notes legal tender were taken by the states. For example, the Council of Safety of Pennsylvania declared in 1776 that anyone who refused to accept the Continental currency would forfeit whatever he refused to sell, and be subject to a penalty. In the same year, Rhode Island made both state and Continental notes legal tender. In addition to providing penalties for not accepting this paper, that state prohibited the buying of specie (gold or silver coins) or differentiating in prices of goods when offered gold or silver instead of paper.

With such Draconian measures to support it, the Continental paper money did circulate. But the more of it that was issued, the more it depreciated. The most noticeable effects of this to the public were general rises in prices. Some of the states then tried to fix prices. In short, they attempted to control the effect—the rise in prices—rather than the cause—the increase of the money supply. Congress recommended that regional conventions be held to set prices. The New England and Middle States held such conventions, but the Southern States south of Maryland did not. The conventions that were held suggested prices for their regions, and it was left to the states to enforce them. Some states adopted strenuous measures to keep prices from rising. The result of these price controls, where they were at all effective, was shortages of goods. John Eliot wrote from Boston in June of 1777: "We are all starving here, since this plaguy addition to the regulating bill. People will not bring in provision, and we cannot procure the common necessaries of life. What we shall do I know not."[32] What they did, of course, is what people ever do in such circumstances: evade the regulations, barter, use money that will be accepted, and so on. Government intervention can hardly prevent the working of the market; it can only make it difficult for people to meet their needs in it.

That aside, however, the major point to be made is that this fiat paper money did not suffice to provide the needs of the army. As more and more of the Continental and other paper currencies were issued, and they declined rapidly in value, they were often refused by sellers and debtors and, when accepted, bought less and less. By 1779 George Washington wrote that "a wagon load of paper money will scarcely purchase a wagon load of provisions."[33] In desperation, the army had to seize—requisition—what it wanted to provide for its needs. As the war wore on, this practice became more widespread. This was a wasteful, inefficient, and costly way to get supplies for the army. George Washington wrote to the President of Pennsylvania in 1782: "A great proportion of the specific articles have been wasted after the people have furnished them, and the transportation alone of what has reached the army has...cost more than the value of the articles themselves."[34] The main cause of these difficulties, and the deprivation of the army, was the attempt to finance the war with paper money.

By early 1780, Congress was on the verge of repudiating the Continental currency. In March 1780 Congress devalued the currency by proclaiming that it should now trade at forty to one of its face value for gold or silver. To finance this exchange, new paper money was to be issued to be redeemed by the states by taxation. An elaborate plan was contrived for the retiring of the old currency and replacing it with the new. The plan did not work. There was no reason why it should. If the new money was more valuable than the old, it would not circulate, according to Gresham's Law, assuming the old money was still legal tender. In fact, the new money quickly fell to the same value as the old, and the whole became virtually worthless by 1781. In March 1781 Congress abandoned the acceptance of its own paper money at face value. It was now to be accepted only on a sliding scale that was supposed to represent its depreciation. Thereafter, it depreciated so rapidly that it ceased shortly to circulate at all. Thus arose the saying, "Not worth a Continental," which is to say, worthless. Specie came out of hiding and replaced paper money as the currency of the land.

Not only did this fiat money inflation fail in its primary purpose of providing the means for conducting the war but it also harmed the American cause generally. The inflation contributed much to the loss of confidence in the Congress, the state governments, and prolonged the agony of the fight for independence. The idea was advanced, when the first issues of paper money were made, that its becoming currency would help to tie people to the cause of independence. Since the fate of the money—its eventual redemption—would depend upon the success of the revolt, those who came into possession of it would be committed to victory. So it might have been, if the Congress had been content with one or two issues, if the states had refrained from issues, and if the governments had then turned to direct taxation. But the effect of issuing more and more was not only to reduce the value of all the notes but also to undermine confidence in the governments which issued it.

Even so, the Americans won the war, but they had to rely increasingly on foreign aid to do so.

Enter the French

Many of the French were enthusiastic for the American cause from the outset, and their desire for its success increased over the years. Britain was the traditional enemy of France, and the Seven Year's War, in which France had lost most of her empire to Britain, was a recent outrage to resent. It was pleasant to many Frenchmen to contemplate the possibility that the Americans might wrest much of that empire from the British. On the other hand, the king, Louis XVI, did not want war with Britain, or anyone else. Nor could he see the advantage to monarchy of encouraging rebellions by republicans.

Even so, Americans received aid from the French almost from the beginning of the conflict. Silas Deane was the first diplomat to arrive in Paris in 1776, after the appointment by Congress. Although he was not received officially, he met with the Count de Vergennes, an important minister in the government, who suggested that he might find help from private parties. Deane met with a playright, Beaumarchais, who did indeed make arrangements to ship supplies to America. Actually, all this was done with the knowledge and support of government, though private businesses made the shipments. Americans received not only military supplies but also French volunteers for the army, more than were wanted of these usually, since they wanted to be commissioned as officers. In addition, American privateers put in at French ports freely when they were preying on British shipping.

In late 1776 Arthur Lee and Benjamin Franklin joined Deane in Paris as representatives of Congress. Franklin was an especially happy choice for the post. At that time, he was the most famous American in Europe.

He had gained much experience in diplomacy as a colonial agent in England. His fame as a scientist and inventor was long since well established. As if being Doctor Franklin were not enough, he effected the simple dress and manners of an American frontiersman, even wearing a coonskin cap. The French loved it. Though he was already in his seventies, Franklin enjoyed the company of women, and the ladies of the court fawned over him.

Even so, the government continued on an official course of neutrality. A loan was arranged in conjunction with Spain, but this was still a behind-the-scenes move. Vergennes was determined not to press for official recognition until the Americans showed that they were determined to overcome the British. The victory at Saratoga in 1777 provided the needed evidence. In January 1778 Vergennes notified the Americans that the government was ready to work out an alliance. Two treaties were drawn in the next several weeks. One provided for commercial relations between the two countries on a most favored nation basis. This was also a clear recognition of the independent status of the United States. The other was a treaty of alliance (the Franco-American Alliance) which would go into effect when and if war broke out between Britain and France. France committed itself to seek no territory on the continent of America and gave the Americans a free hand in obtaining as much territory as they could and would acquire.

Before Congress had approved these treaties, however, Lord North

Silas Deane (1737-1789)

Deane is best known for his diplomatic service in France where he succeeded in getting much needed supplies for America early in the war. He was born in Connecticut, graduated from Yale, and was a delegate to the Continental Congress 1774-1776. In the latter year, he was appointed first a secret agent to France and then a commissioner, along with Arthur Lee and Benjamin Franklin. Deane participated in the making of the Franco-American Alliance, but was recalled to face charges before Congress for the manner in which he kept his accounts. He was under a cloud of suspicion during the remainder of his life, but no evidence of dishonesty ever came to light. In effect, Congress cleared his name, finally, in the middle of the 19th century.

obtained approval of a Conciliation Plan from Parliament to end the conflict between Britain and America. The plan promised the removal of those laws to which the Americans objected, the resolution of differences by a peace commission, and would require that the American states return to the British empire as colonies. Congress gave a cold shoulder to the whole proposal and, when pressed, notified the British that the only thing they wanted to negotiate was the British removal of their armed force from America.

Meanwhile, Congress ratified the treaties with France on May 4, 1778. Hostilities broke out between Britain and France in June, and the full alliance went into effect.

While other European nations did not come into the war on the side of the United States, they did, in varying degrees, take positions in opposition to Britain. In June 1779 Spain entered the war alongside France, but not with the United States. In 1780 Russia proposed a League of Armed Neutrality aimed at the British blockade. She was eventually joined in that effort by Denmark, Sweden, the Netherlands, Prussia, Portugal, and Austria. Britain went to war against the Netherlands late in the year. Thus, the War for American Independence very nearly sparked a world war.

The Unequal Naval Conflict

For most of the war, the British control of the seas was hardly challenged. With only a few exceptions, such naval warships as Congress managed to get under sail operated singly and did not usually challenge British men of war. That is not to say that the British blockade of the American coast was entirely effective in shutting off trade. Many vessels evaded the blockade to take goods in and out. Moreover, American privateers did much harm to British ships. In 1778 a report to the House of Commons indicated that they had taken 733 ships as prizes. The number, however, had declined between 1775 and 1777. It picked up again, however, in 1778, spurred by the French alliance.

The new naval vigor could be attributed in part, too, to the exploits of Captain John Paul Jones. For a few days, Jones, aboard his ship, the *Ranger*, even took the naval battle to the British Isles. He sailed into the Irish sea in April 1778, landed at Whitehaven, England, spiked the guns of the fort there, and burned a ship in the harbor. Off the coast of northern Ireland he attacked the British sloop *Drake* and forced it to surrender. Jones also took two ships as prizes during the course of this foray into British waters. His greatest exploit, however, was in 1779 aboard the *Bonhomme Richard*, a French ship he refitted and named in honor of Benjamin Franklin (*Poor Richard's Almanac*). In the company of several other ships under his command, Jones came upon a

John Paul Jones
(1747-1792)

Jones was the most illustrious American naval commander in the War for Independence. He has sometimes been called the "father of the American navy," because his daring exploits have been an inspiration to the navy. He was born in Scotland with the family name of Paul. John Paul went to sea as a cabin boy at the age of 12 and spent most of the rest of his life in one sea adventure or another. Because of difficulties with the British naval authorities, he left their jurisdiction and changed his name to John Paul Jones. He turned up in Virginia as the war approached, and Congress commissioned him as a naval officer in 1775. He quickly distinguished himself and was given command of a naval vessel. Not only did Jones engage British warships in action, but he also took a large number of merchant ships as prizes. He went to Europe after the war, served for a time in the Russian navy, and died in obscurity.

fleet of merchant ships being convoyed by the *Serapis* and another British warship. The *Bonhomme Richard* attacked the *Serapis*, and at first the battle went heavily in favor of the *Serapis*. However, when he was asked if he was ready to surrender, Jones replied: "I have not yet begun to fight." Indeed, that was the case, for when several hits were made on the British ship, the commander struck his flag. Both the British warships were taken, and Jones and his crew made it into port aboard the *Serapis*, to which they were transferred as the *Richard* sank.

While the exploits of John Paul Jones did much for American morale and became a part of naval lore, the British navy still dominated the American coastline. Nor was it possible to overcome a major British army in an American seaport as long as it had naval support.

The Battle for the South

The French alliance did not make any immediate great impact on the American military situation. Although the French had been concentrating their efforts on building up their navy in the years before their entry into the war, it was more than three years after they entered the conflict before they could bring it to bear against a British fleet in a decisive way. Meanwhile, Washington had little hope of success and avoided attacks of British strongholds. The British did withdraw from Philadelphia on June 18, 1778. The American army at Valley Forge was still small, but it had been much improved in discipline and organization through the efforts of Baron von Steuben. This emboldened Washington to order an assault upon the British army, now under the command of Sir Henry Clinton, as it marched through New Jersey. The result was the Battle of Monmouth Court House. The British were spread out and might have been routed had it not been for General Charles Lee's untimely retreat in the face of British resistance. This enabled Clinton to concentrate his forces, and the best that Washington could do was rally his troops and withstand the assaults. Clinton removed his army from

Baron von Steuben (1730-1794)

Steuben is best known for instilling discipline in and reviving the disheartened Continental Army at Valley Forge. He was born in Prussia (Germany) of noble background. Steuben began his military life at the age of 14 and fought in the Prussian Army during the Seven Year's War. He came to America at the urging of a French count and offered his services to Congress. For his work at Valley Forge he was made inspector general of the army. In 1780 Steuben was placed in command of military forces in Virginia. Although he was replaced in that command by the Marquis de Lafayette, he took part in the siege of Yorktown. His manual on military regulations remained the official book until 1812. He was rewarded both by Congress and the several states for his contributions to the American cause. The picture above shows Baron von Steuben drilling Washington's troops at Valley Forge.

the scene under cover of night and boarded ships for New York. He had no more stomach for taking on the Americans without naval support than they had the foolhardiness to attack the British with theirs. Washington could only encamp in the vicinity of New York City and await an opportunity.

British strategists at home now pushed for the concentration of offensive measures in the South. Having failed to conquer America by attacking the concentrations of population along the northern coast, they advocated attacking at the more spread out and sparser settled South. This strategy had much to commend it. After all, much the more valuable trade items were produced in the South. If Britain could control Virginia and the lower South, plus Canada, it might still dominate the vast eastern Mississippi Valley region. Virginia already 'aid claim to much of the territory west of the Alleghenies; the conquest of Virginia might vouchsafe it to Britain. The approach to Virginia might be made from the lower South, which was the weakest link in the colonial chain. Georgia was the least populous of the states, and a considerable portion of the population of South Carolina was slave. North Carolina was known to have an important Loyalist contingent.

Savannah fell to British forces in December 1778. Early the next year they took over the rest of Georgia and installed a Loyalist government. But the British stationed in Georgia had little success over the next year with their advances into South Carolina. The force sent there was not adequate for such a campaign. Early in 1780, however, General Clinton, who had been reluctant to undertake the Southern campaign, finally did so; he was able to take Charleston on May 12, 1780 with a vastly superior military and naval force. Clinton then returned to New York, entrusting the Southern campaign to Lord Cornwallis. Cornwallis was probably the ablest field commander the British ever had in America. He was daring, decisive, and could win battles when the odds were against him. He did win many battles. In fact, he won most of the battles and lost the war.

For the remainder of 1780, Cornwallis see-sawed back and forth between South and North Carolina with his army. Virtually the whole Patriot army in that region had been surrendered at Charleston, necessitating the assembly of a new force in the deep South. Congress sent General Horatio Gates, the victorious commander at Saratoga, southward with a core of Continentals to do the job. As it turned out, his victory at Saratoga had given Gates a much greater reputation than he deserved. Cornwallis routed his army at Camden in August; Gates fled the scene of battle on the fastest horse he could command, and was 60 miles away before he considered it safe to stop. His army was scattered, and he was in disrepute.

Nathanael Greene assumed command of the Patriot forces in the Carolinas late in 1780, and he proved worthy of the calling. He was as successful at maneuvering as his mentor George Washington, but Cornwallis did not tarry overlong to test his talents. Instead, Cornwallis moved northward into Virginia in 1781, while Greene drove southward into South Carolina. In the course of the year Greene was so successful against British posts that he failed only in retaking Charleston. Indeed, a pattern emerged in the South similar to the one elsewhere on the continent. The British frequently won the pitched battles, but once the main army moved on the post left behind soon fell to the Patriot forces.

Nathanael Greene (1742-1786)

Greene was a general in the Continental Army throughout the war and was at his best in the Southern campaign of 1780-1781. He was born in Rhode Island, the son of a Quaker, served in the legislature, and became greatly interested in military tactics as the war approached. He served in the New York, New Jersey, and Pennsylvania campaigns under Washington, and as quartermaster general until his appointment to command the Southern army. Greene excelled in maneuvering his forces so as to outwit the enemy and is credited with the reconquest of most of North and South Carolina after Cornwallis moved the main part of his army into Virginia.

During the late spring and into the summer of 1781 Cornwallis rampaged across Virginia with a much larger army than the Americans could muster in that state. When the American forces were increased, Cornwallis decided to establish a base near the sea for naval support. He chose Yorktown, which is located on the York and James rivers and which empty into Chesapeake Bay. He set up camp there in early August.

Victory

Virginians had for some time been pleading with Washington to bring his army to save his home state. However, Washington was confronting the largest British army in America in New York; victory over that army would most likely be decisive. He wanted only the help of the French fleet to advance into the city itself. However, when it appeared that the fleet could be made available for a campaign in Virginia, he determined to go there. For this venture, Washington's Continentals were reinforced by a major French army under the command of the Comte de Rochambeau. Washington took pains to tie Clinton's army down in New York by leaving a good-sized military detachment behind and misleading Clinton as to the purpose of his moves. He succeeded well enough that reinforcements to Cornwallis arrived too late to affect the outcome.

Washington's plan for overcoming Cornwallis entailed both coordination between French and American land and naval forces and for the British to stay put. He had to move an army several hundred miles, most of them going by land. His heavy artillery was dispatched by sea, but its timely arrival depended upon the earlier dispersal of the British navy. The French navy had to be available at the right time or Cornwallis might be reinforced or his army transported elsewhere.

For once, all went well with the combined American and French undertaking. Admiral de Grasse, the French naval commander, turned up with the fleet at the right time. He succeeded in luring the British navy out to sea and got the better of the contest. The artillery was available at the right time. Cornwallis stayed where he was; he was hemmed in by water on three sides. The Continentals and the French were joined by the militia to make a formidably superior force under Washington. The attacks on the forward positions of the British army were successful, and they were exposed to artillery bombardment. Cornwallis judged his situation to be hopeless, and he surrendered his army intact.

Yorktown was the great victory of the American War for Independence. It had all, or almost all, of the right ingredients. Washington was in command of the victorious army; after so many years of perseverance in the face of the odds, his hour had come. If Cornwallis did not have the largest British army in America, he had the most seasoned and successful one. Even the surrender was dramatically carried out, though Cornwallis sent a subordinate to do the dishonors. With the French lined up on one side and the Americans on the other, the British marched between them to the tune of "The World Turned Upside Down" to the place where they laid down their arms. The British turned their eyes toward the French, as if in contempt of the Americans. They were roundly jeered by the Americans, who waited to do it, wisely, until the British had thrown down their arms. Thus ended the last great battle of the war.

Two other victories of the Americans, one before and one after this, need to be mentioned. One was the breaking of the British control west

Surrender of Lord Cornwallis at Yorktown, Virginia, October 19, 1781. (From the painting by John Trumbull.)

of the Alleghenies. During the first part of the war, the British, with their Indian allies, had retained control of the area. In 1778 George Rogers Clark led a contingent of Virginians into the region of the Mississippi Valley, and in that year and the next he defeated the Indians and drove out the British. Although he failed to take the British post at Detroit, his victory was so nearly complete that the Americans were able to lay claim by possession to the whole huge area at the treaty negotiations. Less grand in its dimensions but equally important for a smaller area, Georgia was reconquered by the Patriots in 1782; the reconquest was the culmination of a long series of exploits by General Anthony Wayne.

Before this last had been completed, however, Lord North's government had fallen in Britain, and a new ministry had begun negotiations to end the conflict. Before these led to a ratified treaty, the British evacuated Wilmington, Savannah, and Charleston in the course of 1782. All British forces were now concentrated around New York. In early 1783, the Treaty of Paris began to go into effect.

What did not happen toward the end of the war is as important in many ways as what did. Even as the American victory was being solidified by a peace treaty the success of the American revolution may well have hung in the balance. As the British forces withdrew, the Continental Army remained as the only armed force in the country, or much of it. This was the moment for a military *coup d'etat*, if there was to be one, the moment when the American Revolution might have followed the course of so many others. Nor was the provocation lacking. The military had been sorely deprived during the long years of the war. Now that the victory had been won, the army was invited to disband and its members return home without many of the financial rewards they had been promised.

George Washington was almost certainly the key to what would and did happen at this juncture. Had he sought to rally the army to himself and against the Congress, he would almost certainly have succeeded. His prestige had grown during the years of his command, until at the end of the war he was the preeminent American. There is no evidence that he ever seriously contemplated seeking power by grabbing it. On the contrary, he rebuked those who hinted at such things, and persisted in doing his duty as he saw it. His duty, as he saw it, was, having finished his military task, to lay down his sword, following the path he had ever trod of subordination to civil authority, and return to his peaceful pursuits at Mount Vernon. His every utterance, too, confirmed that in this case duty was happily joined to his heart's desire. Moreover, the manner in which he conducted himself in the last months of his service indicates both his desire to avert military takeover and his longing to retire to private life. A little retelling of some of the events will underscore the points.

Two events of early 1783 indicate that there was danger of a military revolt. The first of these is the one known as the Newburgh Address. It was a communication sent around to the officers exhorting them to take matters into their own hands to get what they thought they deserved. Washington ordered his officers assembled, to be presided over by General Gates, who was believed to be sympathetic with the Address. When they were assembled, Washington came into the room and asked to be allowed to say a few words to them. He told them that he well knew how much they had suffered and could sympathize with their wish to be rewarded. But he bade them to keep their faith in and with Congress. They were not visibly moved by this appeal, and Washington said that he had a letter from a member of Congress that might help to restore their faith. However, when he opened the letter to begin reading, he had difficulty making out some of the words. He took out his glasses and put them on—he had not worn them in public before—and looking up from the letter, he said: "I have grown gray in your service, and now find myself growing blind." The eyes of those gathered round filled with tears, for they knew how sturdily he had borne so much for so many years. It was hardly necessary for him to finish what he had to say. When Washington withdrew, the officers adopted a resolution affirming their confidence in Congress and declaring that they rejected "with disdain the infamous proposals contained in a late anonymous address to them."[35]

Of less potential for mischief was an event in June, though it does provide a clue as to what might have been. Fewer than a hundred soldiers of the Pennsylvania Line regiment descended on Congress at Philadelphia and threatened them in such a way that Congress retreated to the quiet of Princeton to hold its deliberations. Washington sent troops to put down this little uprising.

The last major contingent of British forces departed from New York City in early December 1783. Prior to their taking leave the Continental troops moved into the city to see that everything went off in an orderly way. It was an occasion for great rejoicing as the Continentals marched in, for the British had occupied the city for more than seven years. A spectator wrote: "We had been accustomed for a long time to military display in all the finish and finery of garrison life; the troops just leaving were as if equipped for show, and with their scarlet uniforms and burnished arms, made a brilliant display; the troops that marched in, on the contrary, were ill-clad and weather-beaten, and made a forlorn appearance; but then they were *our* troops, and as I looked at them and thought upon all they had done and suffered for us, my heart and eyes were full, and I admired them and gloried in them the more, because they were weather-beaten and forlorn."[36]

The time had at last come for George Washington to take leave of the army he had served for eight and one-half years. He notified the officers he would bid them farewell at Fraunces' Tavern at noon on the day of departure. All who could make it gathered there. It was a moving occasion. Washington was so filled with emotion that he could hardly speak. "With a heart full of love and gratitude," he said, "I now take my leave of you. I most devoutly wish that your later days may be as prosperous and happy as your former ones have been glorious and honorable." So saying, he asked that each of them would come by to shake his hand as a personal farewell. General Henry Knox, who had served him faithfully for so many years, came first; Washington was so overcome with emotion that a handshake would not do. He embraced him as both of them wept. "Once done, this had of course, to be done with all from Steuben to the youngest officer. With streaming eyes, they came to him, received the embrace, and passed on."[37]

When he set out from New York, Washington hoped to make it home by Christmas. But there were many festive occasions to be attended along the way, and he had business to do. He journeyed to Philadelphia to turn in his accounts. Then he went on to Annapolis to resign his commission before Congress. This he did just after 12 o'clock on December 23. The galleries were packed for the occasion, though many members of Congress were absent. One who was there described it this way:

> It was a solemn and affecting spectacle....The spectators all wept, and there was hardly a member of Congress who did not drop tears. The General's hand which held the address shook as he read it. When he spoke of the officers who had composed his family, and recommended those who had continued in it to the present moment to the favorable notice of Congress he was obliged to support the paper with both hands. But when he commended the interests of his dearest country to almighty God...his voice faltered and sunk, and the whole house felt his agitations.

When Washington regained his composure, he concluded strongly:

> Having now finished the work assigned me I retire from the great theatre of action, and bidding an affectionate farewell to this august body under whose orders I have so long acted I here offer my commission and take my leave of all the employments of public life.[38]

As soon as the ceremony was over, Washington left for Mount Vernon, and by hard riding was able to make it home to spend Christmas day with his wife and grandchildren. The American Cincinnatus had returned to his plow.

Chapter 4

Confederation Period

> *His Britannic Majesty acknowledges the said United States ...to be free, sovereign and independent States; that he treats with them as such, and for himself, his heirs and successors, relinquishes all claims to the Government, proprietary and territorial rights of the same, and every part thereof.*
>
> *—Treaty with Great Britain, 1783*

> *And, for extending the fundamental principles of civil and religious liberty...; to fix and establish those principles as the basis of all laws, constitutions, and governments, which forever hereafter shall be formed in the said territory: to provide also for the establishment of States..., and for their admission to a share in the federal councils on an equal footing with the original States....*
>
> *—Northwest Ordinance, 1787*

> *I do not conceive we can exist long as a nation without having lodged somewhere a power which will pervade the whole Union in as energetic a manner as the authority of the State governments extends over the several States.*
>
> *—George Washington to John Jay, 1786*

Chronology

1776-1780—Adoption by states of constitutions.

1783—Treaty of Paris ratified.

March 1785—Mount Vernon Conference.

May 1785—Basic Land Ordinance.

September 1786—Annapolis Convention.

December 1786—Shays' Rebellion.

May 1787—Begin Constitutional Convention.

July 1787—Northwest Ordinance.

The Articles of Confederation did not serve for long as the constitution of the United States. Their ratification was not completed until 1781, and a new government elected under what is now known as the

Constitution of the United States took office in 1789. Thus, technically, the Articles were in effect for only 8 years. But the process of replacing them was begun in 1787, and the independence of the United States was not fully established until 1783. Clearly, then, the Confederation period was only a brief interval in American history, even if we include in it the years from 1776 to 1781 before the Articles were ratified. It is even doubtful that what existed under the Articles was a general government at all. The states governed and from time to time took common action through the Congress of their representatives.

Even so, the Confederation period was important to American history; in many ways, it should rank as the most important period of all. A revolt against Britain was successfully conducted. American independence was achieved. The state governments were reconstituted. The bounds of the territory of English America were expanded. A union of the states was forged, though how firm and lasting it might be was still very much in doubt. Even the United States Constitution itself was achieved during the Confederation period, though Congress acted under pressure to call a constitutional convention. And the United States of America began to assume a place among the countries of the world. Treaties and trade agreements with other countries in the 1780s provide evidence for that.

This chapter will be devoted to two subjects mainly: (1) the achievements under the Confederation, and (2) the weaknesses of the Confederation. It might be supposed that in view of the record of achievement the political arrangements would have been kept more or less intact. But it could be argued that what had been accomplished was in the face of and despite the loose union effected by the Confederation. Much evidence could be assembled to support this view. But by 1787, say, there were few who would venture to try to make a case for the Articles as they stood. There was widespread agreement that the government of the union needed strengthening, though many still believed that they needed only to be revised or amended. Others believed that only a strong national government could maintain the union, act effectively with foreign nations, and keep the peace at home. On this question, there were major differences.

At any rate, the Confederation period became a decision time for the nature of the union. Would it continue as a confederation? Could it continue for long with little more than meetings of representatives of the states to hold it together? The histories of confederacies offered little encouragement. Confederacies tend either to be dominated by the largest state in them or to disintegrate. But if not a confederation, then what? How could a government of the union be devised that was at once effective and yet would not compromise the independence of the states. It was a question to which none knew the answer and which most were afraid even to raise. Yet, in the course of the 1780s, they moved toward grappling with it. That is the context both for the discussion of the achievements of the Confederation and its weaknesses.

The Treaty of Paris

The greatest achievement under the Articles of Confederation was the peace treaty with Great Britain, which was incorporated into the general European settlement of the Treaty of Paris of 1783. By the terms of the settlement with Britain, the states not only attained their independence but also acquired an empire beyond the mountains. The acquisition of this vast domain was probably the greatest diplomatic triumph in American history. That a people who had won so few battles, who had only a loose confederation for common action, who had never managed to bring many of their resources to bear on the prosecution of the war, who were so dependent on aid from other countries, should have such successes at the peace table requires more than a little explanation.

Treaty of Paris — 1783

1. His Britannic Majesty acknowledges the said United States...to be free, sovereign and independent States.

2. Boundaries shall run, as described in some detail, from Nova Scotia to and through the Great Lakes and the Lake of the Woods, thence on a due west course to the river Mississippi, down the Mississippi to the thirty-first parallel, and then east to the Atlantic Ocean.

3. The people of the United States shall have fishing rights and liberties in the waters of British North America.

4. Creditors on either side shall meet with no lawful impediment to the recovery of the full value, in sterling money, of all bona fide debts heretofore contracted.

5. Congress shall earnestly recommend to the legislatures of the respective States that they make restitution for confiscated Loyalist property.

6. There shall be no future confiscations or prosecutions on account of the part that anyone may have taken in the war.

7. Hostilities shall cease, and His Britannic Majesty shall, with all convenient speed, and without causing any destruction, or carrying away any negroes or other property of the American inhabitants, withdraw all his armies, garrisons and fleets from the said United States, and from every post, place and harbour within the same.

The American success can be attributed in part to the precarious position of the British. Britain wanted to end the war, but her leaders were eager to prevent gains by other European powers. The manner in which Lord North's government had fallen in 1782 left little room but for the British to come to terms with the Americans. A motion to make it a crime to advance the idea that the colonies could be restored by war carried in the Parliament. Moreover, Lord North was replaced at the head of the government by the Earl of Rockingham, "the old Whig and repealer of the Stamp Act," who was favorably inclined to the Americans and was pledged to end the war as quickly as possible. He died shortly, and was replaced by Lord Shelburne, who was also well disposed to the Americans. Richard Oswald, who headed the British peace delegation, took the long view that so far as possible the Americans should continue to enrich the British by trade.

John Jay (1745-1829)

Jay was a statesman, diplomat and jurist. He was born in New York City, the son of a prosperous merchant, graduated from King's College (now Columbia University), and practiced law until the troubles with England began to come to a head. He served in the First Continental Congress and was elected to and served briefly in the Second. He headed the committee which drew up the New York state constitution and served for a time on the highest court in that state. However, he was appointed by Congress in 1779 to work out a treaty with Spain. Jay had little success in that undertaking, but from there he went to France to help Adams and Franklin negotiate a treaty with Great Britain. He was a leader in getting the Constitution ratified in New York and was appointed the first Chief Justice to the U.S. Supreme Court. In 1794, he negotiated Jay's Treaty with Britain, and upon his return home he served as governor of New York for the remainder of his political career.

European rivalries and alliances both threatened and provided opportunities for American gains. The Count de Vergennes, who handled French foreign policy, was a wily diplomat who operated behind the scenes to trade away any potential gains by his allies—the United States and Spain—if he could gain some advantage for France. Of course,

France was pledged to American independence, but beyond that anything was fair game for a deal. The French alliance with Spain entangled Vergennes in Spanish territorial ambitions. Nor was France eager to restore friendly relations between Britain and her former colonies. As if all this were not enough, Congress instructed its peace commission to follow the guidance of the French in the treaty making.

Whether the Americans would get an advantageous settlement or be thwarted by French maneuvers, Spanish ambitions, and such British reluctance as existed really depended, however, on their peace commission. The men appointed to negotiate the peace were Benjamin Franklin, John Jay, and John Adams. There was some danger at the outset that these three would fail because of rivalries and suspicions among themselves. Jay and Adams could work well enough together because they distrusted the Europeans, believing them to be corrupt and devious. They also distrusted Franklin, fearing that he had adapted too well to European ways and was under the influence of the French. Actually, Franklin was a superb diplomat, was adept at maneuvering and getting his way by subterfuge, but he was as devoted to American interests as either Jay or Adams, and proved himself to be a tough negotiator when the occasion arose.

Before the negotiations got underway, Jay had learned that the French had indicated to the Spanish their willingness to allow them to have territory south of the Ohio and for the British to keep that north of the Ohio. "If this French proposal, which so pleased the Spaniards, had been adopted, the United States would not have secured from Great Britain title to the region now composing the present states of Ohio, Indiana, Illinois, Michigan, Wisconsin, and Minnesota, and would have lost to Spain the western part of Kentucky and Tennessee, Mississippi, and part of Louisiana, along with most of Alabama."[39] In view of the fact that Spain wanted Gibraltar from Britain and Britain wanted to hold on to Florida, the above might have taken place if all interested parties had gathered around a table to negotiate, or if France had been allowed the role of arbitrator.

This did not happen, however. The Americans negotiated a settlement with British delegates behind closed doors, ignored the instructions of Congress to defer to France, and did not even keep Vergennes informed during the course of the negotiations. They did make their agreement a part of the overall treaty among all the involved powers, thus avoiding the charge that they had made a separate treaty in violation of the Franco-American Alliance. But they did avoid the pitfall of joint negotiations with the French.

In the treaty, the United States got all the territory east of the Mississippi River, south to the 31st parallel, and north to a line bi-

secting the Great Lakes, or south of Canada. The British also conceded
that the people of the United States could use the North Atlantic fisheries off Canada. The independence of the states was affirmed, hostilities were to cease, and Britain agreed to remove her armed forces
"with all convenient speed."

The United States also made some concessions to Britain. The most
contested issue was that of the Loyalists. British negotiators insisted
that the property and rights of all Loyalists be restored. Many Loyalists had fled the country, especially as British troops were removed.
Also, the property of some Loyalists had been taken by states and sold
at public auction. The American peace commissioners pointed out that
the Congress had no authority to compel restoration. Franklin declared
that if the British insisted on full restoration to Loyalists, then the
United States must insist that the British and Loyalists pay for all the
damage they had wrought in America. If these matters were ever looked
into, Franklin pointed out, it would "form a record that must render
the British name odious in America to the latest generations."[40] The
Americans did agree, however, that Congress would recommend to the
states that the rights and property should be restored. Debts of the citizens of one country to those of the other were to be collectible in the
courts. Britain and the United States agreed to the free navigation of
the Mississippi, but Spain, the other country with territory on the river,
did not join in the agreement.

The Treaty of Paris was truly an American triumph. George Washington described its significance this way: "The citizens of America,
placed in the most enviable condition, as the sole lords and proprietors
of a vast tract of continent, comprehending all the various soils and cli-
mates of the world, and abounding with all the necessaries and con-
veniences of life, are now, by the late satisfactory pacification,
acknowledged to be possessed of absolute freedom and independence."[41] Some decades ago, an American historian declared: "On
the part of the Americans the Treaty of Paris was one of the most
brilliant triumphs in the whole history of modern diplomacy."[42] A
more recent diplomatic historian has seconded this opinion: "The
greatest victory in the annals of American diplomacy was won at the
outset by Franklin, Jay, and Adams."[43]

Western Lands

The United States did acquire a vast domain by the Treaty of Paris.
In general, the territory acquired extended from the western side of the
Appalachians to the Mississippi. Although it was several years before
all the disputes were settled, this territory was the possession of and

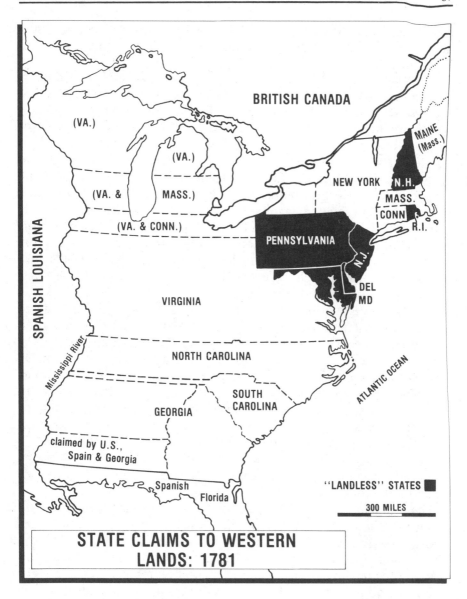

BRITISH CANADA

(VA.)

(VA.)

MAINE
(Mass.)

NEW YORK   N.H.

(VA. &   MASS.)

MASS.

CONN

(VA. & CONN.)

R.I.

PENNSYLVANIA

N.J.

SPANISH LOUISIANA

DEL
MD

VIRGINIA

Mississippi River

NORTH CAROLINA

ATLANTIC OCEAN

SOUTH
CAROLINA

GEORGIA

claimed by U.S.,
Spain & Georgia

Spanish
Florida

"LANDLESS" STATES ■

300 MILES

STATE CLAIMS TO WESTERN
LANDS: 1781

under the authority of the United States, not of the individual states. That is, in theory it was subject to the authority and disposal of Congress. In practice, the situation was much more confused than that sounds. There were still Indian claims to be dealt with in many areas. There were Indian tribes with whom no effective agreements had been made. Land companies laid claim to some of the lands. Veterans of the war had been promised western lands for their services, by some of the states at least. Congress had the authority, but it had no certain means for enforcing its decisions. It could and did pass ordinances, but it would either have to rely upon voluntary compliance, state courts, or the army to enforce its will.

Nevertheless, two important ordinances were passed by Congress during the Confederation period and began to go into effect. The first of these was the Land Ordinance of 1785. This ordinance provided for the surveying and sale of the land in the Old Northwest, i.e., west of Pennsylvania, north of the Ohio, and west to the Mississippi. The land was to be laid out in townships 6 miles square and such fractions of that amount as should occur. Each township, then, would consist of 36 square miles at the maximum. The minimum size of tracts to be sold was 640 acres (a square mile or section), and the minimum price was set at $1 per acre. One section in each township was to be set aside for the purpose of providing schools. Lands were to be sold at public auction to the highest bidder. Since the smallest tracts to be sold were 640 acres, the land was often bought by investors and divided into smaller parcels to be sold to farmers and other buyers.

The Northwest Ordinance of 1787, however, is generally considered to be the most important piece of legislation of the Confederation period. Moreover, it was second only to the Treaty of Paris among the achievements of Congress. The Northwest Ordinance provided for the governing of the territory of the Old Northwest and, equally important, for eventual statehood for the territories. This ordinance was important not only for the Old Northwest but also for the governing of territories generally belonging to the United States. Even as the ordinance was being passed a convention meeting in Philadelphia was in the process of drawing up a new constitution for the United States. But after the new constitution went into effect the Northwest Ordinance was passed into law once again.

The ordinance provided for territories to go through three stages to reach statehood. During the first stage, when there were but few inhabitants, Congress would appoint those who would rule the territory. The second stage would arrive when there were at least 5,000 adult males in the territory. They could then elect representatives to a legislative assembly, who would rule in conjunction with a council of five appointed by the governor and Congress. When there were 60,000 inhabitants, they could frame a constitution and apply to Congress for admission to the United States. New states would then take their place in the union on an equal basis with the older states. Thus, while Congress had acquired a colonial empire, in effect, it provided for the dissolution of that empire by the formation of new states. Eventually, five states—Ohio, Indiana, Illinois, Michigan, and Wisconsin—came into the union from the Old Northwest.

It is important, too, that full civil and religious liberties were guaranteed the residents of the territories. Among the protections of rights and liberties specified were: freedom of religion, the right to a writ of *habeas corpus* (not to be held in jail arbitrarily), trial by jury, to be bailable except for capital offenses, to be subject only to moderate fines and no cruel or unusual penalties, no interference with private contracts, and to be compensated for any service required or property taken for public use. It is of special interest to note that slavery was prohibited in the Northwest territory.

Weakness of the Confederation

Americans tended to be fearful of government and to distrust those who governed at the time of the American Revolution. They were especially fearful of governments any great distance from them, and this fear was amply demonstrated in the Confederation, which was made almost totally dependent upon the states. It was sound instinct, for the powers of government are indeed dangerous. Of course, Americans had learned their politics within the British Empire. The folly of attempts to govern from England had impressed them greatly. They were equally skeptical about placing large powers in the hands of executives, for many of their governors had been appointed from England. Their own legislators they trusted more, but even these they did not trust with power for long.

While the instinct may have been sound, the way they went about putting it into effect at first tended to make weak governments. Undoubtedly, they had it in mind to limit and restrain their governments, but what they did was to make them unstable and lacking in firmness.

1. The State Governments

The basic weakness of the Confederation was that it could not use force; it had neither courts of its own nor police and had to put its own laws into effect as best it could. But the Confederation was an instrument of the states, and its weakness was in considerable measure a reflection of their own instabilities. The state governments demonstrated both the virtues and faults of their revolutionary origins. They had come into being in resistance to British rule and the fact is that they were in the process of losing such self-government as existed in the colonial period. Not only did the states make a strong assertion of control over their own affairs after they declared independence but they also showed considerable determination not to allow any general government any power.

All but two of the states adopted new constitutions after the break from England. The exceptions were Rhode Island and Connecticut, which continued to live under their colonial charters, revised only to delete any references to British authority. Except for Massachusetts, these new constitutions were drawn and put into effect by revolutionary assemblies. Most of the constitutions were hastily devised in 1776, and reflected the sentiments of people in the process of leading a revolt against Britain.

The main features of the new government were frequent elections, weak executives, and a tendency to concentrate powers in the legislative branches. In some of the states there was a revulsion to the title of governor, going back to the colonial period when most governors were appointed from England, but the states continued to have a single executive head. They did not, however, have the power and influence exercised by most colonial governors. Colonial governors had usually possessed an absolute power of veto over legislation. Only in Massachusetts and New York was a limited veto retained. Otherwise a bill became law once it was passed by the legislature. Colonial governors could usually call legislatures into session and dismiss them. All remains of this power were removed except in New York. In eight of the states, the chief executive was elected by the legislatures, and he was made, thereby, dependent upon them. His tenure of office was usually quite brief. In nine states, it was only 12 months, and nowhere was it for a longer period than three years. To prevent the growth of personal power in the hands of the governor, most state constitutions limited the number of terms he could serve in a given period.

The courts generally were made more dependent on legislatures than they had been formerly. The Pennsylvania constitution, for example, described the relationship of supreme court justices this way: "The judges of the supreme court of judicature shall have fixed salaries, be commissioned for seven years only, though capable of reappointment at the end of that term, but removable for misbehavior at any time by the general assembly...."[44] When a judge in Rhode Island declared an act to force people to accept the paper money of that state unconstitutional, he and other judges were examined by the legislature. Those judges who agreed with the opinion were dismissed from office. There were differences from state to state, but judges were more clearly under the power of legislatures than formerly.

Except for Pennsylvania, all legislatures now had two houses of the legislature that were popularly elected. This differed from the colonial period when only one house was usually popularly elected. Indeed, most colonies had not clearly had two houses. The governor's council sometimes served as a kind of upper house, but it was a creature of the governor, not of the electorate. Frequent elections were the rule. In most states, the lower house was elected annually, but in two states elections were held twice a year. In eight of the states the upper house was elected annually, and in the other for somewhat longer terms. In any case, the members of the legislature came in and went out of legislatures almost as if they were revolving doors, contributing much to the instability of government.

Even so, much of the power of government was in the hands of these revolving door legislatures, and it was not much subject to external restraints. Thomas Jefferson complained that in Virginia—

> All the powers of government, legislative, executive, and judiciary, result to the legislative body....An *elective despotism* was not the government we fought for, but one which should not only be founded on free principles, but in which the powers of government should be so divided and balanced among several bodies of magistracy, as that no one could transcend their legal limits, without being effectually checked and restrained by the others.[45]

What Jefferson was saying, in effect, is that frequent popular elections do not provide a sufficient check on the powers of a government.

Yet it was these same shifting state governments which appointed the members to and directed the control over the Continental Congress. Not only did Congress lack effective power, but its members had no assurance of continuing in office from one session to the next. They might even be recalled during a session, and they were prohibited to serve for any long time during any given period of time by some states. The Congress tended to have even less continuity than the state governments.

Moreover, one state government could prevent any change or amendment of the Articles of Confederation. Such amendments required the unanimous approval of the states. There were repeated efforts to amend the Articles, but to no avail. There was widespread agreement that the Congress needed the power to tax in some fashion if it was to meet its obligations. Yet an effort to amend so as to allow Congress to levy a 5 percent tax on imports failed. All the other states approved, but Rhode Island refused to concur. Other attempts fared no better. Not only could one state veto it but also one or more states could attach such qualifications upon their approval that no agreement could be reached. The weakness of the Confederation was part and parcel of the instability of state government.

2. Foreign Relations

The Congress was authorized to conduct foreign relations for the United States, i.e., to make war and peace, to send and receive ministers and ambassadors, to make treaties and alliances, and the like. But it did not have power to make its own citizens adhere to its agreements. And, in commercial relations, the states could levy their own tariffs on foreign goods and regulate the use of their ports. Indeed, there was no power to prevent one state from penalizing goods brought in from another state.

The weaknesses of the Confederation in foreign relations soon became apparent in relations with Britain. The British continued to forbid trade of Americans with the British West Indies. In addition, they continued their trade rules on American goods brought in, almost as if the states were still colonies. Americans continued to prefer British goods and to buy them, but the result was increasing American debt and a drain of coinage from this country to Britain. John Adams became minister to the Court of St. James (Britain) in 1785. He hoped to obtain a commercial treaty that would open British ports in their colonies to American ships. But he found the government unwilling to make any concessions, skeptical about the usefulness of any agreement with the Confederation, and well satisfied with commercial relations as they stood. Instead of being able to make new agreements, Adams found himself occupied with questions about the failure to comply with the terms of the Treaty of Paris.

The British reproached the United States through Adams for not restoring the property and rights of Loyalists. Congress had indeed recommended this to the states, as it was required by treaty to do, but some of the states were more inclined to further retaliation, and none of them was favorable to or made full restitution to the Loyalists. The failure of the states to comply pointed up the weakness of Congress and raised doubts about entering into agreements with it. Nor did the states heed the treaty in allowing British merchants to collect their debts. Virginia, where the debts were most extensive, proceeded to pass laws obstructing their payment. Congress was powerless to compel compliance within states.

The British used the American failure to comply as an excuse for not withdrawing their forces in the Old Northwest according to agreement. They had several military posts on the American side of the Great Lakes. Contrary to the treaty provisions, they did not evacuate them; instead, a secret order to hold them indefinitely went out in 1784. Though the posts themselves were on the edge of American claimed territory, they provided bases for the British to extend their influence on Indians on American territory and for carrying on a prosperous fur trade with them. British connections with the Indians increased the danger to Americans attempting to settle in the area as well.

Difficulties with Spain were, if anything, more pressing than those with Britain. Trading privileges were not at issue, for Spain had opened up her most important colonial ports to America. The major issues were the location of the boundaries between the United States and Spanish territory to the south and west, Spanish relations with Indians in territory claimed by the United States, and the navigation and use of the Mississippi and ports located along it. The difficulties arose out of differences in claims and designs on the Old Southwest. Spain had lately acquired Florida from Britain, and the territory included what was then called West Florida, which extended all the way to the Mississippi. Spain continued its historic claim to the vast territory west of the Mississippi. These territories gave Spain control over all the routes of access to the Gulf of Mexico from the continent of North America. The fact that Britain had ceded territory to the United States did not greatly impress the Spanish, particularly when these same British were clinging to their own former posts to the north in defiance of the treaty.

In 1784, Spain concluded treaties with Indians who lived within the United States territory. Moreover, Spain held onto a military post at Natchez, which she had acquired during the war but which was now within the treaty territory of the United States. It was the position of both Britain and the United States that navigation of the Mississippi River was free to all, but Spain did not accept this position. Nor would Spain grant the right of deposit of goods in New Orleans for transhipment—a right essential to the effective use of the Mississippi—to the United States.

Of course, use of the Mississippi for transport was an absolute requirement for the commercial development of the trans-Appalachian region of America. The expense of hauling freight overland from the west to the east was prohibitive; only lightweight cargo of high value could be considered for such expensive shipment. Even so, Americans poured into the region west of the mountains in increasing numbers in the 1780s. This, despite the fact that to transport their goods they would either have to make private agreements with Spain or become Spanish citizens. John Jay conducted negotiations over a considerable period with the Spanish diplomat, Diego de Gardoqui, but the United States had little to offer and the Spanish had little to fear from the continuation of the deadlock. Jay saw scant hope for settling the dispute favorably to the United States by negotiation and saw little to hope for in going to war. "For," as he said in 1786, "unblessed with an efficient government, destitute of funds, and without publick credit, either at home or abroad, we should be obliged to wait in patience for better days, or plunge into an unpopular and dangerous war with very little prospect of terminating it by a peace, either advantageous or glorious."[46]

Not all the difficulties of the Confederation were with European countries: those people commonly called the Barbary Pirates along the African coast of the Mediterranean disrupted trade in a particularly distressing way. Several Moslem principalities, or whatever they should be called, had long preyed on shipping in the Mediterranean. Countries which wished to avoid their depredations were expected to pay bribes. Once the Americans cut themselves loose from British protection, they were exposed to these pirates. Algeria went to war with the United States, or so rumor had it, seized two American ships, and enslaved their crews. Congress offered to ransom the sailors, but the amount they could and did offer was too small. A "diplomat" from another Moslem principality approached the United States with the proposition that the harassment of shipping would cease if tribute in sufficient amount were paid. As things stood, however, the United States could neither afford to pay tribute nor assemble the necessary force to suppress the pirates.

The United States had plunged into nationhood without providing the means for dealing effectively with other nations or the protection of her nationals in commercial competition.

3. Economic Troubles

The Confederation never was on a sound financial footing. It had no dependable revenues, often could not pay its bills, could not redeem its currency, and made no provisions for retiring its debts. The Congress resorted to first one and then another expediency to raise money: issuing paper money, borrowing from foreign countries, making requisitions on the states, and selling western lands. The issuing of more and more paper money mainly succeeded in destroying its value. Borrowing from foreign countries increased the debt and lowered the credit standing of the country. All this made it not only difficult to conduct foreign relations but also some of the efforts contributed to domestic depression.

Congress attempted to put its financial house in order beginning in 1781. It appointed Robert Morris as Superintendent of Finance. He was probably the leading merchant and financier in the country, and he had great plans for putting finances on a sound basis. The war was still underway, and his first task was to provide funds for the army. He managed to do this fairly well by a combination of foreign loans, requisitions on the state, and borrowing on his own credit, which was better

Robert Morris (1734-1806)

Morris is best known as the financier of the American Revolution. He was born in Liverpool, England, but he came to America in 1747 to become a merchant, and eventually became a partner in a large firm in Philadelphia. He was a member of the Continental Congress and a signer of the Declaration of Independence. Almost from the first, however, he took a leading role in the financial efforts of the Congress, serving on the committee that dealt with finances and after 1781 as Superintendent of Finance. Morris founded the Bank of North America, and was brought before Congress on charges of dishonesty, mainly for intermingling government and private accounts. He was cleared of these charges. He served as a delegate from Pennsylvania to the Constitutional Convention, but did not take an active part in the deliberations. Morris served as United States Senator for six years, and was a supporter of Hamilton's financial policies. He became very much involved in western land sales in his later years.

than that of the Confederation. Morris also was able to get underway what he hoped would be a central bank for America, the Bank of North America. The bank did do well for a time, and he was able to redeem the bank notes (paper money) he issued at face value. But when all efforts to get the states to amend the Articles to provide a steady revenue for the Confederation failed, Morris recognized that the task was hopeless. He resigned with these words, "To increase our debts while the prospect of paying them diminishes, does not consist with my ideas of integrity. I must, therefore, quit a situation which becomes utterly insupportable."[47]

Indeed, the situation was bad, and did not improve with the passage of time. One estimate of the total debt of the Confederacy at the end of the war amounted to over $35,000,000. Far from being retired, the debt continued to grow. Congress received $2,457,987 by way of requisitions from the states between November 1, 1781 and January 1, 1786. Very little was realized from the sale of western lands, and the total was less than one fourth of the amount that would have been needed to pay current expenses and the interest on various debts. Many of the requests for funds from the states fell on deaf ears. Rhode Island sent word that the state was having difficulty meeting its own expenses and that Congress should borrow the money it needed. So it went.

Americans had hardly achieved independence before they were hit by depression. It was probably at its worst around the middle of the decade of the 1780s. The stage for depression was set by the attempt to finance the war by large issues of paper money. The inflation which resulted produced higher prices, but since people had more money it gave the appearance of prosperity for a while. When the paper money depreciated to the point that it was virtually worthless, it was abandoned, and people began trading in specie. There was, of course, much less gold and silver coins than there had been paper money. Hence, the inflation was followed by deflation, as is the usual case. A deflation ordinarily results in what is commonly called a depression. Prices fall as they adjust to the reduced supply of money. Debts contracted during the inflation are especially hard to pay.

Although the paper money was going, or had gone, out of circulation by 1781, the full-fledged depression did not hit until around 1784. Two things helped to defer the deflation. One was that a great deal of money came into the country in 1781 and 1782 from foreign loans. The other was that a great many coins that had been hidden during the inflation came into circulation. The British armies, too, had enriched many Americans with hard money. But after 1783 foreign loans were increasingly hard to get, the British armies had been withdrawn, and the coins were being shipped out of the country. Americans still showed a marked preference for British goods, and once the war was over British goods began to pour in. Americans had an unfavorable balance of trade, however, because the British did not buy nearly as much as they sold. The depression came. As one historian writing about these times has said, "Hard is the lot of one who, burdened with taxes and debts and destitute of cash, is beset by falling prices of the things he makes and sells."[48]

Actually, the falling prices were the main means for coming out of the deflation-depression. Not only did lower prices work to adjust goods to money supply but they would also tend to lure money from abroad. There are at least anecdotal indications that this was working by 1786. Benjamin Franklin wrote in that year: "America never was in higher prosperity, her produce abundant and bearing a good price, her working people all employed and well paid...; and our commerce being no longer the monopoly of British merchants, we are furnished with all the foreign commodities we need, at much more reasonable rates than heretofore."[49] Charles Thompson wrote to Thomas Jefferson in a similar vein at about the same time. "Population is increasing," he said, "new houses building, new lands clearing, new settlements forming, and new manufactures establishing with a rapidity beyond conception, and what is more, the people are well clad, well fed, and well housed." But, he went on, "Yet I will not say that all are contented. The merchants are complaining that trade is dull, the farmers that wheat and other produce are falling, the landlords that rent is lowering, the speculists and extravagant that they are compelled to pay their debts, and the idle and vain that they cannot live at others cost and gratify their pride with articles of luxury."[50]

However all that may be, there is little reason to doubt that debtors were often still hard hit even if conditions generally were improving. Those who had gone into debt on long terms during the inflation were undoubtedly hard put to pay off the debts with the much scarcer money now in circulation. For example, in Worcester County, Massachusetts, over 2,000 suits were taken to court for recovery of debt in one year. Debtors and others brought pressure to bear on state governments to do something.

One way that some states responded was in trying to discriminate against the citizens of other states and in favor of their own in trade regulations. Congress was powerless to regulate either foreign or interstate commerce. Some states jumped into the gap with attempts to regulate both. A situation something like this developed:

> Meanwhile, the different states with their different tariff and tonnage acts, began to make commercial war upon one another. No sooner had the other three New England states virtually closed their ports to British shipping than Connecticut threw hers wide open, an act which she followed by laying duties upon imports from Massachusetts. Pennsylvania discriminated against Delaware, and New Jersey, pillaged at once by both her greater neighbours, was compared to a cask tapped at both ends.[51]

The other approach was pressure on the states to issue paper money. This was taking the hair of the dog that had bit them, for it was unbacked paper money that had started the whole process. Seven states had gone into the paper money business again by 1788. Rhode Island was the most irresponsible of these, not only issuing the money abundantly but also trying to compel its acceptance. The situation was so bad there that creditors fled from people trying to pay their debts in the worthless paper money, and many merchants closed their shops.

Massachusetts resisted the pressure to take such measures. The result was what is known as Shays' Rebellion, which occurred in late 1787 and early 1788. Overt action began when mobs began preventing courts from having their regular sessions. Beginning in early 1786, a succession of courts were disrupted and prevented from conducting business by large groups of armed men: at Worcester, at Concord, at Taunton, at Great Barrington, and at Springfield. Their main object was to prevent foreclosures, but they were also trying to get action from the legislature. When the legislature refused to move, a rebel force was organized with Daniel Shays as a leader. Massachusetts authorized an armed force to put down the rebellion, and the rebels were dispersed January 25, 1787. New Hampshire was threatened by rebels, but Governor John Sullivan, who had been a general during the late war, took decisive action to prevent the rebellion from getting underway.

Actually, all these developments only helped to convince more people that they needed a stronger general government and some restraints on the states. Even before Shays' Rebellion, the movement was well on its way to fruition to do something along those lines.

Toward a Constitutional Convention

Even before ratification of the Articles had been completed, there were those who believed that the powers of the Confederation were not adequate to its task. As early as 1780, Alexander Hamilton wrote, "The fundamental defect is a want of power in Congress....But the Confederation itself is defective, and requires to be altered. It is neither fit for war nor peace. The idea of an uncontrollable sovereignty in each State over its internal police will defeat the other powers given to Congress, and make our union feeble and precarious...."[52] By the middle of the 1780s his view was being accepted by more and more people. The main question that remained was how it could be altered. The task of getting unanimous approval of the states to any change appeared hopeless. The way around this was arrived at indirectly.

The first step toward altering the Articles was taken at the Mount Vernon Conference in 1785. This conference was held between representatives of Maryland and Virginia to deal with navigation on the Potomac River. Since the river flows between Virginia and Maryland, and since Congress was not exercising such powers, they met at the invitation of George Washington at his home at Mount Vernon. They settled the matters for which they had met, but this conference raised the broader question of the need for commercial regulations among all the states. James Madison proposed that a convention with delegates from all the states be held the next year. The Virginia legislature passed a resolution calling upon all the states to send delegates to Annapolis, Maryland.

A meeting was held, sometimes called the Annapolis Convention,

Alexander Hamilton
(1757-1804)

Hamilton was born in the British West Indies and did not arrive in the mainland colonies until 1772. He missed the colonial experience of most of the Founders, and it could be said with justice that he did not sympathetically share, if he understood, some of the basic beliefs of most Americans. Yet he fought for American independence and was a guiding light in the early years of the Republic and one of its brightest stars. Hamilton was a trusted aide to Washington for much of the war, pressed for a stronger general government in the 1780s, and became Secretary of the Treasury under Washington. It was in this last that he exercised the most influence on the new government. His most brilliant writings, however, were written to urge the ratification of the Constitution and were published in book form as *The Federalist*. (Jay and Madison also contributed essays to it.) He was strong-minded and strong-willed and was often involved in controversies. He helped to found the Federalist Party and died as a result of wounds in a duel with Aaron Burr.

in September 1786. Although most of the states appointed delegates, only a dozen from five states attended. (There was not even a delegation from the host state, Maryland.) Those gathered agreed that they were not sufficiently representative to deal with the commercial matters, much less the broader issues of revising the Articles which needed attention. They proposed, then, in a document drawn by Alexander Hamilton of New York, that a full convention be held with the object of rendering "the constitution of the Federal Government adequate to the exigencies of the Union." This report was sent to Congress and to all the states.

In February 1787, Congress recommended to the states that they each send delegates to a convention to be held in Philadelphia beginning in May of that year. The meeting was to be "for the sole and express purpose of revising the Articles of Confederation." Well before Congress acted, Virginia had adopted a passionate resolution authorizing the appointment of delegates to the Philadelphia Convention. The legislature declared that they could "no longer doubt that a Crisis is arrived at which the good People of America are to decide the solemn question whether they will...reap the just fruits of that Independence which they have so gloriously acquired and of that Union which they have cemented with so much of their common Blood, or whether by giving way to unmanly Jealousies and Prejudices...they will renounce the ...blessing prepared for them by the Revolution...."[53]

Over the period of several months before May 1787, twelve states appointed delegates to the fateful convention to be held in Philadelphia.

Chapter 5
The Making
of the Constitution

In framing a government which is to be administered by men over men, the great difficulty lies in this: you must first enable the government to control the governed; and in the next place oblige it to control itself.

—James Madison

It is too probable that no plan we propose will be adopted. Perhaps another dreadful conflict is to be sustained. If to please the people, we offer what we ourselves disapprove, how can we afterwards defend our work? Let us raise a standard to which the wise and honest can repair. The event is in the hand of God.

—George Washington

Fortunate it is for the body of a people, if they can continue attentive to their liberties, long enough to erect for them a temple, and constitutional barriers for their permanent security: when they are well fixed between the powers of the rulers and the rights of the people, they become visible boundaries, constantly seen by all, and any transgression of them is immediately discovered: they serve as sentinels for the people at all times....

—Richard Henry Lee

Chronology

May 1787—Opening of Constitutional Convention
September 1787—Adjournment of Constitutional Convention
September 1787—Congress sends Constitution to States
1787—State Ratifications of the Constitution:
>   December 7—Delaware
>   December 12—Pennsylvania
>   December 18—New Jersey

1788—State Ratifications of the Constitution:

    January 2—Georgia

    January 9—Connecticut

    February 7—Massachusetts

    April 28—Maryland

    May 23—South Carolina

    June 21—New Hampshire (2/3 had now ratified)

    June 25—Virginia

    July 26—New York

January 1789—Presidential Election

September 1789—Bill of Rights submitted to Senate

November 1789—North Carolina ratifies the Constitution

May 1790—Rhode Island ratifies the Constitution

December 1791—Bill of Rights Ratified

Of all the many important gatherings in this era of American political beginnings, the Constitutional Convention must be ranked as the most successful and the one with the greatest meaning for the future. And of all the documents and pronouncements of this epoch the one that came out of the convention at Philadelphia in 1787—*the* United States Constitution—heads the list. It stands alone among them in the impact it has had, in its singular character, and in the role it would play in the lives of future generations. It was a major breakthrough in constitution making, even for a generation already practiced in drawing up such instruments.

What came out of this convention was more than and different from either what had spurred the call or than anyone involved in promoting it had foreseen. Many saw the need for a stronger general government, but none knew how one could be authorized that would meet with the general acceptance necessary for it to work. Even if a masterpiece were produced, some feared it would be rejected by the states. Stranger still, the Constitution actually emerged from the discussions and debates and compromises in the conventions. There were plans drawn by one or a few men, it is true, but these were little more than the vaguest outlines. It is a commonplace that committees produce little of value; yet here, by a group larger than most committees, the exception was made to happen. It has even been described as a miracle. George Washington wrote to Lafayette that it was "little short of a miracle that the delegates from so many different States (which States you know are different from each other), in their manners, circumstances and prejudices, should unite in forming a system of National Government, so little liable to well-founded objections."[54] Catherine Drinker Bowen's book on the convention is titled *Miracle at Philadelphia.* It was surely an extraordinary accomplishment, whatever it should be called.

The Men Who Made the Constitution

Even so, the convention did not get underway any more promptly than other gatherings in that time. It was called for May 14, but there was not a quorum to do business until May 25. It was no easy matter to assemble men from over the length and breadth of the United States; delegates from Georgia, say, had a formidable distance to travel considering the condition of the roads and the state of transportation. Most of those appointed to the convention, too, were men of affairs. They were planters, merchants, businessmen, and farmers, in addition to their professions and other pursuits. In any case, promptness was better calculated in weeks than in hours.

The Virginia delegation was the first appointed by a legislature, and its members began to arrive in Philadelphia before other out-of-staters. It was an impressive delegation, including among its members some of the state's leading citizens: George Washington, Edmund Randolph, George Mason, and James Madison (George Wythe, one of the best legal minds in America, put in an appearance but left shortly to attend his dying wife). Most of the Pennsylvania delegates did not have to make a trip to get to Philadelphia; they were, therefore, available from the beginning. Theirs was an outstanding delegation, for it included Benjamin Franklin, Robert Morris (who did not participate actively in the debates), Gouverneur Morris (no relation), and James Wilson.

The New England states were not only the slowest in appointing delegates but also theirs were among the last to arrive. Rhode Island rejected the invitation to appoint delegates. (The absence of Rhode Islanders was not considered a handicap during the convention, for their political behavior was so universally deplored that men did not gladly seek the counsel of the citizens.) The New Hampshire delegates were exceedingly late—the state had neglected to provide for their expenses; two of the four appointed finally arrived on July 23. New York appointed three delegates—Alexander Hamilton, Robert Yates, and John Lansing, but Yates and Lansing withdrew after a brief period, and Hamilton was absent for an extended period. In fact, Hamilton was not in accord with the other delegates from his state and differed with the other delegates generally.

Overall, 12 states had 55 delegates in attendance at one time or another. The greatest interest and leadership for a stronger general government came mainly from the larger states, New York excepted. Four state delegations were at the forefront in working toward a new constitution, and in this order: Virginia, Pennsylvania, Connecticut, and South Carolina. The delegates from New Jersey and Massachusetts also played a considerable role, and John Dickinson's was a sturdy voice for moderation during the convention. Luther Martin of Maryland and George Read of Delaware would have led if they could have attracted followers.

George Mason (1725-1792)

Mason was a Virginia planter, a neighbor and friend of George Washington, and an early leader in the Patriot cause. Most of his political career was in Virginia, where he served in the House of Burgesses before the Revolution, led Virginia in opposing British taxing policies, and played a major role in drawing up the Virginia constitution and Bill of Rights as Virginia became independent. Although Mason was a slaveholder, he opposed the institution of slavery and looked forward to its abolition. He favored local government over the national government, was more of a Virginian than a nationalist, helped to form the United States Constitution but opposed its ratification in Virginia. He believed that the powers given to the national government were too great and that they endangered not only the states but also the rights of individuals.

The delegates were as well qualified as could have been assembled in America, qualified both by experience and training. Among them were 39 who had served at one time or another in Congress, eight who had signed the Declaration of Independence, eight who had helped draw state constitutions, one, John Dickinson of Delaware, who is credited with the first draft of the Articles of Confederation, seven who had been chief executives of their states, and 21 who had fought in the war. Thirty-three were lawyers, and ten of these had served as judges. About half of them were college graduates, more from Princeton than from any other institution.

Both youth and advanced age were represented at the convention. The youngest delegate was Jonathan Dayton of New Jersey at 26; the oldest, Benjamin Franklin, who was, as he said, in his eighty-second year. The average age was in the low forties. Some of the leaders, however, were rather young: Charles Pinckney of South Carolina was

James Madison (1751-1836)

Madison was the fourth President of the United States, Secretary of State under Thomas Jefferson, served in the U.S. House of Representatives from 1789-1797, and in the Continental Congress for several years before that. However, his most signal achievement was in the making of the Constitution. He is sometimes called the "father of the Constitution," a title more appropriate to him than any other single person. He initiated both the Mount Vernon and Annapolis conferences which set the stage for the Constitutional Convention. Madison constructed a plan for a government in the months before the convention which was the basis of the Virginia Plan. He played a leading role in the debates at the Constitutional Convention, helped in writing *The Federalist*, pushed the Bill of Rights through Congress, and was the leader in getting Virginia's ratification of the Constitution. Along with Jefferson, Madison shaped the Republican Party and became an outstanding spokesman for strict construction of the Constitution. Madison was born in Virginia, educated at Princeton, studied theology and may have intended to become a clergyman, but he eventually concentrated his brilliant mind on political thought and the making of a nation.

only 29; Gouverneur Morris, 35; and James Madison, 36. They were counterbalanced by men of middling years and extensive experience, such as John Dickinson, 54; Roger Sherman, 66; and John Langdon, 67.

George Washington almost did not come to the convention. Although he was as convinced as any and more so than most that a general government with power was essential, he asked that someone else be appointed in his place when he was informed of his appointment. He had, as he pointed out, already declined an invitation to attend the meeting of the Cincinnati Society which would be held during the time of the convention. He had been saddened by the recent death of a brother, his plantation needed his attention, and he was suffering so from rheumatism that he could turn in bed only with the greatest difficulty. But he was urged to attend by those who realized that if the convention were to succeed it needed the support of the most prominent men in America. Reluctantly, he agreed to go.

That done, Washington pitched in with a right good will to get something accomplished. He arrived in Philadelphia before the convention was scheduled to begin. It had long since become difficult for him to go anywhere quietly, and there was good reason this time to let it be known widely that he had come, for it signalled that the convention was an important one. He was met at Chester by a troop on horse and was escorted into Philadelphia where cannons were fired and bells were rung. Washington was elected unanimously (as when was he not) to preside over the convention, an office which he took so seriously that he attended meetings regularly during the most oppressively hot summer in the memory of Philadelphians. Washington was a man of stern visage, impressive physique, and high seriousness; with him in the chair the convention could be expected to go about its business to achieve some results. It was of no small consequence, either, that as the men of the convention were conceiving and fleshing out the office of president they were aware that the man who chaired the convention would also be the first president. This emboldened those who wanted a strong executive to make the office powerful, for they were confident that Washington would not abuse the powers.

Benjamin Franklin was the other most prominent American; his hold on the affections of his countrymen was not so great as that of Washington, but his international fame was such that any gathering which had the benefit of his counsels gained in reputation. Though he was getting old—in fact, was old—his mind was still clear, his vast fund of experience still at his command, and his accomplishments as a story teller still led men to seek his company. He was not only aged but also infirm. He had to be carried in a sedan chair to the sessions, and he wrote out any but the briefest of remarks so that they could be read to the convention by his fellow Pennsylvanian, James Wilson. Aside from his presence, Franklin contributed most to the convention by advising the men there to compose their differences, "to doubt a little of [their] own infallibility," and do their best to arrive at a positive result.

Though the convention was not a large body, a few men did most of the speaking and a great deal of the other work of hammering out the Constitution. The following men generally took the lead: James Madison, George Mason, and Edmund Randolph of Virginia; Gouverneur Morris and James Wilson of Pennsylvania; Charles Pinckney and John Rutledge of South Carolina; Oliver Elsworth and Roger Sherman of Connecticut; Rufus King and Elbridge Gerry of Massachusetts; and William Patterson of New Jersey. According to one tabulation, Gouverneur Morris spoke on 173 different occasions; Wilson, 168; Madison, 161; Sherman, 138; Mason, 136; and Gerry, 119. At the outset, most of those there appeared to be reluctant to rise to speak. Benjamin Franklin called for fuller discussion of the issues, and others urged that members not be timid. As in any assembly, most waited to speak until they could get their bearings, until they could get the sense of what others thought and pick up allies for their position. Before the convention was over, however, some would have been heartily glad to have less speaking.

James Madison has sometimes been described as the Father of the Constitution. That may overstate the case, but there can be no doubt that he mothered the Constitution from the beginning of its inception at the Annapolis Convention through the Constitutional Convention at Philadelphia to its ratification by the states to the adoption of the Bill of Rights and putting it into operation. His dominance owed nothing to his physique. He was quite short and thin and could have been mistaken easily for a clerk. "Little Jemmy," they called him, "no bigger than a half cake of soap." But he stood tall at the convention, based mainly on the superiority of his learning and his tenacity in argument. Major William Pierce, a delegate to the convention from Georgia, said that Madison "blends together the profound politician, with the Scholar. In the management of every great question he evidently took the lead in the Convention, and tho' he cannot be called an Orator, he is a most agreable [sic], eloquent, and convincing Speaker. From a spirit of industry and application, which he possesses in a most imminent degree,

Roger Sherman (1721-1793)

Sherman was born in Massachusetts but spent most of his life as a resident of Connecticut. He studied law, became involved in resistance to British policies, and served in the Continental Congress from 1774-1781. Sherman was appointed a delegate to the Constitutional Convention from Connecticut and became a leader in the development of the United States Constitution. He helped in working out the Connecticut Compromise by which the conflict between the large and small states in the convention was resolved. He served in the first U.S. House of Representatives and, after that, as U.S. Senator until his death.

Gouverneur Morris
(1752-1816)

Morris was a lawyer, a statesman, a financier, a constitution maker, a diplomat, and a
superb speaker and writer. He was born in
New York, educated at King's College (now
Columbia University), served in the New York
Legislature after independence, helped to draw
up the New York Constitution, and served in
the Continental Congress. He moved to
Philadelphia and served the Congress in
managing its finances under Robert Morris.
Morris' most outstanding contribution was as
a delegate to the Constitutional Convention
from Philadelphia. Not only did he play an
active role in the debates which shaped the
Constitution but he also was on the committee which gave it its final form. Later, he
served the new government as a minister to
France and as a U.S. Senator. He is credited
with proposing the dollar as the basis of
American money and was one of the con-
ceivers of the Erie Canal.

he always comes forward the best informed Man of any point in
debate.... Mr. Madison is...a Gentleman of great modesty,—with a
remarkably sweet temper."[55] That he stood out for his learning was no
accident; he spent much of the time in the months before the convention in reading and studying about the history and nature of government, and a letter to Thomas Jefferson in Paris asking for them had
brought many books to augment his own supply.

Gouverneur Morris was, however, the most dazzling speaker in the
convention, an orator whose learning and close reasoning gave an ir-
resistible thrust to his forensic skill. "He winds through all the mazes of
rhetoric," Pierce said, "and throws around him such a glare [of light]
that he charms, captivates, and leads away the senses of all who hear
him.... No Man has more wit,—nor can any one engage the attention
more than Mr. Morris."[56] His weakness was that he shifted from one
train of thought to another without making the transition or showing
any connection from one speech to the next. Even so, he did yeoman
service in the making of the Constitution, including work on style in the
final phrasing of the document.

Impressions tumble over one another of the men during the sessions of the convention: of George Washington presiding from his high-backed chair, leaning forward to try to discern the order of the proposals from amidst the welter of motions made from the floor, forbearing to speak on the issues because it would be improper for the chairman to do so; of James Madison, scribbling away at his notes, taking the floor to make a point, retiring to his quarters at the end of the day to flesh out his notes and review what had been done; of the proud and passionate Edmund Randolph, a young politician already in mid-career, presenting the Virginia Plan to the convention, vacillating on issues as the Constitution took shape, unwilling at last to sign the handiwork of the convention which had been shaped from his proposals; of James Wilson, tenaciously pressing for a national government, rising yet once again to support giving the people a more direct role in the government; of George Read, difficult to listen to but determined to be heard, single-mindedly arguing for a more powerful executive; of craggy Roger Sherman, whose face would stop a clock but whose arguments moved the convention toward the accomplishment of its task; of Charles Pinckney, young, brash, but sufficiently brilliant in debate to command the attention of the others; of George Mason, early and late a defender of the rights of man, working with obvious good will to shape the Constitution, but at last unwilling to sign it; of John Dickinson, theoretician of resistance in youth, coming to fame with his daring employment of reason, now grown older declaiming: "Experience must be our only guide. Reason may mislead us."; and of Jonathan Dayton, the youngest man there, rising to second what had not clearly been a motion by Gouverneur Morris on the evils of slavery, and saying: "He did it...that his sentiments on the subject might appear whatever might be the fate of the amendment."[57]

Though the convention was composed of many of the best minds and most able men in America, some prominent Americans were not there. John Adams was out of the country, doing his best to represent Congress before the royal court in London. Adams had lately published a book in defense of the state constitutions, and it would undoubtedly have had more influence had he been at the convention. Thomas Jefferson was in Paris as minister to France. Any gathering without him was lacking one of the American luminaries, though he did not shine in debate. The pen, not the voice, was his chosen instrument of persuasion. Several firebrands of the Revolution were missing, if not missed, for they were better known for heat than light. Among them were: Samuel Adams who was not appointed; Richard Henry Lee and Patrick Henry who did not choose to attend; and Thomas Paine, who was in Europe trying to promote a project for steel bridges in the interlude be-

Charles Pinckney
(1757-1824)—

Pinckney was born in Charleston, South
Carolina of one of the leading families of
that state. He was studying law when the
War for Independence came, but he left his
studies to serve in several of the military
campaigns in the South. He entered the
South Carolina Legislature in 1779, was captured by the British in the fall of Charleston,
and was a prisoner until the end of the
fighting. Pinckney was chosen as a delegate
to the Constitutional Convention where he
played a prominent role. He presented a plan
to the convention from which much was borrowed, offered several resolutions, and
helped to word some of the provisions. He
served several terms as governor of South
Carolina and a portion of a term in the
United States Senate, as well as being active
in the formation of the Jeffersonian
Republican Party.

tween revolutions. Probably if some of these men, at least, had been
there they would have been so outspoken in favor of a bill of rights that
one would have been included, thus removing what turned out to be *the*
major objection to the Constitution.

The Task of the Convention

The men who assembled at the convention were in general agreement
that Congress acting under the authority of the Articles of Confederation could not perform its duties. Indeed, the convention had been
called to "render the federal constitution adequate to the exigencies of
Government & the preservation of the Union." Nor did anyone in the
convention dispute the assertion that Congress was near to dissolution
and that if something were not done the United States would be no
more. "Between October 1, 1785, and January 31, 1786, Congress had
a quorum on only 10 days, and never were more than seven states
represented. Between October 1, 1785, and April 30, 1786, nine states—
the minimum required to do any serious business—were represented on
only three days."[58] Nor did matters improve in the ensuing months.
Something had to be done.

But how should they proceed? Should they revise the Articles and submit them as amendments? (That would have required the approval of each and every one of the states.) Or, should they devise a new constitution? If the latter, did the convention have the authority to do it? The language of the call by Congress specified that the convention was "for the sole and express purpose of revising the Articles." Some of the states included much the same language in the commissions to the delegates. On the other hand, other states gave a much broader commission. For example, Georgia authorized its delegates "for the Purposes of revising and discussing all such Alterations and farther Provisions as may be necessary to render the Federal Constitution adequate to the Exigencies of the Union."[9]

The question came up several times in the convention, but it was not much debated. While sentiment for revising remained strong among some until the presentation of the New Jersey or Small States' Plan, the question was usually dismissed as soon as it was raised. Many thought that they had the task of coming up with the best plan of government they could devise, that their task was to preserve the union, and they should not be detained from doing so over legalistic questions about their authority. In any case, the convention had no power to impose anything on anyone. Whatever they devised would have to be ratified by the country. Thus, although some of the provisions in the Articles appear in their completed plan, what they produced was essentially a new constitution.

Granted, then, that the convention was assigned a task which in the judgment of many of those assembled required making a new constitution, what would be the form and powers of the new government? Edmund Randolph presented a plan during the early days of the convention, known both as the Virginia Plan or Large States' Plan. It called for a general government of three branches: legislative, executive, and judicial. But there was much to get out of the way before even this much would be agreeable. The most crucial change advanced, and eventually achieved, was to have the general government act directly on the people. The government must have the power to tax if it was to be effective. It must also be able to enforce its laws on individuals. In short, the government must be given the power to use force to collect its taxes and exact obedience to its laws.

But how could this be done? Neither history nor theory provided much help in doing this. As matters stood, the United States was a confederation in which each of the states retained the bulk of its independence and sovereignty. How could the United States government use force on individuals without destroying the independence and sovereignty of the states? There was widespread doubt at the beginning of the convention that it could be done. Several of the leaders proposed at the outset that the powers of government be concentrated in the general government and that the states be made subordinate subdivisions of it. But this would never do. The states must be preserved in their full vigor, as speaker after speaker arose at one time or another to tell the delegates to the convention. Even those who were strongest for a consolidated government admitted the need for strong local governments. Nor could anyone doubt that the people were much more attached to the state governments than to a general one. Yet if the states retained their power, how could the union have the necessary power? Equally important, would they not use that power to break up the union?

A part of the difficulty stemmed from the fact that the more learned members of the convention were struggling with the doctrine of *sovereignty*. They had inherited this doctrine with their European background. The idea of sovereignty was feudal and was bound up with monarchy. That is, the monarch was sovereign, i.e., exercised power over a given territory or country. The theory took hold in that setting that sovereignty could not be divided. There must be one, and only one, sovereign over a land. The states already claimed sovereignty over the territory they controlled. For example, Georgia headed its documents with this claim: "The State of Georgia by the grace of God, free,

Edmund Randolph
(1753-1813)

Randolph was born in Virginia, educated at William and Mary, was in the Continental Army briefly, served in the Continental Congress, was a delegate to the Annapolis Convention, served a term as governor of Virginia, was a delegate to the Constitutional Convention where he presented the Virginia Plan which was a primary basis of the Constitution, was the first Attorney General of the United States and the second Secretary of State. He was a prominent lawyer in his native state, and the son and grandson of men who served as the king's attorneys in Virginia. Although Randolph played a leading role in forging the United States Constitution, he refused to sign and at first opposed its adoption. However, in the Virginia convention he favored and helped to secure its ratification.

Sovereign and Independent.'' If all this be accepted, how could a United States government exercise power over the citizens of a state?

A large part of the task of the convention was somehow to reconcile these conflicting claims. They had to reconcile the claims of the large states as well as the small ones, the North as well as the South, and the east coast as well as the new territory beyond the mountains. Above all, they must find some means to cement the union more firmly. To effect these changes, they needed all the guidance from the past they could bring to the effort as well as much creative imagination.

The convention was organized in such a way as to allow the fullest and freest debate of all questions possible. In effect, the convention was shut off from the outside world. Its deliberations were held behind closed doors; no record of what was said or being considered there was to be released without the approval of the convention. No visitors or reporters were permitted to attend the sessions, and delegates were urged not to provide information to those outside the convention. There was nothing amiss in these precautions or in the secrecy; there was no plot to impose a new government on the country. Their plan for a government could only go into effect after it had been approved in a prescribed manner. What the secrecy enabled people to do was to introduce ideas, abandon them, take positions and change, without being called to account politically for what they had said. Actually, the substance of the debates did not begin to become known until nearly 50 years later, when James Madison's voluminous notes on the debates were released after his death.

Strict rules were adopted so that the convention could go about its work effectively. For example:

> Every member rising to speak, shall address the President; and whilst he shall be speaking, none shall pass between them, or hold discourse with another, or read a book, pamphlet or paper....
>
> A member shall not speak oftener than twice without special leave, upon the same question; and not the second time, before every other, who had been silent, shall have been heard, if he wish to speak.[60]

The convention operated on the rule that no decision on any part of the constitution should be considered final until the whole constitution was complete. That way, new parts could be adjusted to those already considered as the work proceeded.

Voting was by states in the convention, with each state having one vote. If the delegation of a state were equally divided on a question, that state would have no vote on that particular question. If the states were equally divided, the motion would be lost. The decision to vote by states was a concession to the small states at the beginning of the convention.

The Compromises

The Constitution has been described as the result of a "bundle of compromises." So far as it goes, the description is fairly accurate. It would be misleading, however, to conclude that principle was necessarily being compromised. On the contrary, the men often arrived at a high principle by yielding ground on their particular interests. Sometimes, too, principles had to be joined and meshed with others to reach higher ground. For example, the Founders generally subscribed to the doctrine of the separation of powers. Yet if the branches of government were entirely separate, i.e., independent, of one another they would lack the means for checking and balancing one another, which is the overriding purpose of the separation. Thus, they compromised to some extent on the separation in order to make the checks effective.

There were many compromises in the course of the convention. Indeed, hardly a proposal was made that did not come in for more or less extensive debate, and many issues were settled by debate. For example, the length of the term of members of the Senate came up several times. The first proposal to gain much following was that the terms of senators be for seven years. Despite the fact that many thought elections ought to be more frequent and terms shorter, the argument prevailed that one branch of the legislature needed extensive experience to offset the other. Let the members of the House stand for election frequently, and the Senate for a much longer term. However, those favoring frequent elections were partially satisfied by having one-third of the Senate elected periodically. That decided, seven-year terms would not be appropriate, since seven is not divisible into three whole numbers. Both six- and nine-year terms were then proposed. Nine-year terms were reckoned to be too long, and the motion for that failed to gain a majority of the states. Thus, six years was finally arrived at as a compromise figure.

One issue that came up time after time and looked as if it would never be settled was who should appoint or elect the president. A whole range of possibilities were canvassed, from appointment by the Congress or one or the other houses to appointment by the governors of the states to appointment by the state legislatures to election by the voters to election by an especially chosen electoral college. The compromise finally reached was an intricate one. The president is chosen by an electoral college, themselves elected on a basis determined by the legislatures of the states. Each elector was to vote for two persons, one of whom must be from a different state than the elector. The person receiving the highest number of votes, provided he had a majority, would be president, and the one receiving the next highest number would be vice president. However, if there was a tie, or if no person received a majority, the election would go to the House of Representatives, which would elect a president from among the candidates voting by states. Each state is allowed a number of electors equal to the number of senators and representatives combined from that state.

But the one issue which appeared to be beyond compromise, which threatened to bring the convention to a standstill, was that of whether representation in Congress should be by states or in proportion to population (or wealth). All other issues were dwarfed by this one question. The Virginia Plan, which was presented first, called for some sort of proportional representation in both houses. The New Jersey Plan, presented by William Patterson, was really only a revision of the Articles of Confederation. It provided for representation by states, as in the Congress that then existed. Much was involved in this question. The larger states were hardly prepared to give a government the power to tax in which neither wealth nor population were represented. On the other hand, the smaller states were determined to maintain their equality in the union. The very existence of the states, and especially the smaller ones, would be threatened by a union in which only population was represented.

The debate on this and related matters went on for weeks with no resolution in sight. Some began to despair that anything would ever be worked out. Benjamin Franklin proposed at that juncture that the daily sessions of the convention be opened by prayer. Franklin pointed out that:

> In the beginning of the Contest with Great Britain when we were sensible of danger we had daily prayer in this room for the divine protection. —Our prayers, Sir, were heard, & they were graciously answered.... And have we now forgotten that powerful friend? Or do we imagine that we no longer need His assistance? I have lived, Sir, a long time, and the longer I live, the more convincing proofs I see of this truth—*that God Governs in the affairs of men.* And if a sparrow cannot fall to the ground without His notice, is it probable that an empire can rise without His aid? We have been assured, Sir, in the sacred writings, that "except the Lord build the House they labour in vain that build it." I firmly believe this....[61]

Probably, most of the men gathered in convention firmly believed it, too, but they adjourned for the day without taking action. Still, these stirring words must have had some impact. A compromise was worked out. It is known as the Great or Connecticut Compromise. It resolved the question of representation by having the members of the House of Representatives apportioned on the basis of population and each of the states having an equal representation in the Senate.

Another sticky question was whether or not slaves should be counted as a part of the population. Since they could not vote or otherwise participate in political activities, a good case could be made that they should not be counted at all in the census. But since they might be subject to a tax, either as property or on the basis of a per capita (head, poll) tax, there was strong feeling in the lower Southern states that they be counted. Many from the North objected, but a compromise was reached. Each slave was to be counted as three-fifths of a person. There was widespread objection to giving slavery constitutional standing by mentioning it in the Constitution, so slaves were referred to as "other Persons." The decision to count them as three-fifths of a person was a pure compromise; any other fraction would have made as little and as much sense. A similar compromise was worked out about importing slaves. There was to be no restriction on importing such persons as any state might wish until the year 1808. The only thing going for that particular year was that it was 20 years from the date the Constitution might be expected to go into effect.

The Form of the Government

The United States Constitution was a major breakthrough in the establishment of government. It was a breakthrough in that it clothed the government authorized with governmental powers yet limited them to those granted. It was a breakthrough in that it went beyond the confederation to a new form of government. It was a breakthrough in that it limited the powers of the states. It was a breakthrough in that it provided for bringing new territory into the union by admitting new states on an equal standing with the old.

That is not to say that the delegates gathered at Philadelphia in 1787 created something entirely new out of thin air. On the contrary, they relied heavily on past experience, their own and that of others recorded in history. They borrowed forms from their own state constitutions, from colonial charters, the listing of powers from the Articles of Confederation, from the British constitution, and from much that had been done in modern and ancient Europe. But the Constitution was not simply a hodgepodge of old and new elements thrown together haphazardly. Rather, it was a judicious combination of the old with carefully crafted innovations. The stately, but simple, rhythms of the Constitution as it came from the committee on style meshed old and new into a symphonic whole, providing the plan for an empire for liberty.

1. A Mixed Government

Although it is not customary to refer to the United States government as a mixed government, it helps to understand the government that was provided. The Founders understood the idea, for there were many indirect references to it in the convention. The formulation was made by thinkers in ancient Greece. They maintained that there are three pure forms of rule or ways to be governed. There is monarchy, rule by one; aristocracy, rule by a few; democracy, rule by many. A mixed government is one which combines elements from each of these, and Aristotle held that a mixed government is best.

The three elements appear clearly in the executive and legislative branches. The executive branch is *monarchical* in character. That is, it has one head, the president, and he is responsible for the decisions and actions of the executive branch. If the powers of the president are increased, the government is made more monarchical and tends toward monarchy (though not necessarily hereditary monarchy). The Senate was conceived as the *aristocratical* branch, for its members are few. The House of Representatives was thought of as the *democratical* branch, for it was more numerous than the others, was based on population, was frequently elected, and was elected by the voters.

The Founders did not, of course, provide for or intend to create either a monarchy, aristocracy, or democracy. They were, almost to a man, opposed to monarchy. Indeed, if there was one feature of British government they despised most, it was that of a hereditary monarch. They were equally opposed to a hereditary aristocracy, and took care to guard against one arising in the United States. As for a direct democracy, they believed the extent of the country too great to permit. Besides, they did not think popular rule desirable. Alexander Hamilton said, "The voice of the people has been said to be the voice of God; and, however generally this maxim has been quoted and believed, it is not true to fact. The people are turbulent and changing; they seldom judge or determine right."[62] Moses Ames of Massachusetts, who had experience with direct popular rule in town meetings, declared in the ratifying convention held in his state: "It has been said that a pure democracy is the best government for a small people who assemble in person.... It may be of some use in this argument...to consider, that it would be very burdensome, subject to faction and violence; decisions would often be made by surprise [hastily], in...passion, by men who either understand nothing or care nothing about the subject; or by interested men [hoping for personal gain].... It would be a government not by laws, but by men."[63] In short, they wanted a government that would be neither a monarchy, aristocracy, nor democracy. Instead, they wanted a mixed government with features drawn from each but in which none of these would predominate.

To prevent the domination of one branch by another and enable them to check one another effectively, the Founders came to believe that each body or branch should have a separate and distinct source of power. Only thus would they be sufficiently independent of one another. Yet what electorates could they have so as to have distinct sources? In England there were classes: the monarchy was hereditary; the lords spiritual and temporal composed the House of Lords; and townspeople and gentry were the source of power in the House of Commons. But Americans neither wished to nor had a hereditary class system. What they hit upon was this. The House of Representatives would be chosen by the people generally; the Senate by the state legislatures, thus representing the state governments; the president by an electoral college, chosen for the purpose and in a manner directed by state legislatures. To complete the system, members of the Supreme Court were to be appointed by the president with the advice and consent of the Senate. By these devices, they provided for a mixed government.

2. A Federal System of Government

Our federal system of government was invented, so to speak, at the Constitutional Convention. No such system had existed before 1787. Even the word "federal" changed in meaning in 1787-1788 to accommodate the new system. "Federal" is derived from confederation, and before this time it was used as an adjective to describe a confederation. For example, Richard Henry Lee, in opposing the ratification of the new Constitution, said that the "object has been all along to reform our federal system...."[64] He could only have been referring to the system under the Articles of Confederation. What happened can be described this way. Those who favored ratification of the Constitution tried to downplay the extent of the innovation involved in it. Therefore, they referred to it as federal and themselves as federalists. The name stuck, and as the understanding increased that it was a distinctive system of government, a federal government began to be contrasted with a confederation. What the Founders did was mingle elements of a national government with those of a confederation and call it federal. A present-day writer notes that the "United States is regarded by many students as the archetype of a federal system....Even general definitions of the term seem to derive from the American model."[65] That is as it should be, for Americans invented it.

Actually, the federal system of government comprises both the general or central and state governments. Although the general or national government has come to be called *the* federal government, that does not accurately describe the relationship. Both the state and national governments are full-fledged governments. The powers of government are *dispersed* in the United States. This system extends the check and balance (or separation of powers) idea to coordinate governments, each exercising the power of government over the citizens. The national government checks the states by exercising certain powers itself, and the Constitution prohibits the states to exercise specified powers. The states check the central government both by its dependence upon them (for elections and the like) and by having powers reserved to them alone.

The most important check of the states upon the central government, however, was supposed to be that the state legislatures elected the members of the Senate and that each of the states was represented by an equal number of senators. The idea was that the state governments (not simply the states as geographical units) would be represented in the Senate. In the debates in the convention, election of the Senate by state legislatures was several times explained as a means for the states to defend themselves from and check the national government. Hugh Williamson of North Carolina "professed himself a friend of such a system as would secure the existence of the State Governments." George Mason of Virginia declared himself strongly in favor of "allowing the State Governments the [means of] self-defence. If they are to be preserved," he said, "as he conceived to be essential, they certainly ought to have this power, and the only mode left of giving it to them was by allowing them to appoint the 2nd branch of the National Legislature."[66] Earlier he had argued the same point on the grounds that "The State Legislatures...ought to have some means of defending themselves against encroachments of the National Government. In every other department we have studiously endeavored to provide for its self-defence. Shall we leave the States alone unprovided with the means for this purpose?"[67] The convention did not, of course, for it provided for the Senate to be elected by the state legislatures.

Within this federal system of counterpoised state and national governments, the convention settled the question of divided sovereignty, so far as it was settled. The Constitution does not grant sovereignty to any government. The general government's acts are, of course, the "supreme law of the land" when they are done in keeping with the Constitution. But the United States government is a government limited to the enumerated powers granted to it. In a similar fashion, the state governments are denied many of the powers and are limited governments. Neither is sovereign. In one of the earliest Supreme Court decisions, Chief Justice John Jay argued that sovereignty resides in the people of the country. "Here we see the people acting as sovereigns of the whole country," he said; "and in the language of sovereignty, establishing a constitution by which...the state governments should be bound...; and the constitution of the United States is likewise a compact made by the people of the United States to govern themselves as to general objects...."[68] It might be most appropriate to say that in the United States the general government has a *jurisdiction* and that each of the states has a jurisdiction, but that sovereignty, so far as it exists, remains with the people.

3. Republican Government

The world is very nearly full to overflowing with republics today. Except for the Scandinavian and Low countries and the United Kingdom, which are still called monarchies, virtually every country in the world styles itself a republic now. The situation was quite different in 1787. Then, about the only country in the world that might have been called a republic was Switzerland. Indeed, the Founders looked back to ancient Rome, to the days of the republic, for their main model for a republic. At the time of the writing of the Constitution, republics were contrasted with monarchies or kingdoms. They could also be contrasted with direct democracies.

The Founders took great care that the government provided in the Constitution conformed to republican principles, and they were so devoted to the idea that they also included a provision requiring that the United States guarantee that the state governments should be republican in character. A republic is "a state in which the supreme power rests in the body of the citizens entitled to vote and is exercised by representatives chosen directly or indirectly by them." The essential features are: (1) that the government be *popular* in origin, and (2) that power be exercised by *representatives*. James Madison said, "we may define a republic to be...a government which derives all its powers directly or indirectly from the great body of the people, and is administered by persons holding their offices during pleasure, for a limited period, or during good behavior."[69]

For a government to be republican in character, it must be based on popular consent from the governed. On this point, all were agreed. But above all what the Founders wanted was to establish a good government. And to do that they generally believed it was necessary to bring to bear upon governing the best ideas, the best minds, and men of the highest capabilities and motives. Madison called the process by which this was to be done "the policy of refining the popular appointments by successive filtrations."[70] Therefore, in the plan they devised they provided not only for representation but also a filtering of the popular will through successive electoral and appointive checks. For example, the members of the Senate were to be chosen by state legislatures. The state legislatures themselves were chosen by popular vote. Thus, a filtering, so to speak, could be expected to take place, or so they thought. The filtering to arrive at judicial appointments was even more extensive. The president, who appointed judges, was to be elected by an electoral college, whose members might be appointed by state legislatures, themselves chosen by popular vote. Their appointment would go through further straining by the advice and consent of the Senate which was necessary to its completion. This filtration and straining was an essential part of republican government, as conceived by the Founders.

Ratification of the Constitution

The debates of the convention were finally over. The committee on style had rendered the Constitution into its final form. The state delegations present and voting in the convention gave their unanimous approval by states to the finished product. Only a very few individuals could not bring themselves to sign the document. According to James Madison's account, Benjamin Franklin made the last public remarks of the gathering. They were words of hope from the oldest person present. Madison described it this way:

> Whilst the last members were signing it, Doctor Franklin looking toward the President's Chair, at the back of which a sun happened to be painted, observed to a few members near him, that Painters have found it difficult to distinguish in their art [between] a rising [and] a setting sun. "I have," said he, "often in the course of the Sessions, and the vicissitudes of my hopes and fears as to its issue, looked at that behind the President without being able to tell whether it was rising or setting: But now at length I have the happiness to know that it is a rising and not a setting sun.[71]

The date was September 17, 1787. All who would having signed, the convention adjourned *sine die.*

The convention sent its work, the Constitution, to the Congress. It was accompanied by a resolution requesting the Congress to submit the Constitution to each of the states, asking that they hold conventions and that delegates to the convention be chosen in an election. When nine of the states ratified it, the two-thirds required, they further recommended that the Constitution be put into operation by holding elections for officers to serve under it. Congress submitted the Constitution to the states September 28, 1787, and most states scheduled elections and

REDEUNT SATURNIA REGNA.

On the erection of the **Eleventh PILLAR** *of the great Na-*
tional DOME, we beg leave most sincerely to felicitate " OUR DEAR COUNTRY."

The *FEDERAL EDIFICE.*

ELEVEN STARS, in quick succession rise—
ELEVEN COLUMNS strike our wond'ring eyes,
Soon o'er the *whole,* shall swell the beauteous DOME,
COLUMBIA's boast—and FREEDOM's hallow'd home.
  Here shall the ARTS in glorious splendour shine !
And AGRICULTURE give her stores divine !
COMMERCE refin'd, dispense us more than gold,
And this new world, teach WISDOM to the old—
RELIGION here shall fix her blest abode,
Array'd in *mildness,* like its parent GOD !
JUSTICE and LAW, shall endless PEACE maintain,
And the " SATURNIAN AGE," *return again.*

A Federalist Cartoon. *The Massachusetts Centinel* of Boston, August 2, 1788,
ran the above cartoon after New York's ratification of the Constitution. Only two
of the thirteen states have yet to ratify. A hand is shown lifting the North Carolina
"pillar" into place, and the caption says "Rise it will." The Rhode Island pillar
is broken but the caption says "The foundation [is] good—it may yet be saved."

conventions quickly. Only two states held out for any extended period
of time: North Carolina held a convention in the middle of 1788, but it
adjourned without taking action; Rhode Island refused to call a convention until 1790, well after the new government was operating.

Most states ratified quickly and with impressive majorities. Delaware
was first to ratify in early December, and the vote was unanimous, 30-0.
Pennsylvania followed a few days later, ratifying by a majority of
46-23; before the end of the month, New Jersey voted for ratification,
39-0. The day after the beginning of the New Year, 1788, Georgia gave
its unanimous approval, 26-0; Connecticut approved overwhelmingly
on January 9, 128-40. The vote was close in Massachusetts, 187-168,
but ratification was achieved on February 16. The Maryland vote in
favor of ratification was not even close—it was 63-11, despite the fact
that some of the delegates had opposed many of the measures approved
every step of the way in the convention. Those in favor of ratification
on South Carolina won handily, 149-73, on May 23; New Hampshire
followed on June 21, 57-47.

Nine states had now ratified, and the Constitution could go into effect. But without New York and Virginia, there would be gaping holes

in the Union. New York had been a question mark from the beginning; the state had been only barely represented in the convention, and that only on occasion. Probably, the greatest exposition of the Constitution, *The Federalist*, was written mainly to persuade New Yorkers of the desirability of supporting and ratifying the Constitution. It was published first as a series of newspaper articles and then as a book. The articles were unsigned, but Alexander Hamilton wrote many of them, James Madison several, and John Jay a few. Though the articles were written under the press of circumstances, they have remained as one of the highest achievements in political thinking ever composed.

The Virginia debates were the most extensive and thorough of those held in any state. James Madison took the lead in pressing for ratification, and he was ably assisted by John Marshall as well as others. Patrick Henry was the most tenacious opponent of ratification. The highlights of the convention were Madison's careful and close reasoning matched against Henry's sparkling rhetoric. The convention met for most of June 1787, and when the vote was finally taken, it was 89 to 79 for ratification. New York finally voted for ratification by an even closer vote, 30-27, on July 26. North Carolina finally ratified the Constitution in November 1789, only after a Bill of Rights had been submitted to the state, but by a lopsided vote of 194-77. With all the other states in and under the threat of a boycott, Rhode Island finally held a convention in 1790 which proceeded to ratification by the narrowest possible margin, 34-32.

A Bill of Rights

Although many objections were raised to the Constitution, only one led to a change or really excited the delegates to the state conventions. That one objection was that it did not contain a bill of rights. There were strenuous objections in several conventions to ratifying without such a listing being made a part of the Constitution. Several conventions attached lengthy lists of rights which they urged in resolutions should receive early consideration as amendments.

Alexander Hamilton, in *The Federalist*, number 84, made as complete an answer as he could to those who wanted a bill of rights. He pointed out that, in the first place, important traditional rights were indeed protected in the Constitution, such as the right to a writ of *habeas corpus* and to trial by jury. Moreover, he argued, bills of rights had originally come into being as devices for restraining monarchs, and they did not appear to be so necessary in a republic. But the most ingenious part of his argument is contained in the following:

I go further and affirm that bills of rights, in the sense...they are being contended for, are not only unnecessary in the proposed Constitution but would even be dangerous. They would contain various exceptions to powers which are not granted; and, on this very account, would afford a...pretext to claim more than were granted. For why declare that things shall not be done which there is no power to do? Why, for instance, should it be said that the liberty of the press shall not be restrained, when no power is given by which restrictions may be imposed?[72]

On the other hand, in the Virginia convention Patrick Henry argued that a specific bill of rights was essential. He said that governments regularly assumed all powers not prohibited to them. "It is so in Great Britain," Henry said; "for every possible right, which is not reserved to the people by some express provision or compact, is within the king's prerogative....It is so in Spain, Germany, and other parts of the world."

Whatever the merits of these arguments, and both cases could indeed be made with considerable evidence to back them, there is no reason to doubt that the makers of the Constitution had made a tactical error in omitting a bill of rights. In any case, soon after the first Congress under the new Constitution met, the movement got underway to do something about the omission. James Madison was the spark plug of the effort. He examined the numerous proposals that had come from the state conventions, pondered the question of which rights were in greatest need of protection, and as a member of the first House of Representatives kept bringing the matter up until the House consented to act upon them. Moreover, Madison served on the committee which drew up the proposals as well as on the joint House-Senate committee which gave final form to the amendments. He took much of the responsibility for reducing the number and took the lead in the effort, as he said, to "confine ourselves to an enumeration of simple, acknowledged principles," for by so doing, ratification will meet with but little difficulty."[73]

The Bill of Rights was submitted to the states in September of 1789 and got enough state ratifications to go into effect in December of 1791. Twelve amendments were submitted, but two were not approved. The first of these dealt with apportioning representatives in the Houses and would have fitted poorly in a bill of rights. The second laid down rules about determining the pay of members of Congress and would have been equally ill-placed at the head of an enumeration of rights and privileges. Madison had hoped to get an amendment passed which would have restricted the states as well as the general government from violating basic rights, but this proposal was turned down in the Senate.

Chapter 6

The Fruits of Independence

We the People of the United States, in order to...secure the Blessings of Liberty to ourselves and our Posterity, do ordain and establish this Constitution *for the United States of America.*

—Preamble to the Constitution

Interwoven as is the love of liberty with every ligament of your hearts, no recommendation of mine is necessary to fortify or confirm the attachment.

—George Washington, 1796

Liberty, in its genuine sense, is security to enjoy the effects of our honest industry and labors, in a free and mild government, and personal security from all illegal restraints.

—Richard Henry Lee, 1787

Freedom of trade, or unrestrained liberty of the subject to hold or dispose of *his property as he pleases, is absolutely necessary to the prosperity of every community, and to the happiness of all individuals who compose it.*

—Pelatiah Webster, 1791

The Constitution of 1787 was a culmination. It was the culmination of a decade of constitution making in the states and for the United States. It was the culmination of several long traditions. For one, it was the culmination of a British tradition of having written acknowledgements and guarantees of rights and liberties. For another, it was the culmination of a colonial tradition of having governments based upon charters. And for yet another, it was the fruition of the Judeo-Christian and Protestant practice of appealing to the precise written word. The Constitution brought to fertile fruition, too, the natural law philosophy. The natural rights doctrine, which held a central place in the justification of revolt against British rule, now served as a basis for protecting rights and freeing people under independence.

That is a way of saying that liberty was the great motivating theme of these years. The desire to preserve and extend their liberty moved the

Patriots to break from England, to fight a War for Independence, and to establish their own governments. The constitution making of these years was animated by the determination to establish liberty more firmly upon these shores. Of course, those who participated in these activities were under the sway of a whole range of motives, ranging from the noble to ordinary to sometimes base ones, as people always are. But what distinguished them, surely, was the steadfast determination to establish liberty.

An Empire for Liberty

After the adoption of the Constitution of 1787 the United States was in some respects like a nation and in others like an empire. In the political terms of the time, it was a federal union. It resembled a nation in that there was a central government which could act directly on the people, and they on it, in limited ways. It resembled an empire in that it was composed of several states with their own governments, and these were often distinct from one another in the ethnic makeup of the inhabitants, in prevailing religious practices, in their different products, and in at least some of their customs and traditions. In these latter respects, it was not simply a nation. But the United States was not conceived as an empire, either, on the pattern of the Roman Empire, say, or the British Empire. Although there was a large area of the trans-Appalachian west which the United States controlled in the manner of an empire, there was no intention to perpetuate the area as a subordinate region. This was made clear from the outset.

Actually, the basic arrangements in the Northwest ordinances were not disturbed in the United States Constitution. But what should be done with the western territory was still treated as a live issue. The most basic issue that was discussed was whether new states in the west would be admitted as equals with the original states. For example, Gouverneur Morris argued vigorously in the Constitutional Convention that they should not. He feared that in time the western states would outnumber the eastern states; "he wished therefore to put it in the power of the latter to keep a majority of votes in their own hands." He summed up such case as he could make this way: "The busy haunts of men not the remote wilderness are the proper school of political talents. If the Western people get the power into their hands, they will ruin the Atlantic interests. The back [country] members are always averse [opposed] to the best measures."[74]

On this occasion, however, Morris was outpointed by the leaders of the Virginia delegation. George Mason said: "If the Western States are to be admitted into the Union, they must be treated as equals and subjected to no degrading discriminations. They will have the same pride and other passions which we have, and will either not unite with or will speedily revolt from the Union, if they are not in all respects placed on an equal footing with their brethren.'' Edmund Randolph declared that it was entirely inadmissible "that a larger and more populous district of America should hereafter have less representation than a smaller and less populous district.'' Madison agreed that "with regard to the Western States he was clear that no unfavorable distinctions were admissible, either in point of justice or policy.''[75] So, when new states come into the union they would come in on the same terms as existed for the original states.

In the usual sense of empire, then, the Constitution provided for the dissolution of empire by admitting new states into the union. But in a larger and less precise sense, the Founders of the United States had a vision, as historians Dumas Malone and Basil Rauch described it in the title of a textbook, of an *Empire for Liberty*. Or, in the words of Thomas Jefferson, they sought to provide for "Such an Empire for Liberty as...has never [been] surveyed since the Creation.'' That is, it would be such a land composed of numerous and diverse states in which peoples of many backgrounds, faiths, and pursuits could live in liberty and at peace with one another.

Limited Government

The Founders believed that for people to have liberty and enjoy their rights governments must be limited and restrained. They believed that government is necessary, of course. It is necessary because men without government would do violence to one another; the strong would prey upon the weak; the clever would take unjust advantage of others; disorder would prevail. Or, to put it another way, man is a fallen creature and must be restrained from harming others. But governments are made up of men as well, and those who govern are given unusual power over others. It is especially important, then, that government be limited and restrained. If men were angels, Madison observed, they would have no need of government. And if they had angels to govern them, there would be no need of limiting the government. But those are not the conditions that prevail: there are fallible men to be governed and fallible men to govern them. That being the case, they believed that government should be limited.

Indeed, there probably have never been a people more jealous of their rights or more aware of the dangers of government to them than were Americans in the late 18th century. The documents of this period are replete with warnings about the dangers of extensive or unrestrained government power. John Dickinson stated that it was his conviction "that every free state should incessantly watch and instantly take alarm on any addition being made to the power exercised over them." Thomas Jefferson maintained that "The natural progress of things is for liberty to yield and government to gain ground."[77] John Adams wrote Thomas Jefferson in 1777 congratulating him on the fact that Virginia had been able to fill its quota for the Continental Army without resorting to the draft, for he said that a draft "is a dangerous Measure, and only to be adopted in great Extremities, even by popular Governments." He had observed, he said, that kings gathered armies in this fashion as a means of realizing their own ambitions.[78] Power was the danger, not simply the form of government, according to Richard Henry Lee. He thought "that unbridled passions produce the same effect, whether in a king, nobility, or a mob. The experience of all mankind has proved the...disposition to use power wantonly. It is therefore as necessary to defend an individual against the majority in a republic as against the king in a monarchy."[79]

The dangers of government were fully rehearsed in the Constitutional Convention. For example, Rufus King of Massachusetts objected to setting a date for Congress to meet each year because he "could not think there would be a necessity for a meeting every year. A great vice in our system was that of legislating too much."[80] Roger Sherman wanted to make the President absolutely dependent on Congress because "An independence of the Executive...was in his opinion the very essence of tyranny...."[81] Benjamin Franklin opposed salaries for those in the executive branch because, he said, "there are two passions which have a powerful influence on the affairs of men. These are ambition and avarice; the love of power, and the love of money. Separately, each of these has great force in prompting men to action; but when united... in the same object, they have in many minds the most violent effects. Place before the eyes of such men, a post of *honour* that shall be at the same time a place of *profit*, and they will move heaven and earth to obtain it."[82]

James Madison pointed out the dangers of unrestricted majority rule: "In all cases where a majority are united by a common interest or passion," he said, "the rights of the minority are in danger."[83]

Some feared that the Congress might extend their power if it were not restrained. Gouverneur Morris favored an absolute presidential veto over legislation. "It is necessary, then," he said, "that the... [President] should be the guardian of the people...against Legislative tyranny...."[84] On the other hand, Madison saw a need for "defending the Community against the incapacity, negligence or perfidy of the chief Magistrate [President]. The limitation of the period of his service, was not a sufficient security. He might lose his capacity after his appointment. He might pervert his administration into a scheme of... oppression. He might betray his trust to foreign powers."[85] In the Virginia Convention, Patrick Henry spoke the fears of those who did not want a strong central government when he declared that "The government will operate like an ambuscade [an ambush]. It will destroy the state governments, and swallow the liberties of the people."[86]

This awareness of the dangers of governmental power, an awareness sharpened by the history of the abuse of those powers over the years, provided the framework for the American limitation of government. It was this that so moved them to separate the powers of government into three branches—the legislative, executive and judicial—, to divide the legislature into two houses, to give the states a check on the government through the Senate, and to disperse power between the general government and the states. But the Founders went beyond separating and dispersing power; they made it necessary for branches to act in concert to accomplish their ends and required a *consensus* for great and important changes.

Legislation has to pass each of the houses separately and be approved by the President to become law. In addition to that, any act is supposed to be in keeping with the powers granted under the Constitution, and the courts may refuse to enforce it. Thus, ultimately, all acts may require the approval of all three branches. That would be majority rule, however. But if the President vetoes a bill, it can only become a law by being passed in each house by at least two-thirds of those voting. That moves closer to the requirement of censensus for government action. For major changes in the government—constitutional changes—there is, in effect, a required consensus. The ordinary route of amendment is for each of the houses to approve a proposed amendment by two-thirds of those voting. Then, the amendment must be submitted to the states, and three-fourths of them must approve the change. All these are procedural requirements which limit the government.

The United States government is limited in two other ways by the Constitution. First, it is a government of enumerated (named) powers. The government is not clothed with all powers but only such as are named in the Constitution or necessary to put into effect those that are named. James Madison described the situation this way: "The powers delegated by the proposed Constitution to the federal government are few and defined. Those...will be exercised principally on external [foreign] objects, as war, peace, negotiation, and foreign commerce; with which last the power of taxation will, for the most part, be connected."[87]

All legislative powers in the United States government are vested by the Constitution in the Congress. Thus, the powers granted to the government are mostly named in the grant of these powers. They are listed in Section 8 of Article I, and include the following:

> The Congress shall have Power to lay and collect Taxes....
> To borrow Money on the credit of the United States;
> To regulate Commerce with foreign Nations, and among the several States, and with the Indian Tribes;
> To establish a uniform Rule of Naturalization....(See the Constitution in the Appendix for other powers granted both to Congress and the other branches.)

The going assumption at the time of the drawing and ratification of the Constitution was that the general government had only such powers as were granted. But it was not left as an assumption; the 10th Amendment spells out the point. It reads, "The powers not delegated to the United States by the Constitution, nor prohibited by it to the States, are reserved to the States respectively, or to the people."

The second way the United States government is limited is by specific prohibitions. For example, taxation is limited in various ways in the Constitution. It required that all direct taxes be apportioned on the basis of population (altered later by the 16th Amendment). Other taxes must be levied uniformly throughout the United States. All taxation must be for the common defense and/or general welfare of the United States, which was not a grant of power but a limitation upon it. Section 9, Article I contains these among other limitations:

> The Privilege of the Writ of *Habeas Corpus* shall not be suspended, unless when in Cases of Rebellion or Invasion the public Safety may require it.
> No Tax or Duty shall be laid on articles exported from any State....
> No Title of Nobility shall be granted by the United States.

In addition to such prohibitions as these the Bill of Rights or first ten amendments to the Constitution consists of limitations on the United States government. As already noted, the fear of government generally, and especially of a central government, resulted in the move for a bill of rights. Many were emphatic about the need for such a list to limit the new government. Thomas Jefferson declared that it was a matter of principle with him "that a bill of rights is what the people are entitled to against every government..., and what no just government should refuse."[88] Patrick Henry insisted that "If you intend to reserve your inalienable rights, you must have the most express stipulation...."[89]

At any rate, the Bill of Rights specifically restricts and limits the United States government. The first Amendment begins in a way to make that crystal clear: "*Congress shall make no law* respecting an establishment of religion, or prohibiting the free exercise thereof; or abridging the freedom of speech," etc. (Italics added.) The others do not point to a specific branch of government that may not act, but it is clear from the language that government is being restricted by them. For example, the fourth Amendment states that "The right of the people to be secure in their persons, houses, papers, and effects, against unreasonable searches and seizures, shall not be violated, and no Warrants shall issue, but upon probable cause...." Since governments are the only body that may legally do such things, the article clearly is limiting government. So it is with the other parts of the Bill of Rights.

Not only is the United States government limited by the Constitution, but the state governments are as well. They are limited, in the first place, by the grant of powers to the United States government, powers which, ordinarily, states may only exercise, if at all, with the approval of Congress. Second, some powers are absolutely denied to the states, e.g., "No State shall enter into any Treaty, Alliance, or Confederation; grant Letters of Marque and Reprisal; coin Money; emit Bills of Credit; make any Thing but gold and silver *Coin* a Tender in Payment of Debts; pass any...Law impairing the Obligation of Contracts, or grant any Title of Nobility."

The central feature of the United States Constitution, then, is the limitation of government.

Freeing the Individual

A major fruit of independence was the freeing of the individual from a variety of government compulsions. Governments were restrained that individuals might be free. That was the thrust of the making of constitutions during these years. The state constitutions were already limiting state governments before the United States Constitution was written. States frequently had their own bills of rights which had as their main purpose the protection of their inhabitants from government. Moreover, many of the restraints which had been imposed under British rule were removed as independence was achieved. Indeed, Americans used the occasion offered by the break from England to remove those restraints on the individual that did not accord with their outlook.

One of those restraints on the individual was compulsory church attendance and the associated taxation and other restrictions supporting an established church. In the main, these restrictions were removed by disestablishing churches. The establishment most readily dispensed with was that of the Church of England. While that church was established in several colonies, it was not popular in most of them, many of its clergy remained loyal to England, and dissenters were numerous in most states. The movement to disestablish the Church of England was greatly aided, too, by the fact that it was a national church; membership in it was tied to loyalty to the king of England. Since Americans could not accept that any longer, the church was speedily disestablished. Several states had no established churches: namely, New Jersey, Rhode Island, Pennsylvania, and Delaware. Even so, they used the opportunity afforded by independence to reduce religious restraints.

The established Congregational church was maintained for several decades in Massachusetts, Connecticut, and New Hampshire. There was, however, some lightening of the load of religious restrictions in these states. The Massachusetts constitution of 1780 affirmed that every man had the right to worship in his own way, that all churches were equal before the law, and tax monies could be used to pay ministers of churches generally. However, attendance in some Christian church was still required, and people were still taxed to pay ministers. New Hampshire made much the same provisions as Massachusetts, but Connecticut clung to as much as the leaders dared of the established church. They did allow dissenters from it to avoid payment of taxes if they could present a certificate from an officer of the church showing that he attended. But the days of formally established churches were ending in New England, too, though disestablishment in the last of these states was not completed until the 1830s.

The constitutions of New Jersey, Georgia, North and South Carolina, Delaware, and Pennsylvania provided that none should be compelled to pay taxes to churches nor attend any service except such as they chose. Virginia, however, made the most thorough-going effort to establish freedom of conscience. This might have been a reaction to the fact that Virginia had the oldest established church in English America and the most rigorously established. Thomas Jefferson, James Madison, and George Mason were leading advocates of religious liberty, but they did not succeed in getting their ideas into law until 1786. This was done by the Virginia Statute of Religious Freedom, which proclaimed religious liberty a natural right. The legally effective portion of the statute reads this way:

> That no man shall be compelled to frequent or support any religious worship, place, or ministry whatsoever, nor shall be enforced, restrained, molested, or burdened in his body or goods,

nor shall otherwise suffer on account of his religious opinions or belief; but that all men shall be free to profess and by argument to maintain, their opinion in matters of religion, and that the same shall in no wise diminish, enlarge, or affect their civil capacities.[90]

In large, this was what Americans were coming to think of as religious liberty.

The Constitution of the United States left to the states the power to determine as they would whether they would have an established church or to what extent religious liberty would prevail. The first Amendment simply prohibited Congress to establish a religion or interfere with its free exercise. The states did, however, move to disestablish churches and to reduce religious restrictions, as already noted, thus freeing people in the matter of conscience.

Many of the provisions in the state bills of rights, as well as the Bill of Rights for the United States, were guarantees of legal practices protecting the freedom of the individual that were a part of the British tradition. The Virginia Bill of Rights, adopted June 12, 1776, was both a model for such documents and illustrates the point. It guaranteed trial by jury in both criminal and civil cases, prohibited excessive bail and fines, declared general warrants to be oppressive, and acknowledged freedom of the press. The protections of persons accused of a crime were stated in detail:

> That in all capital or criminal prosecutions a man hath a right to demand the cause and nature of his accusation, to be confronted with the accusers and witnesses, to call for evidence in his favour, and to a speedy trial by an impartial jury of his vicinage [the vicinity of where he lives] , without whose unanimous consent he cannot be found guilty, nor can he be compelled to give evidence against himself; that no man may be deprived of his liberty, except by the law of the land or the judgment of his peers.[91]

In addition to these protections, the Massachusetts Declaration of Rights of 1780 provided for the right to bear arms, the right of peaceful assembly, the prohibition of *ex post facto* laws and bills of attainder, among others. Most of the above provisions are also in the United States Constitution.

There were some major changes from British practice, however, particularly in the matter of ownership of real property. Several feudal restraints on property were removed. Primogeniture—the legal provision requirement that if the owner died without a will the bulk of the estate went to the eldest son—was abolished generally. The most general encumbrance on property was the quitrent, an annual payment due to king or proprietors on land. Such claims as still existed at the time of independence were speedily extinguished, and land thereafter was generally owned in "fee simple." Entail—legal provisions that estates could not be broken up—, where it existed, was abolished. Such royal prerogatives as the right of the monarch to white pines (for shipbuilding) on private land were, of course, nullified.

A part of the freeing of the individual, then, was making real property ownership free of government restraints and disposable at will by the individual. Indeed, property in general was carefully protected both in state constitutions and in the United States Constitution. Some later commentators have claimed that the Founders distinguished between what they call "human rights" and property rights and attached greater significance to the former. The evidence for that does not appear in the documents or pronouncements of the time. If anything, they placed more emphasis on property than on other rights of humans, but they certainly did not declare one variety higher than the other.

For example, the Massachusetts Declaration of Rights states:

> All men are born free and equal, and have certain natural, essential, and unalienable rights; among which may be reckoned the right of enjoying and defending their lives and liberties; that of acquiring, possessing, and protecting property; in fine, that of seeking and obtaining their safety and happiness.[92]

The Declaration went on to provide that "No part of the property of any individual can, with justice, be taken from him, or applied to public uses, without his consent, or that of the representative body of the people...."[93] With even greater clarity, the Virginia Bill of Rights says that people "cannot be taxed or deprived of their property for public uses, without their own consent or that of their representatives so elected."[94]

In any case, the tendency of the declarations and constitutions of these years was the freeing of individuals from governmental control of their affairs and protecting them in their rights. It has rightly been pointed out, of course, that where Negro slavery continued to exist it was a glaring exception to this tendency. Some have even gone so far as to accuse the Founders of hypocrisy in professing to believe in the equal rights of all men and acquiescing in the continuation of slavery. It strikes us as strange that Thomas Jefferson, who penned the stirring statement "that all men are created equal", should have been himself a slaveholder. But even in the case of chattel slavery the trend of the 1780s was toward the freeing of the individual, and if the trend and sentiment in the direction of ending slavery had continued apace the apparent contradiction would have been resolved.

Some states began to act with the purpose of eventually ending slavery almost as soon as independence from Britain was declared. In 1776, Delaware prohibited the importation of slaves and removed all restraints on their manumission (freeing by the owner). Virginia stopped slave imports in 1778; Maryland adopted a similar measure in 1783. Both states permitted manumission. In 1780, Pennsylvania not only prohibited further importation of slaves but also provided that after that date all children born of slaves should be free. Similar enactments were made in the early 1780s in New Hampshire, Connecticut, and Rhode Island. In Massachusetts, the supreme court ruled that on the basis of that state's constitution of 1780 slavery was abolished there. Even North Carolina (the greatest resistance to freeing slaves was in the lower South) moved to discourage the slave trade in 1786 by taxing heavily such slaves as were imported after that time. In order to protect free Negros, Virginia made it a crime punishable by death for anyone found guilty of selling a freed Negro into slavery. As already noted, the Northwest Ordinance of 1787 prohibited slavery in the Northwest territory.

Some of the Founders were open and outspoken in their opposition to slavery. Gouverneur Morris denounced slavery in no uncertain terms in the Constitutional Convention. "He never would concur in upholding domestic slavery," the Pennsylvanian said. "It was a nefarious institution. It was the curse of heaven on the States where it prevailed....Proceed southwardly and every step you take through the great region of slaves presents a desert increasing, with the increasing proportion of these wretched beings....He would," he said, "sooner submit himself to a tax for paying for all the negroes in the United States, than saddle posterity with...a Constitution [which counted slaves in apportioning representatives in Congress]"[95]

George Mason, himself a Virginian, had this to say about slavery in the Convention:

> ...Slavery discourages arts & manufactures. The poor despise labor when performed by slaves....They produce the most pernicious effect on manners. Every master of slaves is born a petty tyrant. They bring the judgment of heaven on a Country. As nations can not be rewarded or punished in the next world they must be in this. By an inevitable chain of causes & effects providence punishes national sins, by national calamities....He held it essential in every point of view that the General Government should have power to prevent the increase of slavery.[96]

Jefferson had written a warning about the continuation of slavery, which he abhored, in his *Notes on Virginia*. It was a violation of their most basic rights to keep some people in perpetual bondage. "And can the liberties of a nation be thought secure when we have removed their only firm basis, a conviction in the minds of the people that these liberties are the gift of God? That they are not to be violated but with His wrath? Indeed I tremble for my country," he said, "when I reflect that God is just: that His justice cannot sleep forever...."[97]

Madison, writing in defense of the Constitution, said that it would no doubt have been better if the slave trade had been prohibited by the Constitution rather than delaying action until 1808, but he looked forward to the time when "a traffic which has so loudly upbraided the barbarism of modern policy...may terminate forever...."[98]

There is no reason to doubt the sincerity of many of the Founders in wishing an end both to slavery and the slave trade. Moreover, at the earliest date that it could constitutionally Congress prohibited the importation of slaves. Although slaveholders in the lower South were still tenaciously attached to slavery, they were holding out against a tide running in the opposite direction in the 1780s. Even in the lower South, the crops which were so dependent on slave labor—rice and indigo—declined in importance once the break from England was made. Unfortunately, for the abolition of slavery, the cotton gin was invented in the 1790s; cotton became an important fiber; and slavery was revived by the expansion into the Old Southwest.

Free Trade

One of the fruits of independence was the freeing of trade both within the United States and with other peoples around the world. Independence from Britain removed British imposed mercantile restrictions in one swoop. That is not to say that Britain did not continue in various ways to limit American trade after the break. They did, well into the 1790s, at least. But British mercantilism was no longer legally binding on Americans; they could trade with whomever they could and would around the world. Initially, too, the states adopted various restrictions which limited trade within the United States. But the Constitution of 1787 put an end to that.

American belief and sentiments were tending more and more to favor free trade. The freedom of people to trade with whomever they would on mutually agreeable terms seemed to them to be of a piece with freedom for the individual in general. Benjamin Franklin said that "it seems contrary to the nature of Commerce, for Government to interfere in the Prices of Commodities. Trade is a voluntary Thing between

Buyer and Seller, in every article of which each exercises his own Judgment, and is to please himself."[99] Pelatiah Webster, an American economic thinker of this period, declared: "I propose...to take off every restraint and limitation from our commerce. Let trade be as free as air. Let every man make the most of his goods in his own way and then he will be satisfied."[100] Jefferson said that "the exercise of a free trade with all parts of the world" was "possessed by the American...as of natural right...."[101]

Actually, the freedom to trade is a corollary of private property. The right to dispose of property on whatever terms he will to whomever he will is necessarily a part of the full ownership of property. At its fully extended development, it involves for the seller the right to find anywhere in the world that buyer who will make the best offer for his goods, his time, or his services. For the buyer of these, it involves his right to locate the most attractive goods at prices he is willing to pay.

Aside from the break from England, the greatest stride by Americans toward free trade was the ratification of the Constitution. The Constitution provided for a common market throughout the United States. The power to regulate commerce among the states was vested in the United States. Thereafter, the states could not obstruct commerce, and the whole country became in effect, a free trading area. Further, the Constitution provided that states may not tax imports or exports, except for carrying out inspection laws, without the consent of Congress. But to discourage any of that, all money collected had to be paid into the United States Treasury.

The Constitution contains several other provisions promoting a common market throughout the country. Congress is empowered to pass uniform bankruptcy laws, set up standard weights and measures, and establish post offices and post roads. A common currency (or money) is also important for trade to take place easily. So far as the Constitution provides for a common currency, however, it does so by indirection. It authorizes the government to coin money and to regulate its value. It does not authorize the passing of any tender laws (laws making any currency or money legal tender or forcing its acceptance), and it prohibits states to make anything legal tender except gold and silver coins.

Paper money had a well deserved bad reputation at the time of the making of the Constitution. Not only did Americans generally have the recent unsettling experience with the Continental currency, which became worthless, but also several states had in the 1780s flooded the market with virtually worthless paper money. When the states, most notably Rhode Island, adopted laws to force the paper money into circulation, it not only obstructed trade but also endangered property in debts. The subject of paper money came up twice for extended discussion in the Constitutional Convention. It arose once over a proposal to authorize Congress to emit bills of credit (issue paper money). The delegates were overwhelmingly opposed to the proposal. The tenor of the opposition may be gathered from these delegate comments. Oliver Elsworth of Connecticut declared that he "thought this a favorable moment to shut and bar the door against paper money....The power may do harm, never good."[102] George Read of Delaware "thought the words [emit bills of credit], if not struck out, would be as alarming as the mark of the Beast in Revelations." John Langdon of New Hampshire "had rather reject the whole plan [the Constitution] than retain the...words."[103] Voting by states, the delegates omitted the power by a vote of 9 to 2.

Paper money came up again in connection with a proposal to permit the states to emit bills of credit with the consent of Congress. That, too, was overwhelmingly rejected. The states are prohibited to issue paper money. Thus, the only provision for a common currency is in the power of the United States to coin money and the reserved power of the states to make those of gold and silver legal tender.

While the Constitution does not specifically provide for free trade with the rest of the world, its provisions lean in that direction. It does provide that "No Tax or Duty shall be laid on Articles exported from any State." Thus, tariffs on exports are prohibited. Congress is authorized to levy tariffs on imports. In any case, the widespread sentiment in favor of freeing trade set the stage for low tariffs in the early decades of the Republic, and many Americans had come to dislike British mercantilistic restraints too much to wish to impose them on their own trade.

The Voluntary Way

The story of America after 1789, until well into the 20th century, is not so much the story of the doings of government as of people generally. It is the story of freed individuals working, building, growing crops, building factories, clearing the land for farms, organizing churches, providing for families, and doing all those things that make up the warp and woof of life. They did this singly as individuals, as families, and in voluntary groups. This is always to some degree true, of course. The world's work is done by people generally and very little by governments. But governments often play a dominant role in the economic, social, religious, educational, recreational, and community lives of a people. This has been so in the European countries from which American settlers came. It has become the rule once again in most places in the world in the 20th century.

The constitution making cleared the ground for the triumph of the voluntary way in America in the late 18th century. Governments were restrained and individuals were freed to pursue their own devices alone or in voluntary cooperation with others. There is no need to exaggerate the extent of this change, however. The British colonists generally enjoyed considerable liberty, as a result of British tradition and law, of British neglect, and of the remoteness of many people from the oversight of government. The Americans continued much of what they considered to be the best of their British heritage under their new constitutions. Nor was everyone freed nor to the same degree under them. Slaves were still in bondage where slavery was continued and could hardly participate in the voluntary way. Children were, as they usually are, under the authority of their parents or other adults. Women generally were still under the protection and in some respects the authority of men—fathers, older brothers, and husbands—, partners, as adults, ordinarily to men, though in some ways subordinate ones. But these last were family matters, not things under the direction of government.

In large, then, the voluntary way triumphed. Governments still issued charters for some undertakings, but these more often confirmed some voluntary undertaking than initiating it. Even the registry of births and deaths was much more apt to be done in the family Bible than in some government office. As churches were disestablished, religion became a voluntary affair. Attendance, participation, the payment of the clergy, what structures would be built, what services would be held, were matters left to individual and family choice and voluntary cooperation. Education had never been firmly established by government in America. There had been some faltering attempts to do so in New England and New York, but not much came of them. The education of children was largely left to parents, and schools and colleges were set up, when they were, by churches or other voluntary associations or simply by some schoolmaster. So it was, too, in the matter of providing for those in temporary or some longer term need. Most often, extended families provided for orphans, for widows, for the sick, and for the disabled. Institutional charity, such as it was, was most apt to be provided by churches or private gifts.

Under mercantilism, governments had attempted to direct economic activity for their own ends. The British had not only restricted and controlled economic activity but also granted monopolies to chartered companies to engage in specified production or trade. American colonies had sometimes imitated some of these mercantilistic practices. There were still residues of mercantilism at the time of the founding of the United States, but in general Americans preferred voluntary economic activity to that which was government directed. Mostly men started and operated businesses without asking the leave or aid or charters from government. They built ships and plied the seas in trade as they could and would. In short, they tended to follow the voluntary in their economic life.

How America flourished and grew by voluntary cooperation is a story to be told in detail elsewhere. Suffice it to say here that numerous voluntary societies came into being, that religious denominations multiplied and congregations were organized in virtually every community, that schools and colleges became commonplace, and that there were no more enterprising people in the world than were Americans in the 19th century.

Chapter 7

Establishing the Government

[I]t would be...improper to omit in this first official act my fervent supplications to that Almighty Being who rules over the universe, who presides in the councils of nations, and whose aids...can supply every human defect, that His benediction may consecrate to the liberties and happiness of the people of the United States a Government instituted by themselves....

—George Washington's First Inaugural, 1789.

While the observance of good faith, which is the basis of public credit, is recommended by...political expediency, it is enforced by considerations of still greater authority. There are arguments for it which rest on the immutable principles of moral obligation.

—Alexander Hamilton, 1790.

There shall be a firm, inviolable and universal peace, and a true and sincere friendship between his Britannic Majesty, his heirs and successors, and the United States of America....

—Jay's Treaty, 1794.

Chronology

April 1789—Congress organizes.

July 1789—Outbreak of the French Revolution.

September 1789—Federal Judiciary Act.

1790—Hamilton's Report on the Public Credit.

1791—Bank of the United States chartered.

February 1793—France declares war on Great Britain.

April 1793—Washington issues Neutrality Proclamation.

December 1793—Jefferson resigns from Cabinet.

June 1794—Congress passes Neutrality Act.

September 1794—Whiskey Rebellion.

November 1794—Jay's Treaty.

1795—Pinckney's Treaty.

September 1796—Washington's Farewell Address.

December 1796—Adams elected President.

The new government began slowly to take shape during the early months of 1789. Electors who would choose the first President were elected mostly in January of that year. They cast their ballots on February 4. Meanwhile, elections of Representatives and Senators proceeded within the states. Congress was supposed to meet in the city of New York, where the government was then located, on March 4, 1789. But only a few members of either house had arrived by that date. A week later, only six Senators had put in their appearance, and a circular letter was sent around to the others who had been elected urging their attendance. Two weeks more elapsed without a quorum in either house. "The people will forget the new government before it is born," wrote Fisher Ames, an impatient member of Congress from Massachusetts. "The resurrection of the infant will come before its birth." This was unduly pessimistic, however, for both houses had quorums by April 6.

Nor could a President take office until the Senate was organized, for that body had the duty of counting the electoral votes and certifying the election. This was done on April 6, and the Senate confirmed that

Fisher Ames (1758-1808)

Ames was born in Massachusetts, graduated from Harvard, and set up in the practice of law in his native state after the War for Independence. He worked for the ratification of the Constitution and was elected to the House of Representatives in the first and several succeeding Congresses. Ames was a partisan Federalist almost from the beginning, played an active role in verbally flaying Republicans, and generally supported Washington and Adams. His speech in support of Jay's Treaty helped overcome Republican opposition in the House to making the appropriation necessary to put it into effect. His collected writings were published shortly after his death, and they have provided historians with quotable pithy but acid comments on the political activities of that time ever since.

George Washington had been unanimously elected President, and that John Adams would be the first Vice President, though the vote for him had been less than half that for Washington. (At that time, each elector had two votes, but each was cast for a different person, not a different office, as for president and vice president.)

A few days later, April 16, Washington set out by carriage from Mount Vernon to journey to New York City for the inauguration. Along the way on his trip north Washington was greeted with pomp and ceremony and by throngs of people. The Governor of Pennsylvania, Thomas Mifflin, greeted the President-elect at the border of his state and escorted him into Philadelphia with a troop of cavalry. Thousands assembled to cheer Washington on his way. Trenton, New Jersey, however, provided him the most elaborate welcome. There a triumphal arch composed of 13 flower-bedecked pillars straddled the road. In front of it stood 13 maidens in white, each with a flower basket on her arm. As the great man rode into view, now astride a white horse, the maidens burst into song:

> Virgins fair and matrons grave,
> Those thy conquering arm did save,
> Build for thee triumphant bowers;
> Strew, ye fair, his way with flowers,
> Strew your hero's way with flowers.[104]

New York, too, prepared for quite a spectacle for the inauguration on April 30. A splendid procession formed at Washington's residence to escort him to Federal Hall, the place of inauguration. He took the oath of office in front of a crowd, and then went into the Senate chamber, where both houses of Congress were assembled, to deliver his inaugural address. Washington had taken great pains in preparing this address and had practiced the delivery of it before leaving Mount Vernon. Even so, he appears to have had great difficulty giving it utterance. Fisher Ames noted that the President was "grave, almost to sadness; his modesty, actually shaking; his voice deep, a little tremulous, and so low as to call for close attention." Senator Maclay of Pennsylvania declared that "this great man was agitated and embarrassed more than ever he was by the leveled cannon or pointed musket. He trembled, and several times could scarce make out to read."[105]

It is certain that Washington was no orator, nor was he comfortable in attempting to fill the office. But there was more than that involved. There is good reason to believe that he was awed by the office he had undertaken. He was confident of his abilities as a military commander, but he had neither experience nor inclination to be a statesman. Yet nothing would please many of his countrymen but that he serve in the office. Those who approached him about it he tried to discourage. At the age of 56, he said, he had no "wish beyond that of living and dying an honest man on my own farm."[106] But modesty and inclination aside, there was the fact, as he wrote General Knox, that as the man at the helm he faced "an ocean of difficulties."[107]

The Problems of the New Government

The most extensive problem in 1789 was to translate the Constitution into a government. The Constitution was, after all, still a "piece of paper," as they would say, an important piece of paper, no doubt, a paper on which some of the best minds in America had worked diligently. Would it work as they had tried to foresee? It had many experimental features. It contained a vision, a hope, a dream, if you will, or whatever elegant words might be applied to it, but the government which it described was only in the early stages of becoming a reality. Would people obey this government? Would they support it? Would those who came to power in it adhere to the Constitution? These are always vital questions for a government, but they were especially pressing for one that was yet only a plan and a prospect.

One thing was certain: If the Constitution did give rise to the reality of an effective government, it would be done by men. It would be men who breathed the breath of life into the government, who provided the flesh to the bones of the Constitution, who in their contests with one another held the government in check, and who gave impetus and direction to it. But it was neither the majority of men who did this nor even of those who held office in the government. Madison's comment after looking over the roll of those elected to the first Congress may have been somewhat harsh, but it was much to the point: he said that there were not many of them who would take an active part "in the drudgery of the business."[108] That would be done by that few with the tenacity, the ambition, the drive, and the determination to make the government work. Critics abound; those who will labor long and hard are few.

The government under the Constitution inherited little of positive value from the Confederation. Indeed the Confederation was bankrupt in all but name. As L.D. White, who made extensive studies of the early administrations, says: "The government of the Confederation had steadily run down until its movements had almost ceased." Washington "took over almost nothing from the dying Confederation. There *was*, indeed, a foreign office with John Jay and a couple of clerks to deal with correspondence from John Adams in London and Thomas Jefferson in Paris; there *was* a Treasury Board with an empty treasury; there *was* a 'Secretary at War' with an authorized army of 840 men; there were a dozen clerks whose pay was in arrears, and an unknown but fearful burden of debt, almost no revenue, and a prostrate credit. But one could hardly perceive in the winter of 1789 a government of the Union.''[109]

The very extent of the country and the rudimentary conditions of travel was a major problem itself. Although the first census in 1790 revealed that there were less than 4 million people to be governed, they were spread over a vast area. True, the bulk of the population was concentrated on or near the seaboard, but the seaboard stretched for hundreds of miles from Maine to Georgia. Along this great stretch of coast popuiation was located mostly in clumps, but these were frequently separated from one another by great distances. Back of the Atlantic coast was a huge area, generally sparsely inhabited, split by the Appaachians, much of it inhabited by Indians and still in its primeval condition, most of it not even surveyed. Travel, except by boat along the coast, was still a precarious adventure, uncertain and uninviting. "A trip that President Adams made in 1800 from Philadelphia to the new capital site in Washington consumed three full days, and in heavy rain or snow would have been impossible without resorting to horseback."[110] Whether any general government could be extended over so vast a domain was a serious question.

The United States did, indeed, "have a fearful burden of debt." Even after the repudiation of the Continental currency the debts left from the war were large and growing, for not even the interest was usually being paid. The Constitution stated that these debts were to remain valid. In 1790, Alexander Hamilton estimated that the United States owned to foreign creditors $11,710,378, of which $1,640,071 was interest. The principal of the domestic debt he declared was $27,383,917 to which would be added interest arrears in the amount of $13,030,168. States had debts which had been contracted to help in the war effort, too, and there were those who believed that they should be assumed by the United States. The government would only have revenue to deal with these and other expenses when taxes had been levied and collected.

To these difficulties were added those of dealing effectively with foreign powers. The United States had not yet gained the respect of foreign nations, nor would this be easy to do for a republic in a world dominated by monarchies. The prevailing view was that republics were unstable, and especially those over large territories. British troops still held sway in the Old Northwest from forts on the Great Lakes. The Spanish dominated much of the Mississippi River as well as outlets from it. As if all this were not enough, a mob in Paris stormed the Bastille (a prison) on July 14, 1789, signaling the onset of the French Revolution. At first, events in France could be taken as a sign favorable to America. Not only had the French supported the Americans in their contest with England but in its initial stages the French Revolution moved toward representative government. Moreover, they used a rhetoric of natural law and natural rights which bore a family resemblance to that used in America. Moreover, the revolutionaries proclaimed France a republic in 1792, and it looked for a while as though America might have company in that undertaking.

But the differences between the French Revolution and the American were great. It was not only bloody but also turned to the destruction of the basic institutions in France. The governments were short-lived and unstable, and France became aggressive in spreading its cause to other lands. War broke out in 1793 and continued with only brief intervals of peace until 1815. Every effort was made to draw the United States into the quarrels and conflicts, and the early years of the Republic were made exceedingly difficult by the European conflicts.

Establishing the Branches of Government

The Congress had the most immediate tasks involved in getting the government underway. Not only did it have to pass revenue measures to provide money but it also had to provide for departments for the executive branch and set up such a system of courts as it might reckon necessary. Once Congress had been organized, the first order of business was revenue. Appropriately, then, the first act was a tariff on imports, passed July 4, 1789. Though there were some protectionist features to it, the average duties were only 8 percent, making it a tariff for revenue primarily. The going assumption in the Constitutional Convention had been that the government would be financed primarily from proceeds from a tariff, and for many years that was to be the case (along with the sale of public lands). To supplement this levy, a Tonnage Act passed on July 20. This was a tax on goods unloaded from ships in American ports. The rate was 50 cents per ton on foreign shipping and 6 cents a ton on domestic. James Madison took the leadership in getting these and other measures passed from his vantage point as a member of the House.

These things done, the Congress busied itself with fleshing out the executive and judicial departments. The first departments were State, War, and Treasury, in that order, and these were followed shortly by the authorization for a Postmaster General and an Attorney General, although these dignitaries did not yet oversee departments. A Federal Judiciary Act was passed on September 24, 1789, which provided for a Supreme Court with a Chief Justice and five associate justices. Three circuit courts were authorized, each of which was assigned two Supreme Court justices. (In the early years, members of the Supreme Court rode circuit around the country as well as holding court at the seat of the government.) Thirteen district courts were also authorized. This was a decisive move by the Congress. While the Constitution gave the power to set up such courts, the Congress did not have to exert it. It remained an open question until it was done whether state courts would serve as trial courts for Federal cases or whether the United States would have its own trial courts. The decision had now been made.

Washington was determined to get the most able men he could find to fill the posts he had available. One other thing was foremost in his mind: They must be men attached to the new Constitution and determined to make it work. In a word, they must be Federalists. Not Federalists in the sense of a political party, for none existed at that time, but Federalists in the sense of commitment to the new government. He chose Thomas Jefferson to be the first Secretary of State. Among those with experience in foreign affairs and available for the job, Jefferson stood almost alone. Franklin and John Adams both had broader experience, but Franklin was too aged and infirm to be considered, and Adams had been elected Vice President. John Jay was perhaps equally well qualified, but he was destined for another post. Besides, Jefferson was one of the most prominent Americans of his time.

Alexander Hamilton was chosen for what turned out to be the most sensitive position, that of Secretary of the Treasury. Robert Morris recommended him for the post, and Washington was favorably disposed because he had worked with Hamilton during the war. Henry Knox continued in a position he had occupied in the War Department under the Articles of Confederation, now as Secretary of War. He had been Washington's most trusted general and, though Washington had long since become used to the "loneliness at the top," it undoubtedly pleased him to have someone in whom he might confide near at hand. Edmund Randolph, who had finished his term as governor of Virginia, was selected as Attorney General.

John Jay was named as Chief Justice of the Supreme Court. But actually the court did not play a large role in national affairs in the 1790s. Only a few decisions were made on constitutional questions, and no act passed by Congress was nullified. In *Chisholm vs. Georgia*, citizens of South Carolina sued the state of Georgia for the recovery of confiscated property. The Supreme Court rendered a decision against the state, over Georgia's protest that the court had no jurisdiction. It was a futile decision, however, for the decision was followed by the passage of the 11th Amendment, which denied jurisdiction in such cases to the Federal judiciary, and the amendment was eventually ratified. The court was not yet the force it would become under John Marshall.

The major precedents for establishing the government were set in Congress and especially in the executive branch in the 1790s. This was as it should be. While it was generally understood, though some accepted the idea grudgingly, that the courts might nullify acts of Congress and sometimes play a deciding role in constitutional interpretation, the 20th century notion that the courts alone could interpret the Constitution had not even dawned. After all, virtually every decision by Congress and the executive in the early years involved the interpretation of the Constitution. And, interpret it they did, and out of these interpretations arose the government.

These early decisions were most important for they often became precedents for how to do things. Some of the precedents appear trivial now, others more significant. For example, the Senate spent some time under the spur of the presiding officer, John Adams, discussing a proper form of address for the President. A Senate committee actually recommended that Washington be addressed as "His Highness, the President of the United States of America, and Protector of their Liberties." Many in the House of Representatives were outraged, and under Madison's leadership, that body insisted that he be addressed as the Constitution implies, namely as the President of the United States. And so he has been ever since.

There were other questions that could not be answered by a reading of the Constitution. For example, the document says that treaties are to be by the President "by and with the advice and consent of the Senate." But how should the President go about getting the advice of the Senate? Should he go to that body, tell them what he has in mind, then listen to and incorporate their advice into the proposed treaty? That is what Washington thought at first. He went twice to the Senate chamber to discuss a treaty. The Senate was too awed by his presence, however, so that instead of offering advice then and there the treaty was referred to committee. Washington vowed he would not return to the Senate on such a mission, and he did not. He had treaties prepared thereafter, and submitted the completed work to the Senate for approval or rejection. That has been the practice ever since.

The Constitution is silent on the matter of a cabinet for the executive branch. It authorizes Congress to establish departments, for the President to appoint heads with the consent of the Senate, and empowers the chief executive to require their opinions as he sees fit. The cabinet, then, is strictly a presidential institution. It began to take shape during the Washington administration, when Washington met from time to time with two or more of his department heads. However, the cabinet has only such power as the President grants to it, and the President is ultimately and solely responsible for the executive branch and its operation. Washington set the example for this, and his example has generally been followed ever since.

One other example of a precedent set in the early years may illustrate further the importance of these early actions. This one has to do with the number of terms a President serves. There was much concern at the Constitutional Convention about limiting the terms not only of Presidents but also of other elected officials. Fears were expressed that once a man was elected to the presidency, he might have the office for life. Others believed, however, that it was desirable to attract outstanding and ambitious men to high office and that to disqualify them for further service might work harm. Washington's example did serve to restrain those who might have considered seeking the office term after term, though no restrictions were put into the Constitution. He decided to retire after two terms and announced the decision before the election. Every other man who had the opportunity stepped down voluntarily for the next 144 years. Franklin D. Roosevelt was the first President to serve for more than two terms. The precedent was still so highly valued, however, that the two term limit has since been made a part of the Constitution.

Hamilton and Economic Policy

George Washington did not conceive any grand program of governmental action and make an attempt to push it through Congress. Indeed, no President did so on any scale until the 20th century. In his messages to Congress, Washington went no further than to suggest subjects for consideration, refraining from any effort to direct the result. "Motives of delicacy," he wrote, "have uniformly restrained the P[resident] from introducing any topic which relates to Legislative matters to members of either house of Congress, lest it should be suspected that he wished to influence the question before it."[111]

His Secretary of the Treasury, however, was not restrained from pushing his programs by any such delicate feeling. Alexander Hamilton was the man with a plan, a plan he expected to put into effect if he could. Hamilton was brilliant, daring, and determined, determined to see that the new government acted with sufficient energy to gain a hold on the American people. He was for bold action in the economic realm, and he did not even restrict himself to that area. His economic ideas were distinctly mercantilist; otherwise, he was a nationalist and became the leading spokesman for a broad construction of the Constitution.

Hamilton conceived a financial program which he hoped would provide the sinews of a nation. His task would have appeared hopeless enough if he had aimed only to get revenue to run the government. Americans were not, after all, known for their enthusiasm for paying taxes, and their politicians had thus far shown considerable willingness to delay as long as possible the necessity for levying taxes. But Hamilton wanted much more than a revenue. He wanted to establish the credit of the United States, when bankruptcy or repudiation was the obvious outlet. And, he wanted to do so in a way that would tie men of wealth and position to the government, influence the people to view the United States government as *the* government, and make it clear that the general government would take care of national concerns.

Hamilton's programs were made public in a series of reports to Congress. These reports dealt with the subjects of public credit, a national bank, and manufactures. It should be said that these reports were composed at the request of Congress, that members of Congress were generally glad to have his direction, and that they did not, themselves, constitute executive interference with the affairs of Congress. It is also true, however, that Hamilton did aggressively push his programs through contacts with Representatives and Senators. "Nothing is done without him," according to Senator Maclay of Pennsylvania. Indeed, when the funding bill was up for consideration, Maclay wrote in his diary, "Mr. Hamilton...was here early to wait on the Speaker, and I believe spent most of his time in running from place to place among the members."[112] Hamilton not only proposed but also disposed, as much as he could.

His report on the public credit was presented to Congress January 14, 1790. In it, he argued vigorously that the domestic debt as well as the foreign debt should be taken over at the full face value. There was general agreement on his proposal for dealing with the foreign, but the domestic debt was another matter. Many of the debt certificates had been bought by speculators from the original lenders at a fraction of their stated value. There was much objection to enriching these buyers. But Hamilton insisted that the government had an obligation, and that if it was going to establish its credit on a sound basis it must meet it fully. "By what means," he asked, "is the credit to be established? The ready answer to which question is, by good faith; by a punctual performance of contracts. States, like individuals, who observe their engagements are respected and trusted, while the reverse is the fate of those who pursue an opposite conduct."[113] He carried his point; new certificates of indebtedness were issued to the holders of the old for the full extent of the obligation.

In the same report, Hamilton proposed that the United States government should assume the state debts contracted during the War for

Independence. They were, he said, debts contracted for the prosecution of the war and thus should fall on the whole people. Assumption was much more controversial than the other proposals. The United States was already taking on a heavy debt; why burden itself with those of the states? Besides, the state debts were unequal in amounts, even when population differences were taken into account. The Southern states did not owe nearly as much in proportion as those to the north. Adjustments were made that made the differences less glaring. Beyond that, Hamilton promised Jefferson that if he would persuade Madison to drop his opposition to assumption, he would do his best to get the capital located on the Potomac. The bill was passed, and the capital is located on the Potomac.

Although the national debt was now even larger than it had been before, Hamilton argued that if it were managed properly it could be a "blessing" to the country. This, despite the fact that a large portion of the Federal revenues would go for interest and principal. Hamilton's point was that if the new certificates, or securities, could trade at par, or near to it, they could be sold by holders or used as security for borrowing money. That way, there would be much more capital for investment in enterprises, and the country might prosper. A sinking fund was authorized to enable the government to go into the market and buy its securities to make sure that they did trade close to par.

But Hamilton did not trust to chance that the government securities would augment the capital funds in the country. On December 13, 1790, he submitted his proposal for a national bank. He called for a Bank of the United States to be chartered which would be jointly owned by the government and private investors. As chartered by act of Congress in 1791, one-fifth of the capital stock was to be subscribed by the government and four-fifths by private investors. The private stock was all subscribed within an hour after orders for the stock began to be taken. The bank was authorized to receive deposits, make loans, and issue paper money to the total amount of its capital stock. The paper money was to be redeemed in gold and silver coins at face value. The bank was inflationary—increased the money supply—, and this new money did set off an inflationary boom in the 1790s. (Such booms are followed sooner or later by deflations or depressions, and some of the enterprises that got underway were not long in crashing.) The bank was chartered to run for 20 years.

Hamilton's most ambitious and extensive program was contained in his Report on Manufactures, which he presented to Congress in December of 1791. In it, he made what can probably be considered the most attractive argument for government intervention in the economy. He held forth a vision of an America—North and South, East and West—

drawn together by economic bonds through the interdependence of manufacturers, merchants, and farmers. Few were likely to disagree with Hamilton, either, when he pointed out the advantages of a division of labor, of American independence of foreign countries, or even that there was reason to draw immigrants to American shores along with foreign capital. All of this, however, was attractive background to an argument for government aid to manufacturing. "Such aid," he said, "must consist of protective duties against competitive foreign manufactures, bounties for the establishment of new industries, premiums for excellence and quality of manufactured articles, exemptions of raw materials from abroad from import duties..., the encouragement of inventions, improvement in machinery and processes by substantial grants..., and, finally, the construction of roads and canals for a...flow of physical goods and materials."[114] In short, Hamilton favored the reestablishment of the main lines of mercantilism in America.

With such a program Hamilton had bit off more than Congress could chew or swallow. The tide for free trade was swelling, and this would be a step backward. Besides, where was the authority for such programs in the Constitution? Hamilton argued that it could be found in the general welfare clause. If this were so, Madison declared, then "everything from the highest object of state legislation to the most minute object of policy would be thrown under the power of Congress."[115] Thus, Congress refused to pass the most ambitious of Hamilton's plans.

Though many of Hamilton's policies were divisive, he did contribute much to the establishment of the United States. Not only did he get the debts fully assumed, but he also established the Treasury Department, provided a paper currency, got a Federal revenue at last, put the credit on a solid footing, and put into effect some means of managing the debt. If his audacity sometimes outran his brilliance and his quest for power emerged as a threat to freedom, he nonetheless acted to give energy to a new government.

Independence in a Hostile World

The American colonies were dependent upon Great Britain throughout the colonial period. In the early years of settlement, they were dependent for supplies. During the whole period, that dependence was maintained for trade, for protection, for settlers, and as a source of many of the amenities of civilization. America was dependent upon European powers, too, in the successful effort to cast off British rule. The French provided the naval power and a considerable army for the winning of the most impressive victory—the one at Yorktown—against the British on the continent. French and Dutch loans, particularly, helped much in sustaining the Confederation during the early years. That several European nations were at war with or unfriendly to Britain made the American victory in war more certain. The favorable treaty gained by the United States at Paris in 1783 was made possible by the cross currents of animosities and jealousies among European powers. Even as the Americans were winning their political independence from Britain, then, new lines of dependency were being laid in relations with other European countries.

On the other hand, there was a great and mounting desire of Americans to reduce the dependence upon Europe so that the United States could act independently in the world. To that end, a new Constitution had been adopted, providing the means for a government of the union to be sustained by revenues, act with greater energy, and take its place among the powers of the world. To the end of a greater economic independence, Hamilton's plans had been submitted and some of them made law. But visualizing independence, even taking steps toward it, was some distance away from establishing it in the 1790s. European powers still viewed the United States as a potential pawn in their contests with one another. The French were inclined to think that they had a special claim on the affections and good will of the United States. The British, on the other hand, could not readily accept anything less than restoring in some measure the old relationship of dependence, especially in trade and as an aid in pursuing their foreign policies. The Spanish were hardly resigned to the dominance by the United States of the eastern portion of the continent. Nor were the United States self-sufficient economically, even if that had been a desirable goal. Americans needed markets abroad for their produce and still wanted to buy goods from other countries.

The French Revolution and the wars surrounding it greatly increased the difficulties of charting and pursuing an independent course in the world. The difficulties came to a head for the first time after France declared war on Britain, Spain, and Holland. The Franco-American Alliance committed the United States to the defense of the French West Indies and not to render aid to France's enemies. The British, on the other hand, sought during this extended war, to bring the former colonies over to their side. The trouble threatened to erupt in 1793. Louis XVI, King of France, was put to death by the guillotine; the French Republic was proclaimed; and Citizen Edmond Genet was appointed minister to the United States. Genet landed in Charleston, South Carolina and acted as if the United States were a possession of France. He fitted out privateers to prey on the British and began to recruit troops even before he had presented his credentials to the government.

Meanwhile, Washington proclaimed, in effect, that the United States was neutral in the conflict. He said that the country was at peace with both Britain and France and warned Americans not to commit hostile acts against either power. When Genet arrived in Philadelphia, the capital at that time, the President notified him that he could not continue to commission privateers or otherwise commit acts contrary to American policy. When Genet persisted, the United States demanded and got his recall by the French government.

There were two questions raised by what were basically Washington's decisions. Jefferson doubted that the President had the authority to proclaim American neutrality on his own. There was the further question about the Franco-American Alliance, and what sort of action it required. The last question was left to hang. Jefferson's question became moot when Congress passed a Neutrality Act in 1794. It forbade citizens of the United States to enlist in the service of foreign powers or the fitting out of armed vessels to serve foreign powers in American waters.

The Genet Affair was part of a cooling of differences between the United States and France, and the differences widened in the ensuing years. Although Jay's Treaty, negotiated in 1794 and approved by the Senate in 1795, brought Britain and the United States closer together, it was preceded by events that could have led to war. When Britain went to war against France, the British navy did its best to drive French commerce from the seas. One result was that with French ships unable to operate as usual, Americans moved in to conduct the carrying trade with the French West Indies. A British Order in Council, issued in November 1793, ordered British naval commanders to seize all neutral ships trading in the French islands. This order went into effect so swiftly that it caught the Americans by surprise, and some 250 American ships were seized; some of them were condemned to be sold as lawful prizes. Madison led a movement in Congress to have the government retaliate against the British. Hamilton opposed any such action, and Jefferson retired as Secretary of State and was replaced by Edmund Randolph, another Virginian.

Instead of retaliation, the Washington Administration sent John Jay to negotiate a settlement with Britain. There were many more differences with Britain, of course, than those involving the rights of neutrals, and earlier differences occupied most of the treaty. Jay's Treaty provided for the withdrawal of British troops from American territory in the Northwest and for joint commissions to be appointed to settle claims of British citizens for pre-Revolutionary debts, to settle American claims for the illegal seizures of ships, and to determine the disputed boundary between Maine and Canada. The trade with each nation was placed on a most favored nation basis, meaning that whatever trade advantages either granted to any country would also be extended to each other. American vessels were to enjoy the same advantages as British ones in trading with Great Britain and the East Indies. However, trade with the British West Indies was still to be so hampered that the United States struck out that part of the treaty. The rights of neutrals were not very effectively clarified. Clearly, however, the United States had moved closer to Britain while that country was at war with France.

Before Jay's Treaty had been ratified, or made public, Thomas Pinckney was sent to Spain to try to work out an agreement with that country. Spain had not fared well in war against France and was considering getting out of the war. This step would hardly please Britain, and thus it seemed a good idea to the Spanish to try to improve relations with the United States. It was conceivable, at least, that if the British and Americans drew closer together they might take concerted action against the Spanish on the American continent. In any case, the Americans were willing to negotiate when the Spanish invited discussions.

Pinckney's Treaty, also known as the Treaty of San Lorenzo, was signed in October of 1795. It settled most of the outstanding issues between the two countries in America's favor. Spain formally recognized

Thomas Pinckney
(1750-1828)

Pinckney was born in Charleston, South Carolina, educated in England, and was admitted to the practice of law in his native colony shortly after his return. Despite his English connections, he fought with the Continental army in the War for Independence, was wounded at the Battle of Camden, and captured by the British. After the war, Pinckney served as governor of South Carolina, presided over the convention which ratified the United States Constitution, and was minister to Great Britain, 1792-1796. While there, he was sent to Spain to negotiate the treaty which bears his name. The success of this effort contributed sufficiently to his fame that he was a Federalist candidate for Vice President in 1796. Since he was not elected, he stood for and was elected to Congress, where he served for several years. His other main public activity was as a general in the War of 1812.

that the territory north of the 31st parallel and east of the Mississippi belonged to the United States. Free navigation of the Mississippi by both countries was recognized, and the rights of Americans to deposit goods for transfer to ocean-going vessels on Spanish territory was established. Both powers agreed to restrain the Indians in the area. Although Spain was slow to put all this into effect, the treaty settled, at least in theory, the main differences between the countries.

Rise of Political Parties

Political parties are unknown to the United States Constitution. No provision is made for them in it, or at least in the original document. As visualized and provided, the President was to be selected by the Electoral College after the members of that body had been elected. Each member was to have two votes which had to be cast for two different persons for President. The person receiving the largest number of votes, assuming these amounted to a majority, would be President, and the one receiving the next highest number would be Vice President. If votes were by party, each candidate of the party would receive the same number of votes, and there would be a tie, as there was in 1800. No more was there any particular provision for parties in the methods of election of members of Congress.

Even so, parties were not long in developing. Indeed, the debates and taking of sides on the ratification of the Constitution laid some of the groundwork for parties. Those who favored ratification called themselves Federalists, and those who opposed were then anti-Federalists. Once the Constitution was ratified, however, that issue was more or less resolved. Moreover, the most basic objections to ratification were removed with the adoption of a Bill of Rights. But the basis of parties remained in the variety of interests in the country and in the different positions that could be taken on issues which arose. Those who feared what the rise of a spirit of party might do to the Republic still recognized that so long as men were free to do so they would differ about many things.

Hamilton's economic programs provoked the initial resistance which gave rise to party differences. His proposal to take over the domestic debt at face value met resistance; the assumption of state debts aroused even more concerted opposition, particularly in the South. But it was the national bank proposal that awakened the opposition on grounds of constitutionality. Washington submitted Hamilton's proposal to the heads of departments for their opinions. Jefferson objected that the power to charter a bank was not granted in the Constitution, and that it was unnecessary to carry out any of the powers granted. It might be convenient for the government to have such an instrument, but if convenience were made a test of constitutionality there was no measure "which ingenuity may not torture into a convenience...to some one of so long a list of enumerated powers."[116] In short, Jefferson believed that if there was to be a limited government there must be a *strict* construction of its powers under the Constitution.

On the other hand, Hamilton argued that the power to charter the bank was implied in the Constitution. The power to tax, borrow money, and spend it was granted in those that were listed. Since a bank would facilitate doing these things, the power was implied. He laid it down as a rule that "If the *end* be clearly comprehended within any of the specified powers, and if the measures have an obvious relation to that *end*, and is not forbidden by a particular provision of the Constitution, it may be safely deemed to come within...the national authority."[117] This is sometimes described as a *broad* construction of the Constitution.

The excise taxes which Hamilton got passed into law provoked a different kind of opposition, particularly the excise on whiskey. The tax was passed in 1791 and was advanced as a means of providing a fund for meeting payments on the debt. Opposition to it arose both in North Carolina and western Pennsylvania the next year. Western Pennsylvanians, particularly, had a major problem in getting their farm produce to market. Heavy produce, to be profitable, would have to be shipped by river to the Gulf of Mexico, but the Spanish made this difficult, if not impossible. Thus, many farmers distilled their grain into whiskey and shipped it to the east for sale. They not only objected to the tax but also the revenue agents appointed, and to the fact that they would be tried in the eastern part of the state for offenses.

The resistance rose to a peak in 1794 in western Pennsylvania, in what was called the Whiskey Rebellion. In July, an armed mob burned the home of a tax collector and mass meetings were held. When a presidential proclamation failed to bring compliance, Washington called upon the states to provide troops, placed Hamilton in command, and an army of 12,000 marched into western Pennsylvania. The army met no opposition groups, and no fighting took place. The best they could do was arrest a few men, two of whom were tried and convicted of high treason. Washington pardoned them. However, the rebellion—if that was what it was—ended, and the power of the general government had been displayed. On the other hand, western Pennsylvania became a stronghold for the emerging Jeffersonian Republicans, and opposition to direct taxes became a plank in the Republican Party platform.

Another focal point for the rise of political parties was the French Revolution and American policy toward the French. Once the First

French Republic had been proclaimed, French revolutionaries set on a course of spreading the revolution to other countries. Secular ideology made its appearance on a large scale in public affairs for the first time in the French Revolution. The thrust of this ideology was to overthrow the powers, institutions, and practices of the past and to place new ones in effect. If the revolutionaries had stopped with establishing a limited monarchy and civil rights Americans would have been wholeheartedly on their side. If they had gone no further than to abolish monarchy and establish a republic, many Americans would have been glad of the company. But they did go much further until hardly anything was left to stand, and much of it was advanced by a Reign of Terror. Moreover, governments were unstable, leadership changed hands quickly, and France went to war to unseat monarchy generally and extend its sway.

A great struggle was going on in the European world between the revolutionary force mounted in France and being spread from that center, and the force of monarchies attempting to preserve the order that had prevailed in Europe. The Republican Party of Jefferson and Madison took shape in this context, and the Federalists of Hamilton and Adams took on the character of a political party. Washington tried to remain above the partisan contest, but it became increasingly difficult to do so from 1794 onward. The Republicans may have deplored the French excesses, but they were determined not to fall back in the arms of Britain in reaction to them. Jay's Treaty, to them was an accommodation with the British, and Pinckney's Treaty, however desirable otherwise, was an accord with a monarch. Some Republicans, at least, sniffed a tainted breeze of monarchism in the policies of the government. This aroused fears for the continuation of republican government, of popularly elected government, and for the liberties that had been lately obtained. On the other hand, the Federalists were determined that the French revolutionary fervor not gain hold and spread in America.

Out of these and related issues parties had formed sufficiently well by 1896 to play a prominent role in national elections.

Washington's Farewell

The new government was well on its way to being well established by 1796. So George Washington must have judged, and he had good reason for doing so. The branches of the government had all been set up and were functioning, each, more or less, in its allotted role. A large debt had been assumed, and funds were being collected to service it and for its eventual retirement. Revenue measures had been passed, and money was coming into the Treasury. Challenges to the authority of the government had been met firmly, and attachments to the government were being formed. Treaties with major European powers were in operation, and the United States was beginning to assume its place among the nations of the world.

There were, of course, problems ahead for the budding nation. War still raged in Europe, and efforts were going on still to embroil the new nation in the quarrels of the Old World. What the impact of the spread of revolution from France would be was as yet far from being determined. The turmoil in France itself was not yet ended, if it ever would be. Also, a contest for political control was building in the country: factions resisted some of the policies of the government; societies were being organized, and the lines of political parties were taking shape. Washington did not, indeed could not, foresee the role that parties would play in the future, that they would even serve the valuable function of limiting government. He feared their contests might rend the Republic, and he rather hoped they would be temporary.

In any case, Washington was eager to retire from office, and he thought that the time was right at the end of his second term. He was conscious as always of the example of his behavior, and he probably relished the opportunity of affording the all too rare example of a leader in power voluntarily retiring. Americans have become used to power changing hands without violence or bloodshed, so they are not generally aware of how unusual such things have been in the course of history. Here again, Washington took the lead in providing the example of voluntary relinquishment of power.

Well before the election, Washington made his decision known to the public. It is known as the Farewell Address, though actually it was not delivered as a speech. Instead, it was published in a Philadelphia newspaper, the *American Daily Advertiser.* It was Washington's mature advice to his countrymen on the management of their common political affairs. Although the issues he addressed were timely, the language in which his advice was cast is timeless. That is, Washington wrote in terms of enduring principles, not momentary partisan positions. He did not speak of France or Britain but of relations with other nations at all times. Although Hamilton aided Washington in the composing of the address, none of his partisan fervor shows through. The address is the wise voice of the elder statesman, yearning to retire finally from his years of service yet still deeply concerned with the unity, independence, and future well-being of his country.

Much of the address is taken up with relations with foreign powers. His greatest concern was that the country not be divided by and drawn into the dynastic and imperial conflicts of Europe. "The great rule of conduct for us in regard to foreign nations," Washington said, "is, in extending our commercial relations to have with them as little *political* connection as possible." That did not mean at all that America should not carry on relations with other nations. "Harmony, liberal intercourse with all nations," he admonished, "are recommended by policy, humanity, and interest." But all this must be carried out impartially, not by choosing up sides, for to choose up sides in foreign relations is to make your nation a prey to and servant of the policies of the nation chosen. Beware, above all, he warned, of being used as a pawn in those policies. "Against the insidious wiles of foreign influence (I conjure you to believe me, fellow-citizens) the jealousy of a free people ought to be *constantly* awake, since history and experience prove that foreign influence is one of the most baneful foes of republican government." In fine, he thought it was in the deepest interest of the United States to pursue an independent course, but a course based on "good faith and justice toward all nations. Cultivate peace and harmony with all. Religion and morality enjoin this conduct. And can it be that good policy does not equally enjoin it?"

The overall theme of the address, though, was the unity of the American people behind the general government. Washington knew that the attachment was as yet incomplete, and he feared the impact of foreign attachments upon it as well as partisan conflicts. Beyond these matters, he recommended a firm adherence to the Constitution as written. Changes might need to be made from time to time, but they should be made by amendment, not by bending the document by construction. Americans, said Washington, should "cherish public credit," and the best means to this end was to use it sparingly. Nor did he neglect to point out the need for religion and morality in the lives of men, and he warned that men ought to take care in indulging "the supposition that morality can be maintained without religion."

On March 4, 1797, Washington attended the inauguration of his successor John Adams at Federal Hall in Philadelphia. He walked to the place of the ceremony without attendants, making his first appearance as a private citizen. The assembled crowd greeted him with tremendous applause. In the next few days, Washington packed his household goods and left the seat of the government, never to return. He spent the couple of years that remained to him at his beloved Mount Vernon.

Chapter 8

The Struggle for Political Leadership 1796-1800

*That if any person shall write, print, utter, or publish...
any false, scandalous and malicious writing...against the
government of the United States,...then such person, being
thereof convicted...shall be punished...by imprisonment not
exceeding two years.*

—Sedition Act, 1798.

*Resolved..., that no power over the freedom of religion,
freedom of speech, or freedom of the press being delegated
to the United States by the Constitution, nor prohibited by it
to the States, all powers respecting the same...were reserved
to the States, or to the people....*

—Kentucky Resolution, 1798.

Chronology

1796—France rejects C.C. Pinckney as American Minister.

1797—XYZ Affair.

June, July 1798—Alien and Sedition Acts.

November, December 1798—Kentucky and Virginia Resolutions.

1800—Convention with France (settlement of dispute).

1801—House of Representatives elects Jefferson as President.

Fate was unkind to John Adams. It fell to his lot to serve mainly as a
bridge between the presidencies of George Washington and Thomas
Jefferson. Indeed, between 1789 and 1840 only two men failed to be reelected to a second term as President, and both were named Adams.
Both were caught in struggles for party and personal leadership; neither
could do more than serve in a transition, which was moving away from
their outlook.

Most likely, anyone who succeeded Washington would have had a
difficult time. He was, as Henry Lee said after his death in 1799, "first

in war, first in peace, and first in the hearts of his countrymen." He occupied a unique place, both for the role he had played and in the estimate of Americans generally. To have served as his replacement would have placed a large enough burden on John Adams, or any other man, but that was only the beginning of his troubles. There was the divisive war in Europe, increasing diplomatic and naval problems with France, and political parties were pressing for dominance.

In the larger sense, Americans had not decisively decided who should lead in 1796. Four men were pressing, or being pressed, toward political leadership during these years. They were John Adams, Thomas Jefferson, Alexander Hamilton, and Aaron Burr. This is not to say that they were all running for President, either in 1796 or 1800. Men did not "run" for President, as we understand the word, until well into the 19th century. That is, they did not go about the country making campaign speeches or otherwise openly seeking the office. What was happening was much different from that; several men were in the public eye as possible leaders, and none had clearly emerged in 1796. Nor had political parties come into clear dominance by that time. The struggle going on was for party dominance out of which a leader could emerge. At any rate, the Adams Presidency was transitional, and looking back on it we can say a struggle for leadership was going on during it.

Election of 1796

The struggle, the party contests, and the lack of dominance of any one party or man appears from the presidential election of 1796. Federalist strength was concentrated in New England and New York, though there were other states in which the party was dominant for the time being. John Adams was generally the choice of the Federalists for President. Thomas Pinckney, whose star was temporarily in the ascendancy because of his success in negotiating with Spain, was the favorite for Vice President, though some electors preferred him for President. Thomas Jefferson was the favorite of Republicans, whose strength was concentrated in Virginia and Pennsylvania. Aaron Burr of New York had some support from both Federalists and Republicans; his reputation had not yet been blackened by involvement in conspiracy, and possibly treason, and he gave the appearance of moderation in his views.

Actually, there was no way for electors to distinguish between their choices for President and Vice President, and no direct means for political parties to effect the choices. The Constitution does not specify how electors are to be chosen. How it is to be done is left to the states. State legislatures generally elected them at that time, though in some states they were popularly elected. But even where they were chosen on party grounds, each elector was free to vote his choice. The complexities of

Aaron Burr
(1756-1836)

Burr was born in New Jersey, the son of the president of Princeton (then College of New Jersey), and of the daughter of the famous theologian, Jonathan Edwards. He graduated from Princeton and began the study of law, but left off to serve with distinction in the Continental Army during the war. Burr resigned from the army in 1779 for reasons of health and completed his studies for the practice of law. His political career began in state government in New York in the 1780s, and he was elected to the U.S. Senate in 1791. Although his political views were never as firm as those of Jefferson and Madison, Burr became a leader of the Republican faction in New York. That led to his election as Vice President in 1800, but he returned to New York in 1804 to run for governor. Hamilton's bitter opposition cost him the office, and he challenged him to a duel and killed him. From that point, he went downhill, was charged with treason, and, though cleared, fled the country and lived in Europe for several years.

the electoral system added to the other difficulties of selecting the man who would preside over the union.

John Adams received 71 electoral votes and was elected President. Thomas Jefferson received 68 votes and became Vice President. They were from different parties, and the vote was unusually close. Thomas Pinckney received 59 votes, and Aaron Burr 30. Most likely, the man was more important than the party for many of the electors.

The Adams Administration

Adams never had a very firm grip on the executive department of the government, although he tightened it somewhat in the last year or so of his administration. For one thing, he brought to office little administrative experience. Much of his political career had been spent in diplomacy, and in those days diplomats were hardly executives. His two terms as Vice President did not add appreciably to his administrative experience. His only job was to preside over the Senate. For another thing, he did not have the kind of personality to which men are given to turning for guidance and leadership. In consequence, he did not have a circle of friends and trusted advisers on whom he could rely. Also, he was away from the seat of government for long periods to attend his ailing wife, Abigail, in Massachusetts.

Above all, though, the Adams administration was, in the first years, mainly an extension of the Washington administration, without Washington, and played upon by the influence of Alexander Hamilton. Adams made what turned out to be a major mistake in keeping several of Washington's department heads in his own administration. Two things misled him into this course. One was that no tradition had yet been established of department heads resigning when a new President takes office. The other was that Adams considered his a continuation of Washington's administration. Due to the resignation of Hamilton, Knox, and Randolph, Washington appointed new heads in 1795. When Adams became President, Timothy Pickering was Secretary of State, Oliver Wolcott, Jr., of the Treasury, and James McHenry of the War Department. They continued in office.

Abigail Adams
(1744-1818)

Abigail was the wife of John Adams, second President; the mother of John Quincy Adams, the sixth President; the grandmother of Charles Francis Adams, a statesman and diplomat of the mid-19th century; and great grandmother of Henry Adams, an outstanding American historian. Thus, along with her husband she founded one of the leading American families. Abigail was the descendant (family name Smith) of a line of Puritans going back to the early years of the colony. Although she had little formal education, she is best known for her many letters, which show a woman of strong mind, a considerable flair for writing, and tender feeling. Her *Familiar Letters* to her husband and correspondence with Thomas Jefferson are particularly noteworthy. Her affection for one of Jefferson's daughters, who stayed with her for a time in London, and her later efforts to commiserate with Jefferson on the child's untimely death is one of the most touching and heart-rending episodes in all literature.

Timothy Pickering
(1745-1829)

Pickering was born in Massachusetts, graduated from Harvard, and was admitted to the practice of law. He had a varied political, military, and diplomatic career, ranging from Massachusetts legislator, to serving in the army during the War for Independence, to planning the military academy at West Point, to negotiating treaties with the Indians. Pickering served in three national posts under Washington: Postmaster General, Secretary of War, and Secretary of State. He continued in the latter position under Adams until 1800, when his reluctance to negotiate with the French eventually led to his dismissal. Afterward, he remained active in politics by serving first as a Senator and then as a member of Congress. His national career was entangled with that of the rise and fall of the Federalist Party, and in many ways mirrored its course.

All three of these men were subject to the influence of Hamilton, especially Wolcott at the Treasury. After his resignation, Hamilton entered the practice of law in New York, but he could not stay out of politics. Nor is this surprising, for the Federalist Party was Hamiltonian in tendency, and the Republican Party came into being in resistance to his policies. By his brilliance and political passion Hamilton tended to dominate those with whom he associated; those whom he could not dominate often became his political enemies. The political offices which Hamilton held were appointive not elective, and his elevation to national leadership stemmed from Washington, not from any broad popularity with voters. That is a way of saying that Hamilton's power came from his influence upon other statesmen and politicians. He not only had strong opinions about what needed to be done but also the determination to sway others to do it.

There was never any great likelihood that Hamilton would either dominate or greatly influence Adams. John Adams was small of stature and somewhat rounded, leading some critics to refer to him disparagingly as "His Rotundity," but he was strong-willed and independent. He was not controlled finally by party, by Hamilton, by his cabinet, nor any who sought to bend him to their will. While others spent their energies at machinations, Adams calmly kept his own counsel and bided his time until he judged that the situation was right for action. By the end of his administration he had emerged as the man in charge; Pickering and McHenry had been dismissed from the cabinet; and Hamilton was, if not a man without a party, a man with only a residue of influence on the American course. However, the Federalist Party would never have another opportunity to direct national affairs. "The party committed suicide," Adams said, and blamed him for its demise.[118]

Actually, Adams strove to maintain American independence and neutrality in an international situation unfriendly to both. He had spent too many years in the struggle for independence to sacrifice it for partisan purposes. Most of his administration was immersed in foreign affairs and in a struggle to come to terms with France without either war or submission. That the country was often divided by the strident claims of political parties only added to the burden of Adams.

The XYZ Affair

Increasing difficulties with the French were brewing even before Washington left office. They began to come to a head when James Monroe, Minister to France, was recalled in 1796. Charles Cotesworth Pinckney was appointed to replace him, but the French government refused to accept him. The French were incensed at the terms of the Jay Treaty; as viewed by the French leaders, the United States had abridged the Franco-American Alliance of 1778 by coming to such terms with the British, and that the adoption of the treaty was a violation of American neutrality. In consequence, the French navy began preying upon American merchant ships at sea. Secretary of State Pickering reported that the French seized 316 vessels flying the American flag between the middle of 1796 and 1797.

President Adams sent a three man commission in 1797 to try to come to terms with the French. It was composed of John Marshall, Elbridge Gerry, and Pinckney, who was still in Europe. The commissioners were neither recognized by the French nor formally received. Instead, Talleyrand, the French foreign minister, sent three agents to treat with them. These agents, known as X, Y, and Z in public reports, demanded that before negotiations could begin that President Adams would have to apologize for statements made to Congress, that a sum of 1,200,000 livres be paid, and that a loan of 32 million florins be made to the French government. In short, they demanded a huge bribe before opening negotiations. The Americans refused, declaring that the American government would not pay one cent. Marshall and Pinckney departed from France, but Gerry remained until he was recalled.

When what had transpired became public knowledge in 1798, the

Charles Cotesworth Pinckney (1746-1825)

Pinckney was born in South Carolina, son of a prominent planter, was educated at Oxford in England, and practiced law in his native state. During the early years of the war he served in the state legislature before going into the army. Pinckney worked both in the making of the United States Constitution and in its ratification in his state. He became Minister to France at the time of trouble with that country and was caught up in the XYZ Affair. It was he who told the French agents that America would not pay one cent as a bribe. He was candidate for Vice President in 1800, and for President in 1804 and 1808, but was elected to none of these offices.

American reaction was spirited and vigorous; anti-French feeling rose to a pitch. The slogan, "Millions for defense but not one cent for tribute," was a popular toast, and President Adams became a popular public figure for once. Among Federalists, at least, there was sentiment for going to war against France. The Hamiltonians were for taking brisk action, and Adams might have been relieved, at least momentarily, if Congress had declared war, though he made no such recommendation. Indeed, the country was ill-prepared for war against the mightiest nation in the world, and there is no evidence that the French intended to provoke any such response.

Instead, the government prepared to retaliate. Indeed, even before the degree of the French insult became public knowledge, Adams had asked for increased military spending. Now Congress acted. A Navy Department was authorized, and Adams appointed Benjamin Stoddert Secretary of the Navy. A much enlarged army was authorized; George Washington was appointed commander, but he turned the actual leadership over to Hamilton. Adams, however, was much more concerned with naval preparations than with the army and did little to encourage its growth, to the chagrin of Hamilton. Government spending rose from $6 million in the year before the crisis to $8 million in 1798, and to $11.5 million in 1800. Taxes, too, were increased, and direct taxes were levied on property, and a stamp tax was passed. These direct taxes provoked resistance, especially from Republicans. But the government proceeded with preparing for naval operations, particularly, against the French. There was an undeclared war, as it has sometimes been called, from 1798 to 1800.

Alien and Sedition Acts

Meanwhile, the Federalists used the furor aroused against the French in 1798 as an occasion to shore up the government's defenses against opposition at home. President Adams did not recommend or request these measures, but Congress passed a series of laws known collectively as the Alien and Sedition Acts. Three of the acts dealt in one way or another with aliens, i.e., those residing in the United States who were not citizens. One act increased the period of residence required for a foreign born person to become a United States citizen from 5 to 14 years. Another authorized the President to order out of the country any aliens whom he had "reasonable grounds to suspect are concerned in any treasonable or secret machinations against the government...." A third act, dealing with aliens, which would go into effect only in case of war, gave the President authority to deport aliens from the hostile country. These acts had only symbolic significance, as it turned out. Since states could and did confer citizenship themselves, the longer residence requirement for United States citizenship probably worked no hardship on anyone. As for the other two acts dealing with aliens, President Adams never had authority, in the absence of hostilities or invasion, to apply one, and he did not avail himself of the opportunity to deport aliens under the other.

The Sedition Act did, however, become a subject of controversy, and it was applied in several instances. There were two sections of the act. Section 1 made combinations and conspiracies to obstruct the laws or such activities as inciting to riot unlawful and made persons found guilty of such conduct subject to fine and imprisonment. But it was Section 2 that raised the ire of Republicans and that became the center of the controversy. It dealt with writing, printing, speaking, and publishing, and prohibited "any false, scandalous writing or writings against the government of the United States, or either houses of the Congress..., or the President of the United States...," or to defame them, bring them into disrepute, or stir up combinations against them. In effect, it was a libel law, as libel was then understood, and it prohibited specifically libels against the government, Congress, and the President. Penalties were not to exceed $2,000 in fines (a large sum in that day) and imprisonment for 2 years. Truth was admitted as a defense, and jury trials were provided. This portion of the act was aimed primarily at newspapers.

Before detailing the controversy Section 2 of the Sedition Act aroused, how it was applied, and the general consequence, it may be helpful to explain the context of its passage. The immediate occasion of the act, of course, was the difficulties with France. Underlying the act, however, were several other important circumstances. One was that the spread of the French Revolution was in part by the spread of ideas. Many Americans believed that they were exceedingly dangerous ideas. Moreover, Congressman Robert G. Harper, one who worked to get the Sedition Act passed, said, in a speech to the House: "Philosophers are the pioneers of revolution. They advance always in front, and prepare the way, by preaching infidelity, and weakening the respect of the people for ancient institutions....They talk of the perfectibility of man, of the dignity of his nature; and entirely forgetting what he is, declaim perpetually about what he should be. Thus they allure and seduce the visionary, the superficial, and the unthinking part of mankind."[119] But this fear of the danger of ideas could only have been background, for the act did not proscribe some category of ideas. Rather, it made libelous attacks on some offices and governmental institutions seditious.

More directly, then, the spirited and often raucous conflicts between political parties underlay the act. It was a Federalist measure; it protected only those in office and in control, i.e., Federalists, and it left the Republicans who opposed them exposed. One of the issues that separated Federalists and Republicans, or at least some of them, was American policies toward Britain and France. Federalists tended to be pro-British, and Republicans pro-French. To which it should be added that the leaders of both parties favored neutrality, but that did not keep them from being more tolerant to violations from one or the other side of neutrality.

At bottom, though, the Sedition Act was aimed squarely at newspapers. Newspapers were at the forefront in fomenting party issues, in exaggerating the differences, and in instigating controversies. Nor did they observe the niceties generally in doing so. Attacks on leaders and personalities were virtually unrestrained; gossip would do in the absence of facts. As one historian has said, "At no time in the history of the country has there existed such a community of quarrelsome, brimstone-tongued, vile-epitheted journalists."[120] The attacks in some of the newspapers were so bitter and personal that the New York *Spectator*, a newspaper itself, quoted the Boston *Mercury* to this effect: "No reputation, however virtuous and unsullied, no station, however exalted, has escaped the shafts of their envenomed malice. Men who have served their country with great ability and integrity, and whose names will descend to posterity as the fathers of the people and the benefactors of the human race, have been vilified and stigmatized as the scourges of society, nay as the most infamous traitors."[121] Nor was it Federalists only who held a low opinion of the press. In a letter written in 1807, Thomas Jefferson declared "that the man who never looks into a newspaper is better informed than he who reads them, inasmuch as he who knows nothing is nearer to the truth than he whose mind is filled with falsehoods and errors."[122] In any case, there is no reason to doubt that newspapers at that time, both Federalist and Republican in allegiance, were all too often guilty, as one newspaper said, of "murdering characters."

The desire to curb these vicious scurrilous attacks in the public press is understandable. A plausible case could be made, too, that some of these attacks might so divide the people and undermine the government that it could not prosecute a war effectively or retaliate against foreign governments which had violated the rights of Americans. In the hands of a French sympathizer, a newspaper might become an effective instrument of propaganda.

But only Section 2 of the Sedition Act was enforced to any extent, and it was done in such a way as to further divide the country and raise the anger of some Republicans to new heights. Twenty-five persons were prosecuted under the act, and ten were convicted, all of them Republican editors and printers. (If parties had been so well organized as to have national chairmen, the Republican chairmen might have denied that some of them were Republicans.) It might have been thought that Republican editors had trouble enough as it was. They were generally denied any share of the government printing business, since governments were generally under the control of the Federalists. Moreover, Federalist postmasters were not above denying some of them the use of the mails. Nor did it make things easier that those convicted were usually tried in the courts of Supreme Court justices. They traveled on circuits and held trial courts, and violations of the Sedition Act came under their jurisdiction. Some of them were highly partisan in their attitude toward Republicans who were indicted. The most notorious was Judge Samuel Chase of Maryland.

Chase declared that, "There is nothing we should more dread than the licentiousness of the press. A republican government can only be destroyed by the introduction of luxury and the licentiousness of the press. The latter is the more slow, but more sure and certain means of bringing about the destruction of the government."[123] Not surprisingly, then, Chase was tough with offenders. He sentenced Tom Cooper to pay a fine of $400 and spend four months in prison. James Thomas Callender got a $200 fine and nine months in prison. Some of the other Supreme Court justices were hardly less lenient than Chase, however.

Kentucky and Virginia Resolutions

There are a goodly number of questions that could be raised about Section 2 of the Sedition Act. At the most practical level, its enforcement neither succeeded in silencing Republican editors nor bringing unity to the country. Some of the sentenced journalists continued to publish their scurrilous attacks even while they were in prison. They had too many sympathizers to be much reformed by their punishment. If the Sedition Act united anything it was the Republican Party. Some Federalists were less than enthusiastic about it. "I hope sincerely the thing will not be hurried through," Hamilton wrote while the act was being considered. "Let us not establish a tyranny."[124] Nor, even supposing the act to have been desirable, it was neither drawn nor enforced impartially. The party and men out of power were hardly protected from libel by this measure. As for enforcement, the whole attention was focused on those of Republican sympathies.

Samuel Chase
(1741-1811)—

Chase was an associate justice of the United States Supreme Court, 1796-1811. He was born in Maryland, admitted to the practice of law in that state, and served for 20 years in the legislature. Chase opposed the Stamp Act, was a signer of the Declaration of Independence, and served in the Continental Congress. In the 1790s he was a judge in the Maryland courts until his appointment to the Supreme Court. His manner of conducting trials on his Supreme Court circuit, plus his obvious eagerness to punish Republicans, made him the personification of judicial excess to many in that party. The House of Representatives indicted him in 1804 on eight articles of impeachment, but the Senate failed to convict by only four votes on the most serious charge. Following the trial, he returned to his seat on the Supreme Court. The failure to remove him from office has generally discouraged Congressional efforts over the years, and Federal judges have generally been permitted to continue in office for the rest of their lives after appointment without serious challenge.

But the gravest question about the act was its constitutionality. There is no power to control or direct the content of the press under the enumerated powers of Congress in the Constitution. More, the First Amendment specifically prohibits Congress to make any law "abridging the freedom...of the press...." In a like manner, freedom of speech is protected. It may have been, as Hamilton argued in *The Federalist*, a mistake to prohibit the exercise of an authority that was not granted. It opened the way for claims that "freedom" of speech or of the press does not include licentiousness, which can and should be regulated. Whereas, if there is no authority to regulate and no prohibition entered, the unconstitutionality of such acts might be clearer.

In any case, the Alien and Sedition Acts brought Thomas Jefferson out into open opposition on constitutional grounds, along with James Madison. Jefferson authorized a statement which was adopted by the legislature of Kentucky (that state having come into the union in 1792), and is known as the Kentucky Resolution. James Madison authored a similar, though much briefer, statement which was adopted by the Virginia legislature. These resolutions were sent to the other states in the hope that they might agree.

The Kentucky Resolution is the much broader and more comprehensive of the two. It questions not only the constitutionality of the Alien and Sedition Acts but also the bank chartering act (particular laws punishing fraud) and of the extent of the taxing power. Jefferson argued that the Constitution is a compact between the states and the United States government and that the states may appropriately decide whether or not an act of the United States is in accord with the Constitution. In keeping with that view, the resolution proceeds to declare that the Sedition Act, "which does abridge the freedom of the press, is now law, but is altogether void and of no effect", and that the Alien Act "assumes power over alien friends not delegated by the Constitution, is not law, but is altogether void and of no force."[125] Less extensively, the Virginia Resolution declares that the Alien Act "exercises a power nowhere delegated to the Federal Government," and that the Sedition Act "exercises...a power not delegated by the Constitution, but, on the contrary, expressly and positively forbidden by one of the amendments thereto...."[126] The Kentucky Resolution refers to a power of the states to "nullify" unconstitutional acts, an idea which would come up again later in history.

The states from Maryland northward replied to the Kentucky and Virginia resolutions. They denied, more or less emphatically, that states could nullify acts of Congress or decide questions of the constitutionality of Federal laws. But, in any case, they stated generally that as far as their opinions had any weight they believed that the Alien and Sedition

Acts were in keeping with the Constitution. The question was never appealed to the Supreme Court, possibly because the Republicans did not wish to give the court the satisfaction of being allowed to make a decision. There was no good reason to doubt, however, that if the court had been given the opportunity it would have confirmed the constitutionality of the acts. Several justices had already either passed over the question or ruled summarily that the Sedition Act was constitutional in their roles as circuit court trial judges.

Many Republicans were hardly content with this state of affairs, but they were more eager than ever to take this and a mounting number of other issues to the electorate in 1800. Political parties emerged as divisive factions, but another and more enduring role for them was in the making. They would become a means of holding the party in power in check and contribute yet another block to the system of checks and balances. Republicans had seen evidence enough of the need for something to check the arbitrary exercise of power by the Federalists.

Undeclared War and the French Settlement

Whatever the future might hold, President Adams was pursuing his own course in 1798-1799, largely oblivious to the Alien and Sedition Acts and the controversy swirling around them. Much of his attention was focused on the conflict with France. He wanted to develop a navy sufficient to protect American shipping from the French and give them some punishing blows if it could be. Adams would not ask for a declaration of war; let the French take that step if they saw fit.

By the end of 1798 there were 14 American men-of-war at sea and a couple of hundred merchant vessels fitted out and authorized to take prizes. By agreement with Britain, transatlantic shipping would be protected by Britain, and the United States would protect both British and American shipping in the Caribbean. Some of the most daring exploits of the undeclared war were made by the *U.S.S. Constellation*, which captured a French frigate in early 1799, and the next year got much the better of more heavily armed French man-of-war in an extended battle, in which the French commander twice struck his colors unnoticed by the Americans. In the various naval battles only one small American warship was defeated, and that by two larger French ships.

Meanwhile the French government was making overtures to the United States to come to terms. The XYZ Affair had simply been the result of some misunderstandings, the government now alleged. Many Federalists were far from being enthusiastic about making any agreement with the French. To them, France was still the center of a dangerous fever of the spirit, so to speak, and America was now on the right side of things. Besides, the Federalists had made large gains in the 1798 elections, and their dominant position owed much to a belligerent posture toward France. This opposition to negotiations and settlement was, if anything, stronger in the cabinet than in the Senate.

President Adams saw matters differently, however. The weight of the future independence of America was on his shoulders, and he had no desire to hazard that by prolonging difficulties with France. Acting without the advance knowledge of his cabinet, Adams nominated a new minister to France in March 1799. Instead of approving the nomination outright, the Senate proposed that three men be appointed to the negotiations. Adams agreed, and sent the nominations of his selections. These were eventually approved, and Adams left the capital for a long visit to his home. In his absence, Secretary of State Pickering delayed sending the appointees to France, an action, or inaction, in keeping with some of the other cabinet members as well. When Adams returned to the capital he sent the mission on its way. By the time they reached France, Napoleon Bonaparte had become the political leader of the country, and the mission had to deal with him or his appointees.

After many months of negotiations an agreement was finally reached in September 1800. It is known as the Convention of 1800; it was more nearly a commercial agreement than a treaty, hence the title. On two main points no final settlement was reached: payments for property damage and the status of the old treaty of 1778 establishing the Franco-American Alliance. The property damages were eventually settled as a part of the Louisiana Purchase payment, and the old treaty was allowed to wither away under suspension. Otherwise, all government ships seized by either country were to be returned, and private property not finally condemned was to be returned to the owners. The commercial shipping of both France and the United States was to have most favored nation status, and France agreed not to interfere with American trade with her enemies, except for ships carrying war goods. In effect, the French agreed to the American position that a neutral country should be permitted to trade freely in the world.

Adams had successfully emerged from the struggle within his own party over control. He had even gained some favor with Republicans by coming to an accord with France. He had taken strong measures against France, yet had avoided outright war while maintaining and strengthening the independence of the United States. He had put his own house in order, too, by removing Pickering and McHenry from the cabinet. Hamilton was far from being reconciled with Adams; he even went so far as to write a pamphlet attacking some of his policies. But Hamilton was the main loser in this; most Federalists stood by Adams in the election of 1800, and Hamilton's influence was definitely on the wane.

The Election of 1800

Even so, there was no relaxation of the tension or lessening of the differences between the parties in 1800. If anything, they were greater than ever. The struggle for leadership, however, may have abated somewhat. Adams was clearly the choice of most Federalists now. Charles Cotesworth Pinckney of South Carolina was the choice for running mate this time, and, except for South Carolina, there was no doubt that Adams was the choice for President. One New England elector even cast one of his votes for Jay, rather than Pinckney, to make certain that Adams and Pinckney did not tie. Nor was there much reason to doubt that Jefferson was the choice of the Republicans for President.

In 1796 Jefferson was a reluctant candidate for any office, and it required some urging to get him to accept the vice presidency. When he resigned as Secretary of State in 1793, he had expressed the hope that he was leaving political life for good. He had no taste for the contest of wills involved in political decision making or for defending himself from attacks in the newspapers. But the Alien and Sedition Acts revived his zeal considerably, and by 1800 his reluctance had all but vanished. Moreover, the Republicans had a bundle of issues by this time. In addition to the prosecutions under the Sedition Act, there were the Hamiltonian economic policies, still more or less in effect, the direct taxes which stirred more opposition generally than violations of civil liberties were likely to do, the penchant of some Federalists for standing armies and large navies, their penchant, as well, for at least the trappings of monarchy, preference for the British. Above all, there was the question of the interpretation of the Constitution. The Jeffersonians had grounds, at least, for their belief that the Federalists would take liberties with the Constitution and interpret it so as to continually expand the powers of the central government. Aaron Burr of New York was Jefferson's running mate.

Although it is referred to as the election of 1800, it was not actually completed until 1801. The electoral vote resulted in a tie between the two top candidates, Jefferson and Burr. They each received 73 votes, Adams 65, Pinckney 64, and John Jay 1. Thus, the decision was thrown into the House of Representatives. The Constitution prescribes that the House elect a President in the event of a tie, voting by states rather than individuals, with each state to have one vote. By February of 1801, when the vote by the House was taken, there were 16 states in the union. In addition to Kentucky, Vermont and Tennessee had been added to the original 13. It required a majority, i.e., 9 states (or 9 votes) to elect a President.

To make matters even more complicated, the task of electing a President fell to the old Congress, not the one elected in 1800. In those days, there was always a "lame duck" session of Congress following a national election. Federalists were especially strong in many states in the old Congress, yet they had the task of choosing a Republican President. The Federalists generally favored Burr, though Burr himself insisted that the intention of the electors was to elect Jefferson as President, and where they were dominant they generally cast the state ballot for Burr. This, despite the fact that Hamilton used every ounce of influence he could muster to persuade them to vote for Jefferson. Not that Hamilton wanted Jefferson in the office, but he wanted Burr even less. All this was to no avail through 35 ballots; neither Jefferson nor Burr received the 9 votes necessary for election. Finally, on the 36th ballot, several votes were changed or voted blank, and Jefferson received the vote of 10 states. Burr then became Vice President.

On the face of it, there was little in the election that would suggest that the struggle for political leadership was over. It was as close as between Jefferson and Adams; if South Carolina had given its vote to the Federalists, which was considered, the outcome would have been different. Jefferson and Burr tied in the electoral vote, and it took the House 36 ballots to resolve the issue. But the election was the climax; the struggle had ended. As it turned out, the triumph of the Republican Party was conclusive. So far as individuals were concerned, the contest ended in 1801, or shortly after. Adams packed his possessions and left the capital even before the hour of the inauguration of Jefferson. He had retired from political life. Hamilton had spent his influence in a futile attempt to maneuver the Adams administration and decide elections. He died as a result of wounds received in a duel with Aaron Burr in 1804. That plus implications in a conspiracy finished Burr's political life. It remained to Jefferson to set the course of the government.

Chapter 9

The Jeffersonian Republicans

Still one thing more fellow-citizens—a wise and frugal Government, which shall restrain men from injuring one another, shall leave them otherwise free to regulate their own pursuits of industry and improvement, and shall not take from the mouth of labor the bread it has earned. This is the sum of good government....

—Thomas Jefferson, 1801

I am firmly of the opinion that, if the present Administration and Congress do not...[pay the debt at the rate proposed], the debt will be...on us and the ensuing generations....

—Albert Gallatin, 1801

In questions of power, then, let no more be heard of confidence in man but bind him down from mischief by the chains of the Constitution.

—Thomas Jefferson, 1798

Chronology

1800—Government moves to Washington.

1801—Judiciary Act.

1802—Excise Taxes Abolished.

1803—*Marbury vs. Madison.*

1804—Impeachment of Judge John Pickering.

1807—Burr Treason Trial.

1808—Madison elected President.

1811—Congress refuses to renew Bank Charter.

1816—Second United States Bank established.

1816—Monroe elected President.

1817—Madison vetoes Bill for Internal Improvements.

1819—Panic and Depression.

1819—*Dartmouth College vs. Woodward.*

1820—Missouri Compromise.

1822—Monroe vetoes Cumberland Road Bill.

There were two great surges which established the direction and character of the government under the Constitution. The first great surge was by those who were called Federalists. The Federalists did not constitute a political party at first. Those who favored the ratification of the Constitution as it was presented applied the name to themselves. By and large, they were made up of those who were most determined to replace the confederation with a government that could act directly on the people. Once the Constitution had been ratified and the Bill of Rights adopted, the struggle of the original Federalists was over.

The struggle over control of the direction of the government, however, had hardly begun. After 1793, that struggle became sufficiently intense to give rise to political parties. The Federalists emerged as one of these parties; Alexander Hamilton and John Adams were its most noteworthy leaders. Washington tried to maintain a position above partisan conflicts, but he contributed to it to some extent in at least two ways. In the first place, from the outset he insisted on surrounding himself with men firmly committed to making the Constitution work. That meant generally that he chose officers in the government from among those who supported the ratification of the Constitution. Second, Washington usually supported Hamilton's programs, which meant that he contributed to the rise of the opposition party, the Jeffersonians as well as to the consolidation of a Federalist Party.

At any rate, the thrust of the Federalists was nationalistic, for a vigorous general government, and a broad construction of the Constitution. Hamilton tended also toward what would now be called a managed economy. His attempts to manage the money supply, promote manufacturing and follow mercantilist policies were in that direction. Federalists were inclined to want to use the general government to hold local government in line and to check licentious tendencies among the people. Some of them, at least, wanted the government to make people do the right thing (a not uncommon attitude of those who have governed at all times). There is no doubt that in the early years these policies contributed to the power and prestige of the new government.

The second great surge was provided by the Republican Party. More specifically, it was provided by the Jeffersonians who governed from 1801-1825. Some books refer to them as Democrats, and the present-day Democratic Party traces its origins, rightly or wrongly, back to Jefferson. But Jefferson preferred to be called a Republican, and his preference will be honored here. The germ of this party can be seen in the anti-Federalists, who opposed the ratification of the Constitution, usually because it lacked a bill of rights at the time and, in the opinion of some, endangered the independence of the states. Once a bill of rights had been adopted, however, resistance to the Constitution disappeared. Moreover, some of those who had been Federalists when the Constitution was under consideration became Republicans. No one labored more diligently than he to make the Constitution and get it ratified. But once it was ratified, Madison became a strict constructionist and joined with Jefferson to build the Republican Party.

The Jeffersonians stood for economy in government, the independent powers of the states (sometimes called state's "rights"), free trade and free enterprise, and a strict construction of the Constitution. Above all, Jefferson and his followers wished to limit government to its essential functions, keep it out of the lives of people, and leave people to pursue their own well-being in their own ways. The surge of the Jeffersonians was to bring the central government into line with the ways of America, not to awe people by the power of the government but to earn their affection by having it reflect the best that was in them. Many Federalists were not quite so certain that people generally had better selves.

It would not do, however, to draw the lines too sharply between the Federalists and Republicans. Jefferson said it well in his inaugural address, as he attempted to draw the country together after the bitter partisan struggle: "But every difference of opinion is not a difference of principle. We have called by different names brethren of the same principle. We are all Republicans, we are all Federalists." He had already asked that his countrymen bear in mind "this sacred principle, that though the will of the majority is in all cases to prevail, that will to be rightful must be reasonable, that the minority possess their equal rights, which equal law must protect, and to violate would be oppression." The important points here, however, were that there was widespread agreement on principles shared by both Federalists and Republicans and that the Republicans brought a different emphasis rather than some sort of revolutionary change to the government. That emphasis was that the government should reflect the character of the country at its best.

The United States in 1800

What was the character of the country? The census of 1800 gives a few indications. It revealed that there were now 5,308,483 persons in the United States. To put it another way, this vast country reaching to the Mississippi had about one-third the number of the much smaller British Isles. About a million of these were black, mostly slaves and were concentrated from Maryland southward. The center of population of the country was located a few miles west of Baltimore and north and east of Washington, D.C., about one-half million of the total population lived west of the Appalachians, but most people still lived near the seaboard, two-thirds within 50 miles of tidewater.

Indeed, it was still not practicable to live far from some navigable stream. Travel overland was difficult enough in itself. Thomas Jefferson reported that to get from his home, Monticello, near Charlottesville in Virginia to the new capital at Washington, he had to cross eight rivers, none of which was bridged. But to transport heavy freight overland was too expensive where it was not impossible. Even west of the Alleghenies, in Pennsylvania, Ohio, Kentucky, and Tennessee, most of the settlements were on large navigable streams, usually the Ohio, Cumberland, or Tennessee Rivers. Overland, what passed for roads were often little more than trails. Nor were there any paved roads in America, only a few city streets, with rough cobblestones or bricks.

These details may serve to remind us that the pace of technological change had barely picked up at the beginning of the 19th century. Many, indeed most, things were done much as they had been done time out of mind. Most Americans were farmers, and their modes of doing things had changed little from those of distant ancestors. Henry Adams reminds us that "The cloth which the farmer's family wore was still homespun. The hats were manufactured by the village hatter; the clothes were cut and made at home; the shirts, socks, and nearly every article of dress were also home-made....The plough was rude and clumsy; the sickle as old as Tubal Cain, and even the cradle [a device for cutting grain] not in general use; the flail was unchanged since the Aryan exodus; in Virginia, grain was still commonly trodden out by horses."[127]

True, the pace of inventions was already beginning to increase even before 1800. The steam engine had been in limited use throughout the 18th century. The first such engines were used exclusively for pumping water, but after 1763 James Watt not only made great improvements in the engine but also developed the means for the engine to turn a shaft and flywheel. But it was after the turn of the century before the engine was used to power transport devices and longer still before it would be used to turn machinery.

In the latter part of the 18th century several inventions were made in Britain which made it possible to spin thread and weave cloth more quickly with machines which could be turned by water power. Eli Whitney invented a cotton gin in 1793, which, though it was at first turned

Two Constitutional Amendments

(Although the 11th Amendment was ratified in 1798, it is clearly connected with the Jeffersonian impulse for state's rights. In Chisholm vs. Georgia (1793), the Supreme Court affirmed its power to make a state a party to a suit. Hence, the 11th Amendment. The 12th Amendment, on the other hand, was a direct result of the election tie in 1800.)

ARTICLE XI
[Declared Ratified January 8, 1798]

The Judicial power of the United States shall not be construed to extend to any suit in law or equity, commenced or prosecuted against one of the United States by Citizens of another State, or by Citizens or Subjects of any Foreign State.

ARTICLE XII
[Declared Ratified September 25, 1804]

The Electors shall meet in their respective states, and vote by ballot for President and Vice-President, one of whom, at least, shall not be an inhabitant of the same state with themselves; they shall name in their ballots the person voted for as President, and in distinct ballots the person voted for as Vice-President, and they shall make distinct lists of all persons voted for as President, and of all persons voted for as Vice-President, and of the number of votes for each, which lists they shall sign and certify, and transmit sealed to the seat of the Government of the United States, directed to the President of the Senate;—The President of the Senate shall, in the presence of the Senate and House of Representatives, open all the certificates and the votes shall then be counted;—The person having the greatest number of votes for President, shall be the President, if such number be a majority of the whole number of Electors appointed; and if no person have such majority, then from the persons having the highest numbers not exceeding three on the list of those voted for as President, the House of Representatives shall choose immediately, by ballot, the President. But in choosing the President, the votes shall be taken by states, the representation from each state having one vote; a quorum for this purpose shall consist of a member or members from two-thirds of the state, and a majority of all the states shall be necessary to a choice. And if the House of Representatives shall not choose a President whenever the right of choice shall devolve upon them, before the fourth day of March next following, then the Vice-President shall act as President, as in the case of the death or other constitutional disability of the President. The person having the greatest number of votes as Vice-President, shall be the Vice-President, if such number be a majority of the whole number of Electors appointed, and if no person have a majority, then from the two highest numbers on the list, the Senate shall choose the Vice-President; a quorum for the purpose shall consist of two-thirds of the whole number of Senators and a majority of the whole number shall be necessary to a choice. But no person constitutionally ineligible to the office of President shall be eligible to that of Vice-President of the United States.

by hand, could separate the lint from the seed many times faster than could be done by hand. The elements of what would later be called an industrial revolution were making their appearance, but they had as yet hardly made a dent in the old ways of producing and transporting goods. The horse drawn vehicle on land and the oar and sail propelled boats on water were still the dominant modes of transportation. And, the most that imaginative Americans could think of doing about improving things would be to build better roads and connect streams and bodies of water to one another by canals. Some day, they might hope, transport in America might attain the level that had existed in Europe for centuries.

Aside from the outermost edges of the frontier, nowhere was the rawness of the country more apparent than in the federal capital itself. A District of Columbia beside the Potomac River, which runs between the states of Virginia and Maryland, had been designated as the site of the capital. The city itself was named Washington. The government had moved there from Philadelphia in 1800, but both the government buildings and the city were much more of a hope, or promise, than a reality. "When in the summer of 1800," as Henry Adams said, "the government was transferred to what was regarded by most persons as a fever-stricken morass, the half-finished White House stood in a naked field overlooking the Potomac, with two awkward Department buildings near it, a single row of brick houses and a few isolated dwellings within sight, and nothing more; until across a swamp, a mile and a half away, the shapeless, unfinished Capitol was seen, two wings with-

Eli Whitney (1765-1825)

Whitney was an inventor, something of a mechanical genius and innovator, and a manufacturer. He was born in Westboro, Massachusetts and graduated from Yale College. While visiting on a plantation near Savannah, Georgia, he learned of the difficulty of separating the cotton seed from the lint by hand. Once he had seen the problem, he went to work and devised a machine—the cotton gin—which could do the work as fast as 25 people could by hand. The gin made it practical to use short staple cotton rather than, or in addition to, other fibers in making thread and cloth, and it was this invention which prepared the way for cotton to become king in the South. Whitney also introduced the principle of interchangeable parts and used assembly line methods in his firearms factory.

out a body, ambitious enough in design to make more grotesque the nature of its surroundings....[T]here were in Washington no shops or markets, skilled labor, commerce, or people."[128] Or, as a poet put it a few years later:

> Though nought but woods and Jefferson they see,
> Where streets should run and sages ought to be.[129]

Although the lines for a fine city had been designed by Major L'Enfant, a French engineer, the whole would be many years in taking shape. Meanwhile the unfinished capital was an excellent symbol of the country and the government from a Jeffersonian point of view.

The Jeffersonians

The Jeffersonians, as the term is used here, consist primarily of those Presidents who composed that line also described as the Virginia Dynasty. They governed from 1801-1825, were all from Virginia; each had served as Secretary of State before becoming President. They were Thomas Jefferson, James Madison, and James Monroe. They are called Jeffersonians, too, because the last two followed the philosophical leadership of Jefferson and were in the Republican Party he founded. Superficially, the description also fits John Quincy Adams (President, 1825-1829), except that he was not from Virginia, did not subscribe to Jefferson's philosophy, and the party was breaking up by the time he became President. Another name should definitely be listed as a major Jeffersonian leader. Albert Gallatin served as Secretary of the Treasury during both of Jefferson's terms and for several years under Madison. Gallatin was foreign born—Swiss—and a Pennsylvanian by choice, but he was a Jeffersonian by conviction and, if anything, superior to Hamilton as a financier and economist.

The Jeffersonian Republicans controlled the Congress as well as the presidency. Only the courts eluded their grasp, but that is a story to be told below. If anything, a large portion of the Congress was now more devoted to Jeffersonian principles than was the administration; particularly, they were disinclined to extend the power of the general government, favored free enterprise, and were inclined to respect the powers of the states. That Congress was little disposed to engage in regulatory adventures appears obvious from the following example. When a committee of the Congress considered legislation to regulate steamboats, it recommended against enactment, declaring that "in a free State, where every one is entitled to cultivate his own vineyard according to the dictates of his own judgment, to require that it should be done in a prescribed form, and with a specific amount of labor, or power, would appear to be an interference with individual discretion, and an encroachment on the rights of the citizen...."[130]

James Monroe (1758-1831)

Monroe was the fifth President of the United States and the last who belonged to the generation that founded the United States. Among the many other offices that he held were: Secretary of State, Senator, Governor of Virginia, and Minister to Great Britain. He had earlier been a delegate to the Virginia convention for ratification of the Constitution, a member of the Continental Congress, and he was often appointed to serve on diplomatic missions, including the one to France which resulted in the purchase of Louisiana. Monroe was born in Virginia, attended William and Mary College, and studied law under Thomas Jefferson. He was a good listener and learner if not a great thinker and, as might be expected from his extensive experience in foreign affairs, the greatest achievements of his administrations were in that field. Specifically, they were the acquisition of Florida from Spain and the Monroe Doctrine.

The Jeffersonians in power changed some things and continued others from the Washington and Adams administrations and from the way they were under the Federalists. In contrast to Adams, Jefferson appointed an entirely new cabinet, with Madison and Gallatin in the most prominent posts. He also replaced a considerable number of lesser officials in the government. Jefferson had a penchant for calling changes revolutions, and in one sense he did effect a revolution. That is, those who had been in control of the government were turned out and new ones appointed generally. But it was a peaceful change, and a most valuable precedent was set for such a change. There were some changes in the judiciary also, but that story belongs elsewhere. Taxes were reduced, and the Jeffersonians made large strides in retiring the debt. The army was reduced in size, and the navy kept to a minimum in size and activity. The Federalists had been accused of building a large military establishment in the course of mustering forces with which to confront the French. The Jeffersonians checked the growth of the military.

The Sedition Act was allowed to expire, and Jefferson initiated no prosecutions under it. Instead, he pardoned one of the more notorious of the offenders. On the other hand, the United States Bank was permitted to continue to operate. In foreign policy, Jefferson was even more adamant about staying out of the political entanglements of Europe than Washington had been.

The most obvious change that came with the Jeffersonians was a change in style, though it signified, too, some changes in direction. The change in style is best characterized as "republican simplicity." Its opposite was formality, pomp and show, and, as the Jeffersonians saw it, aping the ceremonious ways of European courts. Washington held ceremonial receptions, delivered his annual addresses before Congress, and presidential messages for both Washington and Adams were answered by formal replies from Congress. Jefferson entertained informally, made no distinctions between his guests, and observed the rule of "pell mell"—the guest could scramble to get the seats that pleased them—at meals. He abandoned the practice of presenting his annual message in person, and it was not resumed until the time of Woodrow Wilson. He let it be known, too, that he expected no formal reply to any of his messages from Congress.

In many ways, Jefferson was the embodiment of the republican simplicity which he favored. The Secretary of the British Legation described him this way in 1804:

> He was a tall man, with a very red freckled face and gray neglected hair; his manners good-natured, frank, and rather friendly, though he had somewhat of a cynical expression of countenance. He wore a blue coat, a thick gray-colored hairy waistcoat, with a red under-waist coat lapped over it, green velveteen breeches with pearl buttons, yarn stockings, and slippers down at the heels,—his appearance being very much like that of a tall, large-boned farmer.[131]

There was more to all these things than is covered by the idea of republican simplicity, however. Jefferson was a man of essentials, not of appearances. He did many things in the course of his life, but he was above all a thinker, a philosopher, a man concerned with the truth of ideas, not creating an image. He was not an orator, hardly a public speaker at all, and he avoided occasions for demonstrating his incapacity. Beyond that, he did not like confrontations which led to the clash of ideas. He did not even hold cabinet meetings when they could be avoided, preferring to have the opinions of his department heads in writing. When people are assembled in a group, differences of opinion tend to turn into a clash of wills for dominance. Jefferson despised such displays, believing, no doubt, that truth is best arrived at by quiet meditation and thought and expressed in writing. He won followers by the elevation of his ideas and clarity of his thought, not by the assertion of his will. These traits which were an integral part of his philosophical temperament probably contributed to the belief of some that he was secretive and guilty of duplicity. Those who do not wish to engage in contention often give the appearance of agreeing when they are being congenial and avoiding argument. In any case, Jefferson's ideas made a large impact both on his contemporaries and on American history.

The Constitution as Higher Law

No doubt, those who labored to provide the Constitution in Philadelphia in 1787 intended that it should be some kind of higher law. That is, they intended that acts made in pursuance of it should be the supreme law of the land and that it should be higher than acts of the legislature. The very methods they provided for its ratification and the difficulties they put in the way of amending it make it plain that they meant it to stand apart from and above ordinary law. Moreover, Americans were quite familiar with the idea of a higher law. They had been under the British constitution, colonial charters, believed in the natural law, and generally accepted the Scriptures as higher than all man-made laws. But intending is one thing and accomplishment is another. The usual fate of constitutions is for those in power either to ignore them or to construe the powers so generously that they are soon a dead letter. That did not happen to the United States Constitution, not for the first 150 years of its existence anyway.

The main explanation of this is that during the period when the Jeffersonians governed, the Constitution attained its full stature as higher law. There were already signs under Federalist direction that the Constitution was being stretched out of shape and not serving as a brake upon government. In his Farewell Address, Washington warned against "change [of the Constitution] by usurpation; for though this in one instance may be the instrument of good, it is the customary weapon by which free governments are destroyed." But Hamilton's broad construction, if not a usurpation, was certainly capable of being interpreted as a means of expanding the powers of government. More directly, the Sedition Act extended the power of Congress over the control of expression in ways not only not authorized by the Constitution but also apparently specifically prohibited. Granted, the Constitution only prohibits Congress to make laws abridging *freedom* of speech and of the press, and that it is possible to argue that seditious or defamatory statements do not belong in that category. Even so, there is no delegation of power to Congress to make laws dealing with such matters, and a good case could be made that the power to do so was reserved to the states or to the people. In any case, at the beginning of the 19th century the Constitution did not yet occupy that pinnacle as higher law which it held for most of the century.

Two developments in the early 19th century contributed most to producing the change. One was the ascendancy of John Marshall over the Supreme Court. The other was the triumph of the Jeffersonian doctrine of strict construction of the Constitution. Though Marshall was a Virginian, he was hardly a follower of Jefferson. On the contrary, he was a Federalist, was appointed at the last minute by President Adams to his seat as Chief Justice, and was a determined opponent of Jefferson. Moreover, Jefferson was bent on a course of restraining and limiting the courts. Clearly, then, Marshall and the Jeffersonians did not work together to elevate the Constitution to its eminent position as higher law. Rather, it gained this position as a result of the contest between them. This is precisely how the framers intended the Constitution would work. They expected that men in power would contend for more power for themselves and their branches of government. They hoped that they would be counterbalanced by those in other branches so that power would be limited and the Constitution respected. This was the outcome in the contest between Marshall and the Jeffersonians.

Jefferson intended to limit and restrain the courts. The result was a struggle with the judiciary or over judicial matters during his first term in office. The first contest was over the Judiciary Act of 1801. Just before the Federalists left office and turned the government over to the Republicans, Congress (the Lame Duck session) passed a new judiciary act. It reduced the number of Supreme Court justices from 6 to 5, added circuit judges to the federal courts (so that justices of the Supreme Court would no longer have to ride circuit), and added to the number of clerks, marshals, and attorneys in the court system. President Adams filled these new posts in what were dubbed "midnight appointments" with Federalists just before leaving office. The Federalists might no longer control Congress and the presidency, but they were apparently well dug in in the judiciary.

The Republicans, prodded by Jefferson, moved to repeal the act of 1801 and to pass a new judiciary act in 1802. This latest act increased the number of Supreme Court justices to six once again, provided that they should ride circuit as they had before, and permitted the Supreme Court to have only one session annually. What of the men who had received appointments as circuit court judges? Their appointments were for life during good behavior. Yet they no longer had any positions to fill and had, in effect, been removed from office. Could Congress and the President do that? There was considerable debate about this, but none of it changed the fact that they had been effectively removed from office.

There was more from the "midnight appointments," however. Some of them were never delivered. John Marshall had been Secretary for the outgoing John Adams, and he did not receive them in time to deliver them. William Marbury was appointed justice of the peace for the District of Columbia, and Jefferson ordered his Secretary of State, James Madison, not to deliver the commission. Marbury sued in the Supreme Court, asking for a *writ of mandamus* compelling Madison to deliver the commission. Although Marshall, now serving as Chief Justice, had been involved in the appointment, he sat on the case and actually wrote the famous *Marbury vs. Madison* decision in 1803. Before describing its importance, however, some observations about Marshall may be helpful.

The Supreme Court had not emerged as a distinguished branch of the United States government until after Marshall became its head. Indeed, John Jay, who had served for a few years as Chief Justice before resigning, refused an offer to head it once again on the grounds that it was defective as an organization. Nor did it help matters in the late 1790s that several of the justices behaved in an unjudicial manner in their vigorous enforcement of the Sedition Act. Nor did it contribute to the dignity of the court to have its members riding circuit over the length and breadth of the country. No man had yet been appointed to the post who could speak to and for the court in such a way as to elevate both the court and the Constitution to their appointed roles. John Marshall changed that.

Judging by externals, Marshall was an unlikely selection to accomplish those feats. He had but the skimpiest of training in the law, but he managed to make a virtue of that, as we shall see. This description of him was written shortly after he came to the Supreme Court:

> The [Chief Justice] of the United States is, in his person, tall, meager, emaciated; his muscles relaxed, and his joints so loosely connected, as not only to disqualify him, apparently for any vigorous exertion of body, but to destroy everything like elegance and harmony in his air and movements....To continue the portrait: his head and face are small in proportion to his height; his complexion swarthy....His voice is dry and hard; his attitude, in his most effective orations, was often extremely awkward, as it was not unusual for him to stand with his left foot in advance, while all his gestures proceeded from his right arm....[132]

His less than striking appearance was more than offset, however, by a gentle disposition, by the ability to capture the attention of an audience by the manner of his presentation, and by relying on persuasion rather than dramatics in debate. His dignity was inward rather than outward, and it stemmed both from his confidence in his own reasoning ability and faith that his listeners could discern the strength of his case. During his 34 years as Chief Justice he wrote most of the major decisions handed down by the court, and there was rarely a dissent. He achieved this ascendancy by the superiority of his grasp of the issues and his ability to find a resolution in the law that compelled assent.

Two ideas undergirded Marshall's work as a jurist. One was that he was a nationalist. Although he was born and died a Virginian, his mind was attuned to thinking of the country as a whole. In this, he resembled another great Virginian, George Washington, who was a much admired neighbor of Marshall's. Marshall explained the outlook this way: "I had

John Marshall (1755-1835)

Marshall was Chief Justice of the Supreme Court from 1801-1835. His magisterial decisions gave a stature to the court, and through it to the Constitution, which they did not have before. He construed the Constitution carefully so as to give the general government its full measure of power. Marshall was born in Virginia, served in the Continental Army during the war, and began the practice of law in his native state after only a brief study of it. Nevertheless, he distinguished himself as the leading lawyer in the state. He was a spokesman for adoption in the convention which ratified the Constitution in Virginia, served several years in his state legislature, and was elected to the House of Representatives. Although he was active in politics and Federalist in sympathies, Marshall was not eager for national appointments. He declined two offers of position in Washington's administration before he reluctantly accepted an appointment as Secretary of State in the last year of Adams' term. As Chief Justice he relied much more on careful reasoning than upon legal tradition. By so doing, Marshall raised the Constitution to its unique position in American law.

grown up at a time when the love of the Union and the resistance to Great Britain were the inseparable inmates of the same bosom;...when the maxim 'United we stand, divided we fall' was the maxim of every orthodox American. And I had imbibed these sentiments so thoroughly that they constituted a part of my being. I carried them with me into the army, where I found myself associated with brave men from different States, who were risking life and everything valuable in a common cause believed by all to be the most precious, and where I was confirmed in the habit of considering America as my country and Congress as my government."[133]

The other was that Marshall was a constitutionalist. He took his text from the Constitution, so to speak, and expounded it in his decisions. He must have been able to do this much more readily because he was unencumbered by any extensive learning in the law. Had he been trained in the law in England, as many of his contemporaries were, or even in some American university, he might have tried to place the Constitution in the broad and comprehensive framework of the common law. Some of his contemporaries tended to do just that, and in the past century it has become increasingly common to treat the Constitution itself as if it were a common law instrument. Marshall apparently saw clearly that the Constitution lies outside of and above the common law. The common law, so far as it is applicable, must fit within the frame of the Constitution, not the Constitution within the frame of the common law. The Constitution is a written document which changes only by amendment; the common law evolves, changes, and grows with decisions of the courts.

At any rate, Marshall cast his opinions in the framework of the Constitution. He made it not subsidiary to some great body of law, but a higher law itself. As a 20th century legal authority has said, "his opinions show that he adhered closely to the words of the Constitution; indeed no one who has attempted to expound that instrument has confined himself more strictly to an examination of the text. In the proper ...sense he was the strictest of strict constructionists...."[134] That is not to say that his decisions and opinions pleased everyone. The Jeffersonians were not prepared to be pleased by them, but when they differed with him, they were on their mettle to find grounds in the Constitution for their differences, for those were the chosen grounds of Marshall. It may be that he was assisted in choosing that course by the very fact that the Jeffersonians were avowed strict constructionists, and they were looking over his shoulder.

There could be little doubt that the Jeffersonians were looking over his shoulder, as it were, when Marshall made his decision in the case of *Marbury vs. Madison* in 1803. The court held, in the first place, that

William Marbury was entitled to his commission as justice of the peace. He had been duly appointed in accordance with the law. Marshall then examined the question as to whether or not Marbury had applied to the proper court for relief. Specifically, did the Supreme Court have original jurisdiction in such cases? Here, Marshall came abreast of conflicting laws. A provision of the Judiciary Act of 1789 did indeed grant original jurisdiction to the court. On the other hand, the Constitution lists the instances of original jurisdiction of the court, and this was not one of them. Marshall raised the question as to whether the court was bound by acts of the legislature or provisions of the Constitution when the two were in conflict. Marshall put his problem this way: "So if a law [legislative enactment] be in opposition to the constitution; if both the law and the constitution apply to a particular case, so that court must either decide that case conformably to the law, disregarding the constitution, or conformably to the constitution, disregarding the law, the court must determine which of these conflicting rules govern the case. This is of the very essence of judicial duty."[135]

Marshall saw his duty, and he did it, as the saying goes. He declared that the court was bound by the Constitution, and that the court would not enforce, or act upon, the provision of the judiciary act to the contrary. Lacking jurisdiction of the case, the court denied Marbury his writ. The court had declared that as far as it was concerned, at least, that portion of the Judiciary Act of 1789 in question was null and void. This was the first time the Supreme Court had declared an act of Congress void.

Whether it was any part of his purpose or not, Marshall had also avoided a direct clash with the Jeffersonians. There is reason to doubt that even if the Supreme Court had issued the writ that Madison would have obeyed it. Indeed, Jefferson stated his position on the power of the courts to issue such writs forcing other branches to act. They had no such constitutional authority, he said. Specifically, "If the legislature fails to pass laws for a census, for paying the judges and other officers of government...as prescribed by the constitution..., the judges cannot issue their mandamus to them; if the President fails to supply the place of a judge, to appoint other civil or military officers, to issue requisite commissions, the judges cannot force him...."[136]

Let us draw out Jefferson's point a little. What he was saying was this. The House of Representatives cannot force the Senate to pass a measure sent to them. The Congress cannot force the President to accept a bill that has been passed. Neither can the courts force any other branch to act. Each division of the government is, as regards acting, independent of the others. That was the great importance to the Jeffersonians of the separation of powers. It is true, of course, that the branches often depend upon one another to effect an action. For example, in criminal court cases, the executive must act through United States attorneys to bring charges before a trial takes place. This necessity for two or more branches to act concurrently has a powerful limiting effect on the government. Since any branch may independently determine not to act, the government is restrained to those actions in which two or more branches concur.

Moreover, Jefferson held that each branch of the government has the duty and obligation to decide for itself on the constitutionality of matters which come before it. That is, each may interpret the Constitution and act or refuse to act in accord with its interpretation. An idea was already being advanced, one that now holds sway in the 20th century, that the courts have the final word, that their decision on the Constitution is binding on all. Jefferson did not doubt that in applying the law to particular cases the courts might make determinations of constitutionality, and that the decisions of the Supreme Court would govern the lower courts. But the other branches had prior and coordinate responsibilities for determining constitutionality for themselves. Thus, they would check one another and limit government.

The Jeffersonians, both in Congress and the executive, tended to adhere to this view of the Constitution. Both House and Senate made constitutional decisions in the course of legislating. Jefferson, Madison, and Monroe examined bills that came before them to determine if they were constitutional. Jefferson doubted that the Louisiana Purchase was authorized under the treaty making powers, and he favored a constitutional amendment to make certain. He said, "Our peculiar security is in the possession of a written Constitution. Let us not make it a blank paper by construction."[137] However, he allowed himself to be persuaded, in this case that the treaty making power was sufficient and that if he was wrong the voters would have an opportunity to correct him, for he believed the ultimate decisions on the Constitution belonged to the electorate.

Jefferson and his followers tried to restrain the power of the courts by impeachment. The House did impeach District Judge John Pickering of New Hampshire, and the Senate found him guilty and removed him from office. The facts that came out showed him to be intemperate and possibly insane. However, an effort in the same year (1804) to remove Supreme Court Justice Samuel Chase failed. The House did pass bills of impeachment, but the Senate failed to convict by the necessary two-thirds majority. Jefferson concluded after that the power of impeachment was too unlikely to be exercised to serve as much of a deterrent. Actually, however, there is good reason to believe that thereafter judges became more careful about what they said and did on the bench for some time.

In any case, the Jeffersonians continued to watch carefully for the constitutionality of what they did. In 1806, Jefferson could report that the Treasury had a surplus, and he thought that it might be well spent for the "great purposes of the public education, roads, rivers, canals, and...other objects of public improvement...." However, before these things could be done, he said, "I suppose an amendment to the Constitution, by the consent of the States, necessary, because the objects now recommended are not among those enumerated in the Constitution...."[138] No amendment which would authorize these expenditures was adopted, and Jefferson took no other steps. However, in 1817, Congress presented President Madison with a bill which pledged funds for roads, canals, and other navigation improvements. Madison vetoed the bill on constitutional grounds. He explained that, "The legislative powers vested in Congress are specified and enumerated in the eighth section of the first article of the Constitution, and it does not appear that the power proposed to be exercised by the bill is among the enumerated powers, or that it falls by any just interpretation within the ...other powers vested by the Constitution in the Government of the United States."[139]

President Monroe had a similar opportunity when a bill came before him in the 1820s appropriating money for maintaining the Cumberland Road. He vetoed it, declaring that no power was granted in the Constitution for such purposes. But Monroe was not satisfied simply to state the case; he later sent a lengthy paper to Congress explaining his reasons for the veto in detail. In it, he included these words in justification of strict construction. "Have Congress a right to raise and appropriate money to any and to every purpose according to their will and pleasure? They certainly have not. The Government of the United States is a limited Government, instituted for great national purposes, and for those only...."[140]

So it was that the Constitution became widely accepted as a higher law, though the idea of appealing to it was practiced from quite different political perspectives. John Marshall, from the Supreme Court, grounded his decisions in the Constitution to claim the full power of the United States government. In *Dartmouth College vs. Woodward*, for example, he annulled an effort by New Hampshire to alter Dartmouth College's charter, on the grounds that the Constitution prohibits states to impair the obligations of contracts. The Jeffersonians, on the other hand, held fast to a strict construction of the Constitution in defense of the states, the branches of the government, and limited government. Moreover, the Jeffersonian view that the other branches had an equal power with that of the courts to interpret the Constitution and that the electorate were the ultimate arbiters prevailed for many years. As the authors of a constitutional history say, "For more than half a century after *Marbury v. Madison* Congress and the President continued to consider themselves at least the equals of the judiciary in determining the constitutionality of legislation. In several important cases before the Supreme Court the validity of certain congressional acts was challenged, but in each case the Court upheld the act in question. Furthermore, practically every session of Congress was to witness lengthy constitutional debates in which the members could rely upon their own rather than the judges' interpretation. Likewise until after 1865 many more bills were invalidated by Presidents on the ground of their unconstitutionality than were invalidated by the Supreme Court."[141]

Economy in Government

The Jeffersonians were firm believers in government economy. Indeed, they came to office in the first place with that as a major concern, and in general they practiced what they preached. Indeed, the Democratic Party, which was one of the descendants of the Republican Party, was noted for favoring and practicing economy throughout most of the 19th century. Andrew Jackson and Grover Cleveland were outstanding later examples of economizers. It should be kept in mind, however, that the basic power over taxes and expenditures belongs to Congress, and, while Presidents may propose, they do not finally dispose.

There were three basic points in the Jeffersonian economy program. First, they wanted to keep taxes to a minimum. Jefferson had said in his First Inaugural that government should be frugal (thrifty) so as not to "take from the mouth of labor the bread it has earned." He appeared to understand clearly what those in government sometimes appear to forget, namely that government is financed by taxing away what others have earned. Jefferson was especially eager to remove the taxes on whiskey, carriages, and the like. The Republicans referred to these taxes usually as "direct" taxes and opposed them initially as being unconstitutional. The Constitution does permit direct taxes but requires that they be apportioned among the states on the basis of population. This had not been done with the above, and Hamilton evaded the requirement (as had been done ever since) by describing them as excises rather than direct taxes. John Taylor of Caroline, a Virginia thinker and Jeffersonian, proclaimed that the "union...is dissolved; states which impose unequal taxes, are masters, those which pay them, slaves."[142] When David Hylton, a Virginian, refused to pay the tax, the government sued (*United States vs. Hylton*) and won the case, though

Taylor served as his attorney. The Jeffersonians continued to oppose the taxes, though they shifted their grounds somewhat, and when Jefferson came to office he moved as quickly as he could to abolish them.

In a message to Congress, Jefferson said that "there is reasonable ground of confidence we may now safely dispense with all the internal taxes, comprehending excise, stamps, auctions, licenses, carriages, and refined sugars...."[143] It was done. But to keep taxes low, expenses had to be reduced. Gallatin wrote to Jefferson, "I cannot, my dear sir, consent to act the part of a mere financier, to become a contriver of taxes, a dealer of loans, a seeker of resources for the purposes of supporting useless baubles...."[144] True to his ideas, he kept a close watch on expenses. When the navy requested $40,000 in 1803 for contingencies, he reduced the amount to $10,000. Further, he wrote to Jefferson: "I allow three hundred thousand dollars to the Secretary of the Navy for the equipment of the four additional frigates: he wants four hundred thousand, but that is too much...."[145]

Undoubtedly, the Jeffersonians were opposed to any large military establishment, but they were equally opposed to any large civilian establishment in the government. Although it had now been more than a quarter of a century since Jefferson wrote in the Declaration of Independence, that the king had sent hither swarms of officials to eat out the substance of the people, the practice was still fresh in his mind as he thought about the federal government. In his Second Inaugural Address, he could report that the internal taxes which had covered "our land with officers" and opened "our doors to their intrusions," were no more. "What farmer, what mechanic, what laborer," he asked, "ever sees a taxgatherer of the United States?"[146] When Gallatin took over the Treasury in 1801, it had 1,285 employees. In 1826, after the close of Monroe's terms, the total stood at 1,075. That was another way of reducing expenditures.

A second purpose for economy was to reduce and ultimately to retire the debt. Jefferson did not believe that one generation should saddle succeeding ones with its debts. Hamilton had maintained that "the funding of the existing debt of the United States would render it a national blessing."[147] He reasoned that the government securities would rise in price in the market when a fund was set up to pay them and that, therefore, the capital in the country, which could be made available by the pledge of the securities, would increase. Gallatin denied that the debt of the government would increase the capital in the country. In the first place, he pointed out, the war, which had been the occasion of the debt, had consumed an immense amount of potential capital. In the second place, he argued, funding did not increase the total capital of the country. True, those who held or purchased the securities might experience an increase of capital when they appreciated in value. But that was counterbalanced by the loss of potential capital by taxpayers generally who would have to pay the debt. More, it would actually be overbalanced by what would have to be raised to pay the interest. Far from being a blessing, increasing capital, or enriching a nation, "every nation is enfeebled by a public debt," Gallatin said. He gave the examples of Spain and Holland and noted that in France "the public debt...has at last overwhelmed government itself."[148]

The way to reduce the debt, of course, is to have revenues exceed expenditures and use the surplus to apply to the debt. The Jeffersonians managed to do that in most years. Despite the cost of the purchase of Louisiana, Jefferson managed to reduce the debt significantly during his two terms. The cost of the War of 1812 reversed the process for Madison, but Monroe continued in most years to have a surplus to apply to the debt. The debt was not finally retired until the 1830s, but the Jeffersonians got the process well under way.

A third point for economy in government was related to the Jeffersonian strict construction of the Constitution. The federal government had, in their view, only a limited role in governing the country, and one way to see that it kept to that role was to limit revenues and expenditures. On this point, Jefferson said that "the States themselves have principal care of our persons, our property, and our reputation, constituting the great field of human concerns." That being the case, "we may well doubt whether our organization is not too complicated, too expensive; whether offices and officers have not multiplied unnecessarily and sometimes injuriously to the service they were meant to promote."[149] And, as already noted, the Jeffersonians used the veto to keep expenses within the frame of the Constitution.

The Era of Good Feelings

In July 1817, the *Columbian Centinel*, a newspaper in Boston, referred to the times beginning particularly with the presidency of James Monroe as an "Era of Good Feelings." Monroe himself said, after a tour of New England, "I have seen enough to satisfy me that the great mass of our fellow-citizens in the Eastern States are as firmly attached to the union and republican government as I have always believed or desired them to be."[150] Ever since then historians have customarily referred to the years from 1815-1825 as an era of good feelings.

The main, though not only, reason was the decline and virtual disappearance of partisan conflict for a few years. More specifically, it was the demise of the Federalist Party after 1816. The Federalists had been in decline since 1800. After the withdrawal of John Adams from politics and the death of Alexander Hamilton, no national figure had emerged to provide a fresh vision to the party. Indeed, the Federalists were hardly a national party after the early years of the 19th century. In 1804, Thomas Jefferson got a landslide victory over the Federalist candidate, Charles Pinckney, of 162 to 14. James Madison did not do so well against the same candidate in 1808, but he won by an electoral vote of 122 to 47. Madison won in 1812 over DeWitt Clinton by 128 electoral votes to 89.

By this time, the Federalists had become a New England party, in effect, the region in which its greatest strength had always been. The War of 1812 brought Federalist dissatisfaction with Republican dominance and Virginia leadership to a fever pitch. Federalists had inclined to sympathize with Britain in the European struggle over the years. New England leaders had smoldered over the foreign policy of Jefferson during his last two years in office, and President Madison's policies only disturbed them more. In the course of the war, the New England states refused to cooperate with the President in his efforts to call up their militia. Finally, in 1814, a New England Convention was called to meet at Hartford, Connecticut, to confer, as they said, upon "their public grievances and concerns," upon "defence against the enemy..., and also to take measures, if they seem proper, for procuring a convention of delegates from all the United States, in order to revise the Constitution thereof."[151] Delegates came mostly from Massachusetts, Rhode Island, and Connecticut, and though there was some wild talk about a separate peace with Britain, nullification of federal laws, a new constitutional convention, and the like, but the most that came out of the Hartford Convention were some recommended changes in the Constitution.

As it turned out, however, the Hartford Convention was virtually the dying gasp of the Federalist Party. Even before the official report reached Washington, a peace treaty had been worked out with Britain, and the war was officially over. But the Federalist Party was discredited nationally and never recovered. The Federalists did have a candidate in 1816, Rufus King of Massachusetts, to run against the Republican candidate, James Monroe. King lost, receiving only 34 electoral votes to 183 for Monroe, and he got electoral votes in only 3 states: Massachusetts, Connecticut, and Delaware. There was no Federalist candidate in 1820, and Monroe got all the votes except one.

There was more to the Republican triumph than the simple end of the Federalists. As the Federalist Party became regional, the Republicans became more national in scope. They became, in effect, the American Party for a few years and in doing so they absorbed some of the

Federalist ideas. This was indicated by the passage of two laws in 1816, while Madison was still President. One was the chartering of the Second United States Bank for 20 years, thus reviving a Hamiltonian program. The second was the passage of the Tariff Act of 1816. This was the first clearly protective tariff in American history; it contained a provision on pricing of textiles that effectively excluded some foreign goods from the American market. The protective tariff was reckoned as a measure mainly to aid American manufactures, and it had been recommended by Hamilton also.

Henry Clay (1777-1852)

Clay was an orator, a statesman, Congressional leader, and Kentucky gentleman. Although he was born in Virginia and studied law there, his political career was launched from Kentucky. He had little formal education, but he overcame this limitation by study on his own, and became one of the best known speakers in the country. At the age of 22, Clay was elected to the constitutional convention in Kentucky; at 26, to the state legislature; at 29, to the United States Senate, when he was still under age for the position. At 34, he was elected to the House of Representatives and immediately chosen Speaker of the House when he arrived. He served several terms as Speaker of the House, was Secretary of State under John Q. Adams, was often a presidential candidate though never elected, and occupied a Senate seat to finish out his political career. Clay was best known for the compromises he achieved, most notably the Missouri Compromise, the tariff compromise in 1833, and the Compromise of 1850. For his efforts as a peacemaker and to preserve the union, he was known as "the great pacificator."

But now new leaders who were both national minded and Republicans had emerged in Congress. John C. Calhoun of South Carolina and Henry Clay of Kentucky were the two most prominent. Clay became the spokesman for what was called the American System. The dominant idea was that America should be knit together economically by a system of roads and canals, manufactures developed behind a protective tariff, and a national bank to provide a common currency. However, both Madison and Monroe balked at extensive appropriations for roads and canals on constitutional grounds, as already noted. The tariff and bank questions, too, would eventually contribute to the division of Republicans into two parties.

For the time being, though, the mood was more national than regional or sectional. Monroe contributed to this mood by his selection for Secretary of State. His two predecessors had named men for the position who had succeeded them as President, both of whom were Virginians, thus maintaining the Virginia dynasty. Monroe named John Quincy Adams to the State Department, and, as it happened, broke the chain, for Adams was from Massachusetts and did become President. John Marshall continued to contribute to the national mood by his decisions in the Supreme Court. In 1824, he delivered his landmark decision on the commerce clause of the Constitution in the case of *Gibbons vs. Ogden.* Ogden had acquired the exclusive privilege of commercial navigation on the waters of New York state from those who had earlier received them as a grant from the state. Ogden sued Gibbons to prevent him from operating a steamboat between New York and New Jersey, and the suit came to the Supreme Court on appeal. The ruling went against Ogden and his monopoly on the river. In his opinion, Marshall pointed out that the Constitution grants power to Congress to regulate commerce among the states and with foreign nations and that where such commerce is concerned the states may not exercise a conflicting power over it. Thus, he vindicated the national power over that of the states in this case. It should be added, however, that the ruling was on the side of free enterprise, which should have pleased the Jeffersonians, and that Marshall arrived at his conclusion by sticking close to the language of the Constitution.

It would be misleading, however, to emphasize overmuch the absence of political conflict, the extent of national unity, or the decline of regionalism during the Era of Good Feeling. Well before 1824, when they would erupt and lead to indecision in a presidential election, contests over differences within the Republican Party were giving birth to new factions. The revival of mercantilist ideas in Clay's American System did not set well with those in the Jeffersonian line. Moreover, if the old regionalism declined, its place was about to be taken by Southern sectionalism. The Missouri Compromise in 1820 signified both a willingness to compromise to preserve national unity as well as the lack of foresight in establishing a line by law which would eventually divide and rend the union.

Toward the end of the year, 1819, both Maine and Missouri applied for admission to the union as states. Slavery emerged as a key issue in the contest over the admission of Missouri. When the two states applied for admission, there were 11 slave states and 11 free states. There was extended debate over whether slavery should be prohibited in Missouri. Eventually, a compromise was worked out. Missouri was admitted as a slave state and Maine as a free state. Even more important for the future, Congress passed a resolution excluding slavery from the Louisiana Purchase territory north of the line 36°30'. Temporary peace was bought at the price of future calamity.

None of this changes the fact that the Jeffersonians had served to knit the country together behind a program for limiting the federal government to a strict constitutional role.

Chapter 10

Napoleonic Wars and Expansion of the Domain

The day that France takes possession of New Orleans...We must marry ourselves to the British fleet and nation.

—Thomas Jefferson, 1802

British cruisers have been in the continued practice of violating the American flag..., and of carrying off persons sailing under it....American citizens...have been torn from their native country...; have been dragged on board ships of war of a foreign nation..., to be exiled to the most distant and deadly climes....

—James Madison, 1812

We owe it...to candor and to...those powers to declare that we should consider any attempt on their part to extend their system to any portion of this hemisphere as dangerous to our peace and safety.

—James Monroe, Monroe Doctrine, 1823

Chronology

1800—Treaty of San Ildefonso.

1801—War with Tripoli Begins.

1803—Purchase of Louisiana.

1804—Lewis and Clark Expedition.

1806—Nonimportation Act.

June 1807—*Chesapeake-Leopard* Affair.

November 1807—British Orders in Council.

1809—Nonintercourse Act.

1810—Macon's Bill No. 2.

1811—Battle of Tippecanoe.

1812—United States declares War on Britain.

1813—Battle of Montreal.

1814—Treaty of Ghent.

January 1815—Battle of New Orleans.

June 1815—Congress of Vienna.

September 1815—Formation of Holy Alliance.

1819—Acquisition of Florida.

1823—Monroe Doctrine.

Jefferson believed that the main business of the federal government was to conduct foreign relations for the United States. "I believe the States can best govern our home concerns, and the General Government our foreign ones."[152] More broadly, he would agree that the federal government deals with relations among the states as well as those with foreign powers. In any case, the Jeffersonians were much taken up with foreign affairs during the whole period from 1801-1825. It was almost inevitable that they should have disposed much of their energy this way. The independence of the United States, particularly the ability to follow an independent course in the world, was still very much at stake. After 1803 until 1815 the Napoleonic Wars raged over Europe and reached even the shores of America. After 1815, much of Europe was in the midst of a reaction, not only to the revolutionary ideas let loose by the French Revolution but also to republican institutions as well.

The Jeffersonians were generally well trained to deal with foreign relations. Jefferson himself had many years of diplomatic experience in Europe and had served for a term as Secretary of State under George Washington. Madison had no particular experience in diplomacy, but he served for two terms as Secretary of State under Jefferson. Monroe had extensive diplomatic experience ranging over more than 20 years prior to his serving two terms under Madison. Monroe's Secretary of State, John Quincy Adams, had been involved in diplomacy off and on for more than 30 years when he came to that post. Thus, they were men generally experienced in dealing with European nations and skilled in the arts of diplomatic exchange.

If anything, the Jeffersonians were more determined than Washington to steer clear of European quarrels and wars or entangling alliances with any nation. Nor was American independence any less dear to them. But their goals, and those of Americans more generally, brought them athwart the course of European nations. Jefferson, for example, believed in free trade, freedom of the seas, remaining at peace with other nations so far as possible, and that the United States should

John Quincy Adams (1767-1848)

Adams was born in Massachusetts, graduated from Harvard, and trained as a lawyer. He was the sixth President of the United States and the eldest son of the second. His presidency was not especially distinguished; like his father before him he came to office in the midst of a struggle for political leadership and no clear direction had been established. Nonetheless, Adams had a long and distinguished career, in the course of which his presidency was only an interlude. His career of public service began in 1781 and ended with his death in 1848. It began in 1781 at the age of 14, when he went to St. Petersburg as secretary to the Minister of Russia and ended at the age of 80 when he had a stroke on the floor of the House of Representatives. He was a vital force in American diplomacy beginning in the 1790s and culminating with his years as Secretary of State under Monroe (1817-1825). And after his term in the White House Adams shortly thereafter ran for and obtained a seat in the House of Representatives, which he held for many years. Moreover, his lengthy and literate diaries have influenced historians and the telling of early American history since their public release.

follow an independent course in the world. If the rest of the world had been at peace, that would have been a much easier policy, but, of course, during the Napoleonic wars and their aftermath that was hardly the case.

Jefferson's foreign policy may have been influenced to some extent by his agrarian beliefs, as they have sometimes been called. An agrarian usually believes in the superiority of farming as a way of life to that of city and factory life. In 1785, Jefferson wrote:

>...Those who labor in the earth are the chosen people of God, if ever he had a chosen people, whose breast he has made his peculiar deposit for substantial and genuine virtue....Corruption of morals in the mass of cultivators is a phenomenon of which no age nor nation has furnished an example. It is [rather] the mark set on

those, who not looking up to heaven, to their own soil and industry, as does the husbandman, for their subsistence, depend for it on...caprice of customers....While we have land to labor then..., let our work-shops remain in Europe. It is better to carry provisions and materials to work-men there....The mobs of great cities add just so much to the support of pure government, as sores do to the strength of the human body.[153]

This view of things committed him toward the development of foreign trade and the protection of shipping in the sea lanes of the world.

His desire to remain at peace, however, led him to have to make a choice, at least temporarily, between aggressive measures in support of trade or to restrain trade. It was hardly a choice to his liking, or to that of Madison, who succeeded him. Undoubtedly, Jefferson believed in peace. "Peace," he wrote, "has been our principle, peace is our interest, and peace has saved to the world this only plant [the United States] of free and rational government now existing in it." But he denied what his own administrations prove: that he wanted peace at any price. "My hope of preserving peace for our country," Jefferson said, "is not founded in the Quaker principles of nonresistance under every wrong...."[154] Sometimes a choice has to be made.

Americans were confronted not only with difficulty on the seas during these years and the efforts of European nations on one side or the other to draw them into the conflict but also the United States was confronted on three sides by territory belonging to European countries. To the North was Canada controlled by the British. To the west of the Mississippi was Spanish territory in 1800, and to the South as well. The only access to the Gulf of Mexico was through New Orleans, which was Spanish territory. What was then called West Florida extended across what is now South Alabama and Mississippi. The port at Mobile was not available, nor the one at Appalachicola, which is still in Florida. Much of the American activity during the years 1801-1825 can be explained in terms of an effort to be free of the restraints and dangers of dealing with these European powers so near at hand. In any case, it was a period of territorial expansion and of an extended effort to remain independent during the European struggle.

War with Tripoli

Jefferson did not have a long wait after becoming President before making a decision between peace and military action. Several principalities along the Barbary Coast of North Africa were accustomed to exacting bribes from countries whose ships plied the Mediterranean.

Piracy was, in fact, a way of life for these principalities—Morocco, Algiers, Tunis, and Tripoli. American colonial shipping had been protected by the bribes paid by the British. The British could have put these pirates out of business by strong naval action, but they found it to their advantage to have competitors driven from the Mediterranean or forced to pay heavy bribes. At any rate, Congress began paying bribes during the Confederation period, and it was continued during the administrations of Washington and Adams. Jefferson despised the practice. "Tribute or war is the usual alternative of these Barbary pirates," he declared. "Why not build a navy and decide on war."[155]

Actually, Jefferson did not build a navy, but he did slim down the one that had been recently built and bring it up to fighting trim. And it is doubtful that it should be called a war, for Congress did not declare war, and the President did not deign to dignify these outlaws by asking for one. The Pasha of Tripoli, a particularly obnoxious ruffian among these petty rulers, did declare war, in his barbaric manner, by chopping down the flag which flew over the American consulate in Tripoli in May 1801. The American decision was to attempt to bring the Tripolitans to terms by a naval blockade. This was pursued rather ineffectively until 1803, when Commodore Edward Preble took over with an enlarged fleet at his command.

The most stirring episode occurred in 1804. The United States frigate *Philadelphia* had got stuck on a reef, which surrounded and protected the harbor from large ships, and its crew of 300 captured by Tripoli. Not only did the Tripolitans have a large number of captives but also a warship which they might fit out for their own purposes. Commodore Preble, however, conceived a daring plan to thwart these designs by destroying the ship. Lieutenant Stephen Decatur, commander of the sloop *Enterprise*, was placed in charge of what well might have been a suicide mission. The plan was to use a boat captured from Tripoli to carry ammunition and explosives to board the *Philadelphia*, bombard the port, and burn it or any other ships in the harbor. When Decatur asked for volunteers every man in his crew stepped forward, so that it was necessary to select from among these brave men. They did, indeed, manage to board the *Philadelphia*, rake the harbor, and burn the ship; on top of it all, they made good their escape.

Still, the blockade dragged on until 1805 before the Pasha agreed to negotiations. Before that happened, however, an American adventurer, William Eaton, had put together a land operation, under the tacit command of the navy, to make a march with what force he could gather across the desert to Tripoli. Before this expedition reached Tripoli, however, negotiations had begun, and it was called off.

The Pasha still exacted as much as he could to come to terms with the

Stephen Decatur
(1779-1820)—

Decatur was a naval commander. He was born in Maryland, entered the navy in 1798 as a midshipman, was soon promoted to lieutenant, and fought in the undeclared naval war with France. His fearless behavior first brought him to wider attention in the War with Tripoli, in the episode of the foray into the harbor of Tripoli to board the *Philadelphia*. He commanded the *United States* during the War of 1812, and was involved in the naval engagements with the Barbary pirates after that war. He was killed in a duel with Commodore James Barron, also of the United States Navy. Decatur is also credited with the famous toast: "Our Country! In her intercourse with foreign nations may she always be in the right; but our country, right or wrong."

Americans. The crew of the *Philadelphia* had to be ransomed with a payment of $60,000. The United States did cease to pay tribute to Tripoli, but payments to the other Barbary pirates continued until after another naval struggle with them following the War of 1812.

Purchase of Louisiana

Even before the contest with Tripoli was over, Jefferson and his colleagues had managed a much more important coup. They purchased Louisiana from France in 1803. When that happened, France had not even taken possession, physically, of Louisiana, and there was no public knowledge of the extent of the territory. It came about in this way. Napoleon Bonaparte became First Consul, i.e., ruler and virtual dictator, of France in 1799. Napoleon was a successful military commander, and he had visions of restoring the French empire in America. Louisiana had been a French possession until 1763, when it was ceded to Spain. In 1800, Napoleon acquired Louisiana from Spain by the secret Treaty of San Ildefonso, but did not take possession at that time.

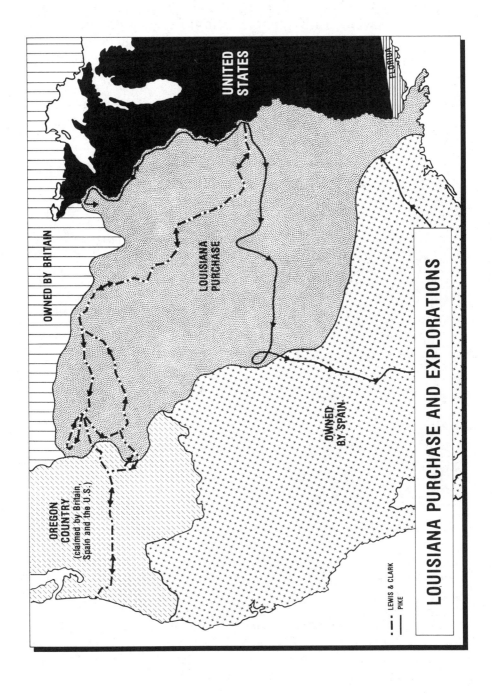

LOUISIANA PURCHASE AND EXPLORATIONS

When word reached the United States about the treaty, the Minister to France, Robert R. Livingston, was instructed to make inquiries of the government to see if the United States could acquire some of the territory, especially East and West Florida. Jefferson was quite concerned that if France controlled the outlets to the Gulf of Mexico, the United States might have to make common cause with Britain to protect her interests. Livingston did inquire, discovered that the cession did not include the Floridas, and that France was not interested in selling any of the territory.

Napoleon Bonaparte (1769-1821)

Napoleon was born in Corsica, an island that had only recently come under French rule. He came to France as a boy, was brought up amidst the ideas that fed the French Revolution, went to military school, came to manhood at the time of the revolution, and put in his early years of military service when both French ideas and French force were spreading over Europe. He began to conceive visions of empire within this setting. The revolutionary ideas resulted in anarchy, and this set the stage for an empire in which a strong man would impose order. Napoleon was that man in France. His military prowess brought him to the fore and in 1899 he became First Consul for life. That did not satisfy his ambition, and in 1804 he was made Emperor, a position he occupied until 1814. Britain and Russia placed limits to the extent of his empire, but he bestrode much of Europe from 1799 to 1814.

While the matter was at that impasse, in 1802 Spain revoked the American right of deposit in New Orleans. Jefferson and Madison were much concerned that westerners, denied access to the Gulf, might move to take New Orleans. Thus, James Monroe was dispatched to France as a special envoy to see if New Orleans and such territory in the Floridas as might be available could somehow be acquired. By early 1803 Napoleon had changed his mind about an empire in America, and in April he instructed his minister of finance to open negotiations with the Americans.

Several things had led to Napoleon's change of mind. For one thing he had given up on Haiti, the possession of which had been tied in with his ambitions in Louisiana. Haiti had been a French possession, and a most valuable one for the import of tropical products. However, a slave rebellion had broken out there in the 1790s and, under the leadership of Toussaint L'Ouverture, a black former slave, the blacks were victorious. Despite the fact that Toussaint was willing to be subject to French rule, Napoleon sent a military expedition to reconquer the island. A combination of black resistance and yellow fever decimated the French army, and Napoleon decided that in view of the destruction that had taken place further efforts at conquest were not worthwhile. Without Haiti, his interest in Louisiana declined. Moreover, he was turning his attention to the domination of the European continent, was about to go to war with Britain, wished to avoid any occasion for joint action by the United States and Britain, and needed the money he might get from the sale of Louisiana for his military adventures. Thus, he offered the Americans all French territory on the continent of North America.

Livingston and Monroe hardly knew how to respond. At first, they told the minister of finance that they only wanted New Orleans and the Floridas, for which they were prepared to pay $10 million. No, the First Consul wanted to dispose of all of Louisiana, they were told. Finally, the Americans agreed, after whittling down the price. The agreement they eventually reached was to pay approximately $15 million ($11,250,000 in direct payments to France, and the assumption of debts owned by the French of $2,500,000). What were the Americans to get for this money? Monroe and Livingston did not know with any certainty. The agreement simply stated that they had bought Louisiana "with the same extent that it is now in the hands of Spain, and that it had when France possessed it...." Livingston asked the foreign minister Talleyrand, "What are the eastern bounds of Louisiana?" "I do not know," answered Talleyrand, "you must take it as we received it." "But what do you mean to take?" asked Livingston. "I can give you no direction," Talleyrand replied. "You have made a noble bargain for yourselves, and I suppose you will make the most of it."[156]

How much territory had the United States acquired? Although claims were to be laid to West Florida, Texas, and Oregon as a result of the purchase, that did not turn out to be the case. However, the territory did include all of the present states of Louisiana, Missouri, Arkansas, Iowa, North and South Dakota, Nebraska, Oklahoma, and most of Kansas, Colorado, Wyoming, Montana, and Minnesota. The size of the United States had doubled with this purchase. A noble bargain indeed!

Exploration of the West

Jefferson sent two exploring expeditions into the Louisiana territory shortly after it was acquired. The first was the Lewis and Clark expedition, which was west of the Mississippi, 1804-1806, and the second was that led by Zebulon Pike into the Southwest, 1806-1807. The Lewis and Clark expedition was the last gasp of the centuries-long effort to find a Northwest Passage by water to the Pacific. That was not, however, Jefferson's official purpose for launching the expedition. He had conceived such an undertaking years before, and asked for a Congressional appropriation even before Louisiana had been acquired. Once Louisiana had been purchased, the expedition had a much stronger justification, for much of it would be through territory lately acquired, something of its extent might be grasped, and if the expedition went all the way to the Pacific it might serve to strengthen the claim to Oregon.

Captain Meriwether Lewis was Jefferson's secretary and first choice to head the expedition. William Clark was a younger brother of George Rogers Clark, a fellow Virginian, and a long time friend of Jefferson. They took command jointly. They spent the winter of 1803-1804 in Illinois overlooking the mouth of the Missouri River, spending their time collecting the party that would go with them. In May 1804, they set out up the Missouri, following its course that year all the way into what is now North Dakota. The next year they crossed the mountains and followed the Columbia River to the Pacific. They came back the following year, following the same route much of the way, and arrived at St. Louis on September 23, 1806.

Not only had Lewis and Clark traversed country never seen before by people of European origin but they had also made numerous descriptions and drawings in their voluminous notes. The two great river systems of the Northwest—the Missouri and the Columbia—had been explored along with much of the northern Rockies. Only one man had lost his life on the expedition, and that probably because of a ruptured appendix. Although the expedition met along the way thousands of Indians, there was only one violent encounter with them. Many of the possibilities for settlers in the Northwest were now known.

Lieutenant Zebulon Pike started out from St. Louis in 1806, only a few miles from the point of the beginning of the Lewis and Clark expedition. His was basically a military expedition, and he had the task of making treaties with the Indians as well as exploring the headwaters of the Arkansas and Red rivers. He went into the Southwest, then, rather than northward. By November the party had reached the Rocky Mountains. With three other men Pike attempted to climb the peak which

Meriwether Lewis
(1774-1809)

Lewis was born in Virginia, served in the state militia, and then entered the army. He was Jefferson's secretary (1801-03) and his choice to explore the territory northwest of the Mississippi River. Although William Clark joined him as head of the expedition, Lewis gave the literary and scientific character to their report. After the Lewis and Clark Expedition, Lewis was appointed governor of the northern part of the Louisiana territory. His life was cut short by his mysterious death in 1809 near Nashville, Tennessee.

bears his name; they did not reach the top, but the effort provided the most lasting memory of his expedition. Since the southern boundary of Louisiana Purchase territory was as yet undetermined, and since the Spanish claimed much of the region, it is not surprising that Pike got into trouble with them. He may have been lost, too, for he marched to the Rio Grande, in what is now New Mexico, but he claimed that he believed it was the Red River.

In any case, Pike and his men were captured by Spanish troops and detained for several months. Finally, they were marched to the Louisiana border and released on July 1, 1807. Pike had taken notes of his explorations and concealed them so that they could not be confiscated. Through them, he provided information about Spanish troops, about the Southwest in general, and about the possibilities of trade in the area. He referred to the region of the plains as a desert, and is credited with originating the myth of the "Great American Desert."

War of 1812

Some wars are appropriately named, others not. But of all the misnomers applied to a war the "War of 1812" must be near the head of the list. Indeed, it was a war; Congress did declare war, and it was fought on a scale that would justify its being called a war. It did begin in 1812, but the last battle was not fought until 1815. There is more than the inappropriateness of the name involved, but it is a singularly difficult war to bring into focus. There was no clear train of events which built up to the war; when the declaration came it was almost as if it were

an afterthought. For the British it was a side war to the titanic struggle with Napoleon going on in Europe. Many Americans, particularly
in New England, were far from enthusiastically behind the war effort.
The British government was close to being ready to end it from the time
it began. They revoked their orders in council—a major provocation—
only days after war was declared. As if that were not enough, the important Battle of New Orleans was fought after the treaty to end the war
had been signed. Swifter communications might have altered the course
of events.

A different name would probably help some to bring the war into
focus. One that has been suggested is the "Second War for American
Independence." That does provide a focus, but it is too sharp to en-
compass the events and purposes involved. True, an important aim of
American policy was to stay clear of European entanglements. But
that was only one of the purposes of the war. A more diffuse and comprehensive focus could be provided by calling it the "British and Indian
War." That tells us, at least, who the Americans were fighting, though
they took a swipe or two at the Spanish as well. But our task is not to
rename the war but rather to get it into a framework in which it can be
understood and to describe it.

The War of 1812 is best seen as an episode in a saga that got underway at least as early as 1803 and did not reach its conclusion until the
acquisition of Florida in 1819, or perhaps the Monroe Doctrine in 1823.
Americans felt the pressure of European nations during the whole of
this period. Europeans hampered the use of crucial waterways and the
seas for commercial purposes. Indians hampered the settlement of the
territory west and south of the Appalachians and east of the Mississippi. Settlement of the Louisiana territory was at least hampered by
the remaining presence of potentially hostile Indians in the older territory. Indians could make raids into the Mississippi Territory and then
escape punishment by fleeing into the Spanish controlled territory. Any
troubles with the British anywhere could lead to British retaliation from
Canada. Actually, the Jeffersonian Republicans had harbored resentments against the British naval behavior since the ratification of Jay's
Treaty in the 1790s. All these resentments and discontents, concerns,
and fears were aroused again during Jefferson's second term and came
to a head during Madison's first term in the presidency.

The pot began to simmer, if not boil after 1805. The British war
against Napoleon and France resumed in 1803. The British fleet destroyed the bulk of the French fleet at Trafalgar in 1805. Thereafter, the
British ruled the seas without serious contest from any other navy. The
American merchant fleet was growing in size and becoming a major factor in international shipping, but the United States had only a few large

warships and could hardly contend with the British. The British did two things that raised the American ire. One was to attempt to prevent American ships from carrying goods to France. The other was the impressment of sailors from American ships. The British navy had great difficulty in keeping sailors, both because of low pay and harsh conditions aboard their ships. American pay and conditions were better, and many British sailors did indeed desert British ships for American ones. The British claimed the right to stop American ships (at least privately owned ones), seize deserters, and impress them into service.

Matters worsened in 1806-07. In 1806, Napoleon attempted to impose what was called a Continental System on Europe. The main purpose was to cut off trade on the continent with any country trading with Britain. The first step in enforcing this system was the Berlin Decree of 1806. It prescribed that no ship coming from a British port could then enter any port of France or her allies on the continent. The British responded in November 1807 with Orders in Council requiring that ships trading with enemy ports would be subject to capture and the goods to confiscation unless they first put into a British port, paid a fee and got a certificate authorizing them to trade with the enemy. This was as much or more a monetary scheme as a part of the direct military effort. Napoleon replied in December of the same year with the Milan Decree. It said, in effect, that any country which complied with the British rules would be considered a British vessel and subject to seizure. On paper, at least, trade with either country had been made an extremely precarious undertaking.

But even before the British Orders in Council were issued, an event occurred which aroused Americans to a fighting pitch. It is known as the *Chesapeake-Leopard* affair. The *Chesapeake* was a United States warship and the *Leopard* a British warship. The *Chesapeake* had just put to sea when it was hailed by the *Leopard* in American territorial waters. The *Leopard* commander wanted to send a party aboard to search for deserters. The American commander refused. At that, the *Leopard* opened fire on the *Chesapeake*, which was unprepared for battle, and had to strike its colors. The *Chesapeake* was then searched and four sailors seized and impressed by the British. Many Americans were infuriated by such an insulting attack on the navy itself, and the prevailing opinion was that Jefferson could have had a declaration of war for the asking.

He elected, however, to settle the matter peacefully, if possible. He ordered all British ships out of American waters and sent James Monroe to make strong representations to the British. The British disavowed the attack, offered to pay for damages, and even agreed to return three of the men taken; the other had been hanged. But no alteration was made in the impressment policy or the interference with neutral shipping. Indeed, the British Orders in Council were issued shortly, followed by the Napoleonic Milan Decree.

Jefferson was not inclined to allow either Britain or France to dictate the terms under which Americans could trade. In any case, as matters stood, it would be necessary to choose one side or the other, or to cease trade. Jefferson and Madison decided for cutting off all trade with foreigners until such time as the warring powers were sufficiently hurt by it to relent. Congress passed an Embargo Act in December 1807. American ships were forbidden to leave port for any foreign country. The Embargo was a failure: it may have injured the French somewhat, the English less, but it had an even more devastating effect on the American economy, dependent as it was on foreign trade.

Under Madison, the Embargo Act was repealed and replaced by a Non-Intercourse Act (March 1809). This act forbade trade with Britain or France but permitted trade with other countries. It also contained a provision that when either country removed its restrictions, trade could be resumed with that country. A tentative agreement was worked out with Britain to the effect that the Orders in Council would not be applied to American ships. The British government, however, rejected this agreement. That having failed, the policy was altered by Macon's Bill no. 2, passed in 1810. Macon's Bill opened up trade to both Britain and France, but promised that if either country removed its restrictions the United States would embargo trade to the other country. This did not work either, though France managed to deceive the United States into reimposing non-intercourse on Britain. Meanwhile, both countries continued their depredations on American shipping.

Two developments occurred in 1811 which pointed America more directly toward war with Britain. One was the coming of new men to leadership in Congress. In the election of 1810, a goodly number of new, and young, men were elected to Congress. Among these men were Henry Clay of Kentucky, John C. Calhoun of South Carolina, Felix Grundy of Tennessee, Langdon Cheves of South Carolina. Henry Clay gained the crucial position of Speaker of the House, from which position he controlled appointments in important committees. John Randolph of Roanoke dubbed these men "War Hawks," and so they have gone down in history. Actually, they were joined in the next year or so by a goodly number of the older Jeffersonians, who had grown weary of indecisive measures, with the obstructions to American trade, and British disrespect for American rights. War came to appear to many a necessary recourse to bring to an end this unhappy state of affairs.

The other development was trouble with the Indians. The Shawnee chieftain, Tecumseh, was busily forming an alliance among the Indians on the frontier. He was supported in his activities by the British appointed governor in Canada, at least at the outset. Tecumseh hoped to stop the piece-by-piece cession of lands claimed by the Indians because they were broken up into many small tribes. He was attempting to form a widespread alliance that would extend from the Shawnees in the North to the Creeks in the South. His activities aroused fears among the settlers on the frontier, and they persuaded the governor of Indiana, General William Henry Harrison, to take the initiative against the Indians. Harrison gathered a force and moved on the main encampment at Tippecanoe Creek, setting up camp about a mile away. Tecumseh was in the South seeking aid when the Indians at Tippecanoe made a surprise dawn attack (November 7, 1811) on Harrison's force. They beat back the Indians and destroyed their village. Harrison gained the fame in the battle which would take him to the presidency nearly 30 years later. On his return, Tecumseh assumed a defensive posture with such of his people as he could muster, but the warfare with the Indians, aided however tentatively by the British, was another thorn in the side of Americans.

Tecumseh (circa 1767-1813)

Tecumseh was an Indian leader, a Shawnee chief, and had ambitions to form an Indian confederation. He was born in Ohio and as a young man became involved in raids on white settlers. Along with his brother, known as "The Prophet," Tecumseh formed a grand plan for uniting all the Indians along the frontier from Canada to Florida. The main object of this military-political confederation was to prevent white encroachment on Indian hunting grounds. He was eloquent, restrained, and exhibited leadership qualities, but however laudable the object his plan was probably doomed to failure. In any case, his aims coincided at the time with those of the British for the United States, and they offered him some encouragement. The Battle of Tippecanoe left his forces in some disarray, and in the War of 1812 he became a brigadier general in the British army and was felled in a battle with an American army.

By 1812, the government in England appeared to be fixed in its determination to pursue its long-term maritime policy and remained unrelenting to the Americans. On June 1, 1812, President Madison asked for a declaration of war against Great Britain. He listed these as major grievances: (1) impressment of American sailors, (2) violation of neutral rights at sea, (3) the blockade of American ports, (4) failure of the British to repeal their Orders in Council despite all efforts to induce them to do so, and (5) the British involvement with the Indians in the old Northwest. The House voted 79 to 49 for war; the Senate vote was much closer, 19 to 13. The opposition to war was greatest from New York northward, and in three states—Connecticut, Delaware, and Rhode Island—not a single Representative or Senator voted for war. On the other hand, in the lower South and in the West, the vote was overwhelmingly for war.

In an appeal for volunteers, General Andrew Jackson stated the case for war this way. The heading of the appeal asked, "For what are we going to fight?" Jackson answered in these words:

> We are going to fight for the reestablishment of our national charactor [sic], misunderstood and vilified at home and abroad; for the protection of our maritime citizens, impressed on board British ships of war and compelled to fight the battles of our enemies against ourselves; to vindicate our right to a free trade, and open a market for the production of our soil, now perishing on our hands because the *mistress of the ocean* has forbid us to carry them to any foreign nation; in fine to seek some indemnity for past injuries, some security against future aggressions, by the conquest of all the British dominions upon the continent of north america.[157]

The focus upon British possessions in America, particularly Canada, both in some of the statements of some of the "War Hawks" and in the actual fighting, has led some historians to conclude that the war was fought to obtain Canada. It is true that the major American military effort during the war was aimed at Canada and that some of those who favored going to war talked of taking that country. It should be kept in mind, however, that Canada was the only place where British forces could be attacked by land. Britain controlled the seas, and there was no other way to reach either her possessions or Britain. Undoubtedly, settlers in the West would have liked to have Britain entirely out of North America, but it does not follow that the purpose of the war was to acquire Canada.

Andrew Jackson
(1767-1845)

Jackson was the seventh President of the United States, a major figure in Tennessee politics, a Southern planter, an Indian fighter, a military commander, and the founder of the Democratic Party. He was born in the back country of the Carolinas, received little formal education, and fought in the War for Independence when he was in his early teens. He studied law, moved to Nashville, Tennessee, helped to frame the Tennessee constitution, and represented that state in the House and Senate at various times. He achieved national fame, however, as a military leader during the War of 1812, during which he defeated the Creek Indians, drove the British from Pensacola, and defeated a major army at New Orleans. In his habits and behavior he remained a frontiersman over the years, had a violent temper, and was involved in several personal gun fights. Even so, and despite the controversial character of some of his actions, he attained great popularity and was a genuine American hero. He represented the essence of the American ideal of rising from poverty to national leadership, of sturdy independence, of the dislike of pomp and ceremony, and the readiness to act decisively when the occasion arose.

The United States was not well prepared for war, nor was the war effort well coordinated. Congress was better at passing resolutions than raising revenue or armies. Except for Andrew Jackson, and perhaps one or two more, there were no bold and capable military commanders of high rank in the country. The navy was the most efficient and well commanded branch of the service, but it was small and hardly a match for the British fleet. The political leaders were hardly accustomed to mustering the goods and people for military purposes. Certainly, President Madison was more adept at the arts of restraining government than he was in mobilizing the country for war.

In any case, the War of 1812 was an indecisive war. The United States did not lose the war, but neither did it win. There were some hard-fought and stirring victories, and there were some losing engagements both on land and sea. The Indians were decisively defeated, most dramatically by Andrew Jackson's forces against the Creeks at the Battle of Horseshoe Bend on the Tallapoosa River in Alabama. Tecumseh joined with the British forces after the beginning of the war, and Harrison led the American forces into Canada in the battle in which he fell. As for the British, such victories as they had brought only temporary gains, and neither side could impose terms on the other at the end.

At the outset of the war, American land forces were deployed in an attempt to strike into Canada. It was to be a three-pronged attack ranging from Detroit eastward to Lake Champlain along the Great Lakes. This effort failed, both because of the timidity of the generals and the fact that Americans had failed to gain naval control of the Great Lakes in the region. There were some naval victories at sea in 1812, however, to offset the military rebuff. The pride of the American fleet were the frigates *Constitution* and *United States*. The *Constitution* engaged the British ship *Guerriere* off the coast of Nova Scotia in August and after a half-hour battle had so badly damaged it that it had to be sunk. The *United States*, under the command of Captain Stephen Decatur, captured the British warship *Macedonian* and took her into port as a prize. A little later, the *Constitution* destroyed another British frigate, the *Java* off the coast of Brazil. It was this sterling performance that earned her the nickname "Old Ironsides." However, from 1813 onward the navy was generally bottled up, as was much of American shipping by the British blockade.

That was not the end of American naval activities, however, but the remaining victories were on the Great Lakes. In June 1813, the United States warship *Chesapeake* was lured out of harbor and beaten by the *Shannon*, boarded and taken as a prize. Captain James Lawrence was killed during the engagement, and his reported last words were, "Don't give up the ship." These words became the rallying cry of the navy, and Captain Oliver H. Perry had them inscribed on his flagship, the *Lawrence*, which led his fleet on Lake Erie. Perry succeeded in September 1813 in clearing the lake of British warships in one of the most intense and extended naval battles of the war. With the lake under American control, the army went on the attack into Canada once again. There were some successes, but before the end of the year American forces were on the defensive once again.

In the spring of 1814 the British finally took the offensive against the United States. The war in Europe was over (except for a brief resurgence in 1815), and the British could concentrate their efforts on what had thus far been a side struggle. The first battles were around Niagara, and the Americans attempted once again to drive into Canada. They were turned back in a fierce but drawn battle with British forces. In like

Oliver Hazard Perry (1785-1819)

Perry was a United States naval officer who is particularly remembered for his exploits on the Great Lakes during the War of 1812. He was born in Rhode Island and entered the service in 1799, following in the footsteps of his father who was a naval officer before him. Perry saw service against the Barbary pirates, during the War of 1812, and commanded the *Java* during the later expedition against the Barbary pirates (1815-16). He put together a squadron of ships on Lake Erie in 1813, and defeated British forces there, making possible extensive land operations in Canada.

fashion the British were turned back in the Battle of Lake Champlain. Neither side could decisively defeat the other.

In August 1814, a British combined naval and army force descended upon Chesapeake Bay and launched a series of raids on the ports and cities on it. British forces marched toward Washington, routed the American army sent to oppose them at the Battle of Bladensburg (Maryland), moved into Washington unopposed, and burned the public buildings, including the White House. They withdrew, boarded their transports, and sailed toward Baltimore. The way to Baltimore was defended at Ft. McHenry, and the bay passage was blocked by the hulks of sunken British ships. The British army disembarked to make a land attack, but American forces, after a brief battle, withdrew to take up defenses on the heights. The British fleet tried to crack Fort McHenry by bombardment, but it failed. That failure is memorialized in Francis Scott Key's *Star Spangled Banner*, which, in the words inspired by the battle, at the end of the bombardment, still flew "O'er the land of the free and the home of the brave." The British gave up, withdrew, and within a month departed the region of the Chesapeake.

But the British had one more string to their bow, or so they hoped. They would take New Orleans, perhaps the whole state of Louisiana, and at least gain bargaining power. But they reckoned without Andrew Jackson and his frontiersmen. Jackson was used to winning, was tough as an "Old Hickory," they said, expected his troops to go where they were told, and stand firm against enemy fire. If they broke and ran, contrary to orders, they might expect summary execution, a lesson he had already found occasion to demonstrate for any who doubted it. He executed a surprise attack on the British forces a few miles from New Orleans. While they were regrouping after that, his forces built breastworks along the line of their advance. The British assault advanced toward the Americans in closed ranks, which was the European way. Jackson's men mowed them down as they came wave on wave. This final battle took place on January 8, 1815. The British lost 2,036 men killed and wounded. The American losses were 8 killed and 13 wounded. This greatest American victory of the war came two weeks after the signing of the treaty that was supposed to end the fighting, but it stood as a symbol for more than a century of the welcome an invading army might expect in America.

Peace negotiations had been going on in Ghent, Belgium since August 8, 1814. The United States sent an outstanding delegation including John Quincy Adams, Henry Clay, and Albert Gallatin. The Treaty of Ghent was signed on December 24, 1814. It provided for a return to the *status quo ante bellum*, i.e., to territorial arrangements as they had been before the war. The treaty provided for the release of prisoners, the restoring of conquered territory, and for a commission to settle boundary disputes. No mention was made of the rights of neutrals, the impressment of sailors, or freedom of the seas. But the war in Europe was over, in effect, and such practices as the British had been following were generally abandoned. Moreover, the British agreed to a commercial treaty

Francis Scott Key
(1779-1843)—

Key was born in Maryland, graduated from St. John's College, studied and then practiced law. His fame derives solely from the fact that he wrote the words to "The Star Spangled Banner," whatever else he may have done. He had gone to the British fleet in 1814 while it was in the Chesapeake Bay in an attempt to obtain the release of a friend who had been captured. The fleet launched the attack on Fort McHenry while he was aboard a British ship, and he was detained until it was over. His fears for the United States during the night of the shelling explain his joy on the morning to see that the Stars and Stripes still flew over Fort McHenry. This fact inspired his verses. "The Star Spangled Banner" became the official national anthem in 1931.

with the United States in 1815 which opened the empire, except for the West Indies, to American trade. American rights to fish off the shores were reaffirmed in 1818, and both powers agreed to disarmament on the Great Lakes (Rush-Bagot agreement, 1817). Americans also struck a blow for freedom of the seas in the Mediterranean by sending warships to punish some of the Barbary states.

The Acquisition of Florida

Florida remained as a troublesome question after the War of 1812, and, though less urgent, so did the southwestern border of the Louisiana territory. Actually, the United States occupied what was then known as West Florida during the War of 1812 and continued to claim it afterward. Spain did not recognize this territorial change, nor the earlier one from the Mississippi to the Pearl River. One of the basic problems was that Spanish authority over the area was not very effectively established. The Seminole Indians roamed at will. They could make raids into the United States and return to Spanish territory with impunity. Some settlement on a more nearly permanent basis needed to be made.

John Quincy Adams, Monroe's Secretary of State, began negotiations with Spain in 1817, negotiations aimed at acquiring all of Florida. They were interrupted, however, by a military foray of Andrew Jackson into East Florida. Jackson was the military commander along the boundary between the United States and Florida. In March 1818, Jackson led an army of 2,000 men into Spanish Florida, defeated the Seminoles, destroyed their settlements, and captured a Spanish fort. Two British agents discovered there were court-martialed and hanged. John C. Calhoun, the Secretary of War, maintained that Jackson had exceeded his instructions. True, he had been authorized to attack the Indians, but not Spanish forts. Monroe's cabinet generally believed that Jackson had overplayed his hand and might provoke retaliations both from the Spanish and the British.

Adams disagreed. Whatever the merits of Jackson's actions, he had demonstrated clearly the weakness of the Spanish hold on Florida and may well have strengthened the bargaining power of Adams. Moreover, the British were in no mood either to tangle with the United States or come to the aid of Spain. In any case, negotiations resumed later in the year, and they bore fruit in the Adams-Onis Treaty of 1819.

By the terms of the treaty, Spain ceded all of Florida to the United States. The United States made no payment to Spain for Florida, but did assume the claims of American citizens against Spain to the extent of $5 million. The United States agreed that Texas would be a Spanish

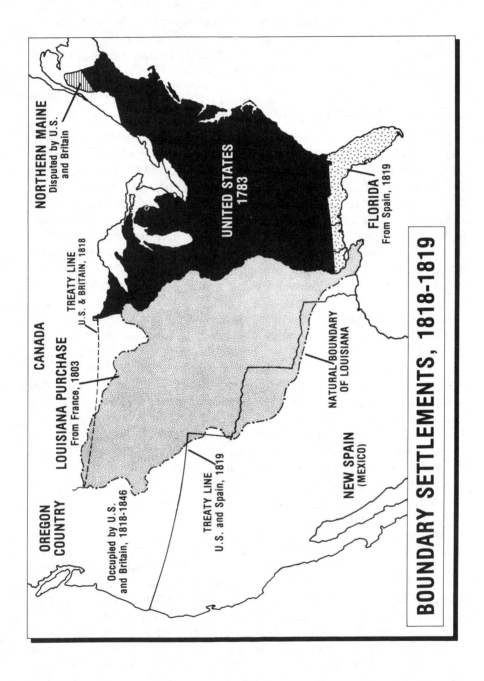

NORTHERN MAINE
Disputed by U. S.
and Britain

UNITED STATES
1783

FLORIDA
From Spain, 1819

CANADA

TREATY LINE
U.S. & BRITAIN, 1818

LOUISIANA PURCHASE
From France, 1803

NATURAL BOUNDARY
OF LOUISIANA

OREGON
COUNTRY

Occupied by U.S.
and Britain, 1818-1846

TREATY LINE
U.S. and Spain, 1819

NEW SPAIN
(MEXICO)

BOUNDARY SETTLEMENTS, 1818-1819

possession and that the southwestern boundary of the Louisiana Purchase territory would run to the north of that state. On the other hand, Spain gave up any claim she might have to the Oregon country. Thus, the United States now had full access to the Gulf from all major rivers in the country that emptied into it as well as at least a claim on territory all the way to the Pacific. The United States was no longer significantly circumscribed by territory of European countries.

The Monroe Doctrine

A new spector arose to haunt republics, such as still existed, in the wake of the Napoleonic Era in Europe. Napoleon had been defeated in 1814; he abdicated power and was exiled to the Isle of Elba. The great powers—Russia, Prussia, Austria, and Britain—in a Quadruple Alliance met at the Congress of Vienna in the hope of restoring order and balance to Europe. They had hardly completed their work, however, when Napoleon returned from exile, gathered a large army, and prepared to do battle once again. An allied force, under the command of the Duke of Wellington, decisively defeated Napoleon at the Battle of Waterloo, and the Alliance completed its work of making a settlement for Europe.

The most basic work of the Congress of Vienna was to restore the order that had existed in Europe before the French Revolution and Napoleon, in general, if not always in detail. Monarchy was restored in most countries. Beyond that, there was a widespread belief among European leaders that republican government had been discredited. Czar Alexander I of Russia called for a Holy Alliance of Christian powers to maintain the peace. Whatever he may have meant, his idea to the extent that it became a reality was a possible threat to republics in general. Moreover, the Alliance, whether Quadruple or Holy, did take steps, at least in Europe, to reinstate monarchy.

This might not have greatly concerned the United States if a series of revolts had not occurred in Latin America. The object of these revolts was to acquire independence from Spain, and, in most cases, to establish republics in the New World. One of the major leaders of these revolts was Simon Bolivar, who banished the Spaniards from large regions of South America. At first, the United States steered clear of any involvement or pronouncements because of sensitive negotiations with Spain. (Spain did not finally ratify the Adams-Onis Treaty until 1821.) However, by 1822, several countries had sufficiently established their independence of Spain that Monroe moved to accord recognition to them. At about this juncture, France invaded Spain, and there was considerable talk about restoring the Spanish colonies.

The British had never displayed any enthusiasm for the idea of a Holy

Alliance, and they were anything but in favor of restoring her former colonies to Spain. They were moving toward a position of free trade, but, that aside, they had no interest in any Spanish monopoly over trade with Latin America. Prime Minister George Canning approached the American Minister to Britain, Richard Rush, about some sort of joint statement by their two countries on the Latin American situation. In a letter dated August 20, 1823, he set forth his ideas, and Rush sent it along to President Monroe. In the letter he declared that "If there be any European Power which...looks to a forcible...reducing [of] the colonies to subjugation, on behalf...of Spain; or which meditates the acquisition of any part of them to itself...by conquest", a joint declaration of disapproval by the United States and Britain might be quite effective.[158]

Monroe seriously considered such a joint declaration, but Adams dissuaded him from that course. There was the fact that the United States was ready to recognize several of the countries, while Britain was not. Moreover, Adams preferred an independent American course to any involvement with Britain. "It would be more candid," he observed in a cabinet meeting, "as well as more dignified, to avow our principles explicitly to Great Britain and France, than to come in as a cockboat in the wake of the British man-of-war."[159]

Monroe eventually agreed. He took the occasion of his seventh Annual Message to Congress (December 2, 1823) to set forth in his section on foreign policy what came to be called the Monroe Doctrine. These are the basic principles: (1) The Americas are not "to be considered as subjects for future colonization by any European powers..."; (2) Europe and America have different political systems, and "We should consider any attempt on their part to extend their system to any portion of this hemisphere as dangerous to our peace and safety"; (3) "With the existing colonies or dependencies of any European power we have not interfered and shall not interfere"; (4) "In the wars of European powers in matters relating to themselves we have never taken any part, nor does it comport with our policy so to do"; and (5) "Our policy in regard to Europe...is, not to interfere in the internal concerns of any of its powers...." In short, the United States would not interfere in European affairs in the Old World, and European countries should not interfere in the affairs of independent countries in the New World.

While technically, President Monroe could only speak for himself and for his administration, there is little reason to doubt that he spoke the sentiments of thoughtful Americans generally. It was for this reason that his policy statement became an American doctrine. Americans had long since grown weary of European wars; the policies of all Presidents to that point had been to do their best to steer clear of them; and they could only look with favor on the expulsion of any European power from America. The independence of the United States, they saw clearly, hinged on not becoming embroiled with Europe, and the more the whole hemisphere became disengaged, the easier that would be.

The 50th Anniversary of Independence

The great themes of the first 50 years of the United States were independence, union, and individual liberty. While these things are never finally won, there can be no doubt that Americans had made great strides in establishing all three during these years. Thus, it is appropriate to conclude this book with some references to the 50th anniversary of the onset of the effort. July 4, 1826 marked 50 years since the signing of the Declaration of Independence. The event was celebrated widely on that day, as it has been over the years.

It is appropriate, too, to recall two men who were still alive at the beginning of that day: John Adams and Thomas Jefferson. No two men had worked more diligently for American independence than Adams and Jefferson. Both had been on the committee which produced the Declaration of Independence, and Jefferson had drafted it. Adams had worked vigorously in Congress in the preceding weeks to gain support for independence. Once independence had been declared, each worked in his own way to achieve it. Both had served as diplomats in foreign lands to advance and defend the American cause. Though neither was at the Constitutional Convention, both supported the document and worked to establish the government under it. Moreover, each had striven in his own way to steer an independent course in the world: Adams to maintain an independence of France and Jefferson of both Britain and France. Yet neither attended any festivities celebrating the 50th anniversary. Jefferson had been invited to attend a special celebration in Washington, but in his last known letter he declined due to ill health.

There is more to the story of Adams and Jefferson that needs to be told, however. They had been devoted friends and co-workers during the early years of the republic. That friendship was strained to and beyond the breaking point by the party differences of the late 1790s. The rupture was so complete that Adams refused to attend Jefferson's inauguration; instead, he packed and left town in the midst. For many years neither man communicated anything to the other. But eventually, at the urging of a mutual friend, they resumed their correspondence and continued it through their last years.

There is a poignancy to the correspondence of these years, as two men grew old together by letter, sometimes recalling those days when they had worked together in a common cause, turning more and more toward the enduring with the years, and at last focusing on the eternal. In 1821, Adams worried about the signs of despotism in Europe, and Jefferson, sharing his concern, declared, "Yet I will not believe our labors are lost....And even should the cloud of barbarism and despotism again obscure the science and liberties of Europe, this country remains to preserve and restore light and liberty to them. In short, the flames kindled on the 4th of July 1776 have spread over too much of the globe to be extinguished by the feeble engines of despotism; on the contrary, they will consume these engines and all who work them...."[160]

But much more often they wrote not of contemporary events but of the stuff of life in the here and the hereafter. Abigail, who also corresponded, wrote to invite Jefferson to visit her and John in Massachusetts. He wrote back that if he could go backward a score of years he would come with alacrity. "But those twenty years! Alas! Where are they? With those beyond the flood. Our next meeting must then be in a country to which they have flown,—a country for us not now very distant. For this journey we shall need neither gold nor silver in our purse, nor scrip, nor coats, nor staves."[161] When Jefferson heard that Abigail had died, he wrote to John Adams offering his sympathy, realizing, as he said, the futility of words in such circumstances, yet reminding him gently that the time was approaching for both of them when they would leave "sorrows and suffering bodies, and to ascend...to an ecstatic meeting with the friends we have loved and lost, and whom we shall still love and never lose again."[162]

No, Adams and Jefferson attended no festivities on the 50th anniversary of the Declaration of Independence, not on this earth anyway. Both died on July 4, 1826. Adams was 90 years old, well on his way to 91; Jefferson was 83. They had lived to see the labor of their young and middle years for American independence brought to fruition and rounded out. They lived, too, to compose their differences and to see their life's work taken up by a new generation. But perhaps they had gone to a more lasting celebration, as Jefferson promised in his last letter to Adams, "when we meet again, in another place, and at no distant period."[163]

Notes

1. Clinton Rossiter, *The Political Thought of the American Revolution* (New York: Harcourt, Brace and World, 1963), p. 52.

2. Edward Dumbauld, ed., *The Political Writings of Thomas Jefferson* (New York: Liberal Arts Press, 1955), p. 22.

3. *Ibid.*, p. 32.

4. *Ibid.*, pp. 19-20.

5. See Jack P. Greene, ed., *Colonies to Nation* (New York: McGraw-Hill, 1967), p. 225.

6. See Anne H. Burleigh, *John Adams* (New Rochelle, N.Y.: Arlington House, 1969), pp. 122-29.

7. Richard B. Morris, *The American Revolution* (Princeton: D. Van Nostrand, 1955), p. 114.

8. John Braeman, ed., *The Road to Independence* (New York: Capricorn Books, 1963), p. 275.

9. Nelson F. Adkins, ed., *Thomas Paine* (New York: Liberal Arts Press, 1953), p. 10.

10. *Ibid.*, p. 18.

11. *Ibid.*, p. 34.

12. *Ibid.*, pp. 43-44.

13. Quoted in John R. Alden, *A History of the American Republic* (New York: Alfred A. Knopf, 1969), p. 243.

14. See Catherine Drinker Bowen, *John Adams and the American Revolution* (Boston: Little, Brown and Co., 1950), p. 602.

15. Russell Kirk, *The Roots of American Order* (Lasalle, Illinois: Open Court, 1974), p. 408.

16. Dumbauld, *op. cit.*, p. 190.

17. Quoted in John C. Miller, *Triumph of Freedom* (Boston: Little, Brown and Co., 1948), p. 426.

18. Quoted in Merrill Jensen, *The Founding of a Nation* (New York: Oxford University Press, 1968), p. 663.

19. Quoted in Piers Mackesy, *The War for America* (Cambridge: Harvard University Press, 1965), p. 91.

20. John R. Alden, *The American Revolution* (New York: Harper Torchbooks, 1954), p. 85.

21. Mackesy, *op. cit.*, p. 36.

22. Samuel E. Morison, *The Oxford History of the American People* (New York: Oxford University Press, 1965), p. 244.

23. Quoted in Douglas S. Freeman, *Washington*, Richard Harwell, abridger (New York: Scribner's, 1968), p. 374.

24. Miller, *op. cit.*, p. 223.

25. Albert S. Bolles, *The Financial History of the United States*, vol. I (New York: D. Appleton, 1896, 4th ed.), p. 193.

26. Curtis Nettels, *The Emergence of a National Economy* (New York: Holt, Rinehart and Winston, 1962), p. 42.

27. Miller, *op. cit.*, p. 458.

28. William G. Sumner, *The Financier and the Finances of the American Revolution,* vol. I (New York: Dodd, Mead and Co., 1891), p. 274.

29. Nettels, *op. cit.*, p. 24.

30. Bolles, *op. cit.*, p. 39.

31. Nettles, *op. cit.*, p. 25.

32. Sumner, *op. cit.*, pp. 56-57.

33. Bolles, *op. cit.*, p. 132.

34. Quoted in Sumner, *op. cit.*, p. 243.

35. John Fiske, *The Critical Period of American History* (New York: Houghton Mifflin, 1916), p. 111.

36. Quoted in Freeman, *op. cit.*, p. 506.

37. *Ibid.*, p. 507.

38. Quoted in Morison, *op. cit.*, p. 269.

39. Samuel F. Bemis, *The Diplomacy of the American Revolution* (Bloomington: Indiana University Press, 1957), p. 219.

40. Quoted in Miller, *op. cit.*, p. 637.

41. Greene, *op. cit.*, p. 437.

42. Fiske, *op. cit.*, p. 34.

43. Bemis, *op. cit.*, pg. 256.

44. Greene, *op. cit.*, p. 343.

45. Quoted in Nelson M. Blake, *A History of American Life and Thought* (New York: McGraw-hill, 1963), p. 100.

46. Quoted in Andrew C. McLaughlin, *The Confederation and the Constitution* (New York: Collier Books, 1962), p. 75.

47. *Ibid.*, p. 51.

48. Nettles, *op. cit.*, p. 65.

49. Merrill Jensen, *The New Nation* (New York: Vintage Books, 1950), p. 249.

50. McLaughlin, *op. cit.*, p. 63.

51. Fiske, *op. cit.*, p. 145.

52. Richard B. Morris, ed., *Alexander Hamilton and the Founding of a Nation* (New York: Dial Press, 1957), pp. 91-92.

53. Charles C. Tansill, ed., *Formation of the Union of the American States* (Washington: Government Printing Office, 1927), p. 69.

54. Quoted in Charles Warren, *The Making of the Constitution* (New York: Barnes and Noble, 1937), p. 737.

55. Tansill, *op. cit.*, p. 105.

56. *Ibid.*, pp. 101-02.

57. James Madison, *Notes of the Debates in the Federal Convention of 1787,* Adrienne Koch, intro. (Athens, Ohio: Ohio University Press, 1966), p. 412.

58. Forrest McDonald, *The Formation of the American Republic* (Baltimore: Penguin, 1965), p. 140.

59. Tansill, *op. cit.*, p. 82.

60. Madison, *op. cit.*, pp. 25-26.

61. Tansill, *op. cit.*, pp. 295-96.

62. *Elliot's Debates*, Bk. I, vol. 1, p. 422.

63. *Ibid.*, vol. 2, p. 8.

64. Richard W. Leopold, *et. al.*, eds., *Problems in American History* (Englewood Cliffs, N.J.: Prentice-Hall, 1966), p. 134.

65. Richard H. Leach, *American Federalism* (New York: Norton, 1970), p. 2.

66. Tansill, *op. cit.*, pp. 276-77.

67. *Ibid.*, p. 173.

68. *Chisholm vs. Georgia* (1793).

69. Benjamin F. Wright, ed., *The Federalist* (Cambridge: Harvard University Press, 1961), pp. 280-81.

70. Tansill, *op. cit.*, p. 126.

71. Madison, *op. cit.*, p. 659.

72. Alexander Hamilton, *et. al.*, *The Federalist Papers* (New Rochelle, N.Y.: Arlington House, n.d.), pp. 513-14.

73. Quoted in Broadus and Louise Mitchell, *A Biography of the Constitution* (New York: Oxford University Press, 1964), p. 196.

74. Warren, *op. cit.*, p. 594.

75. *Ibid.*, pp. 594-95.

76. John Dickinson, *Letters from a Farmer in Pennsylvania* in *Empire and Interest*, Forrest McDonald, intro. (Englewood Cliffs, N.J.: Prentice-Hall, 1962), p. 73.

77. Dumbauld, *op. cit.*, p. 138.

78. Lester J. Cappon, ed., *The Adams-Jefferson Letters*, vol. I (Chapel Hill: University of North Carolina Press, 1959), p. 5.

79. Greene, *op. cit.*, p. 562.

80. Madison, *op. cit.*, p. 398.

81. *Ibid.*, p. 48.

82. *Ibid.*, p. 53.

83. *Ibid.*, p. 76.

84. *Ibid.*, p. 322.

85. *Ibid.*, p. 332.

86. Quoted in Moses C. Tyler, *Patrick Henry* (Boston: Houghton Mifflin, 1887), p. 289.

87. Hamilton, *op. cit.*, p. 292.

88. Alfred Young, ed., *The Debate over the Constitution* (Chicago: Rand McNally, 1965), p. 49.

89. Tyler, *op. cit.*, p. 290.

90. Greene, *op. cit.*, p. 391.

91. Henry S. Commager, ed., *Documents of American History*, vol. I (New York: Appleton-Century-Crofts, 1962, 7th ed., 1962), p. 104.

92. *Ibid.*, p. 107.

93. *Ibid.*, p. 108.

94. *Ibid.*, p. 104.

95. Madison, *op. cit.*, pp. 411-12.

96. Tansill, *op. cit.*, p. 590.

97. Greene, *op. cit.*, p. 398.

98. Hamilton, *op. cit.*, p. 266.

99. Quoted in Virgle G. Wilhite, *Founders of American Economic Thought* (New York: Bookman, 1958), p. 308.

100. *Ibid.*, p. 172.

101. Dumbauld, *op. cit.*, p. 19.

102. Tansill, *op. cit.*, p. 557.

103. *Ibid.*

104. Nathan Schachner, *The Founding Fathers* (New York: Capricorn Books, 1954), p. 6.

105. *Ibid.*, pp. 11-12.

106. Quoted in John C. Fitzpatrick. "George Washington," in *The American Plutarch*, Edward T. James, ed. (New York: Scribner's 1964), p. 51.

107. Quoted in Morison, *op. cit.*, p. 317.

108. Schachner, *op. cit.*, p. 33.

109. Leonard D. White, *The Federalists* (New York: Macmillan, 1948), p. 1.

110. Stephen G. Kurtz, *The Presidency of John Adams* (Philadelphia: University of Pennsylvania Press, 1957), p. 8.

111. Quoted in White, *op. cit.*, p. 55.

112. *Ibid.*, p. 58.

113. Morris, *op. cit.*, p. 290.

114. Quoted in Schachner, *op. cit.*, p. 187.

115. Quoted in John C. Miller, *The Federalist Era* (New York: Harper & Row, 1960), p. 66.

116. Marvin Meyers, *et. al.*, eds., *Sources of the American Republic*, vol. I (Chicago: Scott, Foresman and Co., 1960), p. 197.

117. *Ibid.*, p. 199.

118. Quoted in Stephen G. Kurtz, "John Adams," *America's Ten Greatest Presidents*, Morton Borden, ed. (Chicago: Rand McNally, 1961), p. 56.

119. John C. Miller, *Crisis in Freedom: The Alien and Sedition Acts* (Boston: Little, Brown and Co., 1951), p. 74.

120. Schachner, *op. cit.*, p. 431.

121. *Ibid.*

122. Dumbauld, *op. cit.*, p. 95.

123. Miller, *Crisis in Freedom*, p. 117.

124. *Ibid.*, p. 71.

125. Commager, *op. cit.*, vol. I, p. 179.

126. *Ibid.*, p. 182.

127. Henry Adams, *The United States in 1800* (Ithaca, N.Y.: Cornell University Press, 1957), p. 12.

128. *Ibid.*, pp. 21-22.

129. Samuel E. Morison and Henry S. Commager, *The Growth of the American Republic* vol. I (New York: Oxford University Press, 1942), p. 385.

130. Quoted in Leonard D. White, *The Jeffersonians: A Study in Administrative History* (New York: Macmillan, 1951), p. 24.

131. Quoted in Henry Adams, *History of the United States During the Administrations of Jefferson and Madison*, abridged by George Dangerfield and Otey M. Scruggs (Englewood Cliffs, N.J.: Prentice-Hall, 1963), p. 14.

132. Quoted in Edward S. Corwin, *John Marshall and the Constitution* (New Haven: Yale University Press, 1919), pp. 39-40.

133. *Ibid.*, pp. 29-30.

134. William Draper Lewis, "John Marshall," *Encyclopedia Britannica* (1955), vol. XIV, p. 969.

135. Commager, *Documents of American History,* vol. I, p. 194.

136. Dumbauld, *op. cit.,* p. 153.

137. *Ibid.,* p. 144.

138. James D. Richardson, *A Compilation of the Messages and Papers of the Presidents,* vol. I (New York: Bureau of National Literature, 1897), pp. 397-98.

139. *Ibid.,* vol. II, p. 569.

140. *Ibid.,* p. 736.

141. Alfred H. Kelly and Winfred A. Harbison, *The American Constitution* (New York: Norton, 1955, rev. ed.), p. 231.

142. Quoted in Miller, *The Federalist Era,* p. 181.

143. Richardson, *op. cit.,* vol. I, p. 316.

144. E. James Ferguson, ed., *Selected Writings of Albert Gallatin* (Indianapolis: Bobbs-Merrill, 1967), pp. 325-26.

145. Quoted in White, *The Jeffersonians,* pp. 142-43.

146. Richardson, *op. cit.,* vol. I, p. 367.

147. Morris, *op. cit.,* p. 319.

148. Ferguson, *op. cit.,* p. 40.

149. Richardson, *op. cit.,* vol. I, pp. 316-17.

150. Quoted in Allen Johnson, *Jefferson and His Colleagues* (New Haven: Yale University Press, 1921), p. 266.

151. Quoted in Morison and Commager, *The Growth of the American Republic,* vol. I, p. 428.

152. Dumbauld, *op. cit.,* p. 148.

153. Vernon L. Parrington, *The Colonial Mind, 1620-1800* (New York: Harcourt, Brace and Co., 1954), p. 353.

154. Dumbauld, *op. cit.,* pp. 181, 185.

155. Quoted in T. Harry Williams, *et. al.,* *A History of the United States,* vol. I (New York: Alfred A. Knopf, 1959), p. 248.

156. Johnson, *op. cit.,* pp. 76-77.

157. Quoted in Reginald Horsman, "The Conquest of Canada a Tactical Objective," *The Causes of the War of 1812,* Bradford Perkins, ed. (New York: Holt, Rinehart and Winston, 1962), p. 100.

158. Commager, *Documents of American History,* vol. I, p. 235.

159. Quoted in Morison, *The Oxford History of the American People,* p. 413.

160. Adrienne Koch and William Peden, *The Life and Selected Writings of Thomas Jefferson* (New York: Modern Library, 1944), pp. 702-03.

161. *Ibid.,* p. 678.

162. *Ibid.,* p. 690.

163. *Ibid.,* p. 717.

Glossary

Agrarian—has to do with land and agriculture and connotes a belief both in the importance of the cultivation of the soil and of farming as a way of life. In this sense, Jefferson was an agrarian, but he believed in free trade and free enterprise, not that government should subsidize farming or direct its development.

Alien—a person who is not a citizen of the country in which he resides. The Alien Acts of 1798 denied some of the rights of citizens to aliens.

Attainder, Bill of—an act of a legislature prescribing the punishment of a particular person. For example, a person might be declared by a legislature to be an outlaw, his property and rights taken from him, and a punishment set for him when he should be captured if he were a fugitive. Such bills were frequently used in 16th and 17th century England. They are prohibited in the United States Constitution and in those of most states. The great importance of the prohibition is that it helps to ensure due process before a person is convicted.

Bills of Credit—are, in effect, unredeemable paper money. They are used by government to borrow money by increasing the money supply. The result of issuing such bills is to reduce the value of the money in circulation. States are prohibited by the Constitution to issue such bills, and the United States government is not authorized to issue them.

Blockade—is the closing of a port or harbor by hostile ships. In international law, it has generally been claimed that a blockade to be legal must be effective. That is, there must be hostile ships patrolling the harbor to enforce the blockade. This is often the subject of dispute between nations in times of widespread war.

Broad Construction—is a phrase used to describe a position toward interpreting the Constitution. It favors considerable latitude in construing the powers of the government. Hence, a broad construction is used in an effort to expand the powers of the Federal government under the Constitution. It usually makes use of the idea of *implied powers*.

Capital—is one of the elements of production in economics, and refers to wealth used to produce goods. It may be money, buildings, machinery, raw materials, or what not. Capital goods are also described as *productive* as opposed to *consumer* goods.

Confederation—an alliance or league of otherwise independent states, nations, or countries. The United States was a confederation constitutionally from 1781-89. Confederations are usually formed for particular purposes, such as war or defense, and each of the states retains its independence of action otherwise. The federal system of government in the United States is an expansion and further development of the confederation idea.

Congress—a meeting or gathering. The word was used in Europe to refer to a formal meeting of representatives of independent nations, as at the Congress of Vienna. The American Continental *Congress* had much the same meaning, a meeting of independent states or nations. Under the present Constitution, the national legislature continues to be called a Congress, though the states do not retain their former independence.

Consensus—a general agreement. The word can refer to constitutional arrangements requiring more than a simple majority for action. An example would be the requirement for the concurrence of two-thirds of those voting in both houses of Congress and three-fourths of the states to amend the Constitution. Consensus requirements tend to limit government.

Consulate—the building occupied by consuls, i.e., representatives of foreign nations within a country. The Foreign Service of the United States is divided into diplomatic and consular branches. Diplomats deal with political relations and consuls with commercial affairs.

Continental System—a system which Napoleon attempted to impose on Europe during the French wars against Britain. It aimed to cut off all the trade of the continent of Europe with Britain or any country that traded with Britain. The Berlin and Milan Decrees were efforts to enforce it.

Deflation—occurs when the money supply in a country is reduced drastically. Prices must fall to balance goods with money, and until this has happened there may be a depression. The falling prices, however, are an adjustment to deflation, not the cause of the depression.

Despotism—the rule of an absolute, arbitrary, and unrestrained authority; a tyranny. Related words are despot (referring to a ruler) and despotic (referring to the character of the acts of a government). In the 20th century, a despot would most likely be called a dictator, and despotism dictatorship.

Direct Tax—is a tax levied directly upon the taxpayer. Examples are: a real estate tax, sales tax, income tax, head tax, and the like. The United States Constitution originally required that any direct tax be apportioned among the states on the basis of population.

Electoral College—the body which elects the President of the United States. Electors are chosen by states, each state having as many electors as the combined number of its Representatives and Senators. The Constitution does not specify how or by whom the electors are to be chosen, so that decision is left to the states.

Embargo—an order from a government prohibiting ships to enter or leave its ports. In short, it is intended to stop shipping either into or out of the country.

Enumerated Powers—are power of government that are listed or specified in the Constitution. For example, the power of the government to borrow money on the credit of the United States is *enumerated* in the Constitution. Strict constructionists usually insist that any power exercised must either be enumerated or be necessary to carry out one that is.

Established Religion—one which is supported by or receives favored treatment from government. The Constitution prohibits Congress to establish a religion for the United States, or to interfere with the exercise of religion. Historically, the phrase has usually been "established church," not "established religion." Probably, the different language was adopted because there was talk at the time of establishing the Christian religion in America.

Federalism—a system of government in which the powers are divided between the general government and of territorial division governments, both of which have jurisdictions on people within their bounds. The United States is the prime example of a country in which such powers of government have been divided; indeed, the Founders of the United States invented the system.

Federalist Party—a political party led by Alexander Hamilton and John Adams. It was the first party to hold power in the United States, and at the height of its following in the last years of the 18th century, it was strong throughout the country. However, after 1801, its following began to decline and, after that, was concentrated mostly in New England. After 1817, it was no longer a major factor in national politics.

Fiat Money—is money by decree of a government. It is usually paper money, forced into circulation by government tender laws, and is good only in the country of its origin. By contrast, money of gold, silver, and other precious metals is accepted in most places in the world, not requiring the force of any government to be accepted.

Funding the Debt—a fund set aside from revenue to support or retire a debt. Usually, it involves earmarking particular revenues to be applied only to the debt. Hamilton promoted tax measures for the purpose of providing such a fund for the national debt.

Gresham's Law—an economic law which holds that bad money drives good money out of circulation. This works when there are tender laws forcing the acceptance of the bad money. Then, people tend to hide the good money. This happened during the War for Independence when the Continental currency drove gold and silver coins out of circulation.

Inflation—occurs when the money supply is increased. Prices usually rise as the money declines in value, and some refer to this as inflation, but the price increase, if any, is the result, not the cause.

Jurisdiction—the extent, area, or range of political or judicial authority. It can refer either to a territory or to the government or courts having authority in particular cases. For example, state courts and United States courts have jurisdiction over the same people in the same area. But state courts enforce state laws and United States courts enforce national laws.

"Lame Duck"—a person or thing that is disabled or ineffective. Thus, a member of Congress serving out his term after he has been defeated is sometimes called a "lame duck." Also, a Congress holding a session after the elections may be a "lame duck."

Legal Tender—refers to money that must be accepted in payment of any bill. Such paper money usually bears the legend that it is "legal tender for all debts public and private." Legal tender is a device used by governments to force their chosen money into circulation.

Letters of Marque and Reprisal—a license from a government to a private shipper to capture and confiscate the merchant ships of another nation. Letters and licenses of this kind were granted in time of war or naval conflict only, as a rule.

Loyalist—usually a person who remains attached to the established government when its authority is challenged by a revolt or rebellion. Those who remained loyal to King George or the British government in the colonies when they declared their independence were called Loyalists.

Militia—a body of citizen soldiers who do military drills and exercises from time to time and may be called on by the government when an armed force is needed. They were important to the American cause in the War for Independence. The National Guard has supplanted the militia in the United States.

Naturalization—the process by which a foreign born person becomes a citizen. It may involve a declaration of intent, a term of residence, the passing of a test, and meeting other requirements.

Neutrality—a status of not being involved or taking sides in a war. International law accords rights to neutrals.

Nullification—the act of making null and void, or of no effect. The doctrine of nullification was the view that states acting singly or in concert with others could nullify an act of Congress contrary to the Constitution. It was advanced both in the Kentucky Resolution and by some at the Hartford Convention.

Original Jurisdiction—refers to the order in which a case may come before a particular court. A case is brought first to the court with *original* jurisdiction. It may then go to other courts which have *appellate* jurisdiction.

Patriots—are persons who love their country. In the War for Independence those who favored independence for the colonies and joined their side were called Patriots.

Per Capita Tax—is a tax on each person. It is also a direct tax and may be called by such other names as head or poll tax. It does not necessarily have anything to do with voting, however.

Privateer—a privately owned ship fitted out with arms to do battle. Usually, privateers received letters of marque and reprisal and could keep enemy prizes which they took.

Quorum—the number of members of a legislative body, for example, required to be present for the body to act.

Republic—a popularly elected representative government of a country. It is contrasted with a direct democracy, on the one hand, and monarchy on the other. The people do not rule, but are governed by representatives chosen directly or indirectly by them. The United States is a republic.

Republican Party—a political party founded by Thomas Jefferson and James Madison. This Republican Party lasted until 1828, when it proceeded to break up into the Democratic and Whig parties. The name was revived in the 1850s in a new Republican Party which elected Abraham Lincoln as its first President.

Requisition—an order for goods or services by some government organization. For example, an army may requisition food, transportation, and other goods to meet its needs. The root word is "require," not "request."

Revolution—the overthrow of an established government. A rebellion is an effort to do so; a revolution succeeds. During the past century the word has become loaded with meaning and is used to refer to complete changes throughout a society or nation.

Sedition—to arouse discontent with or incite rebellion against the government.

Libelous comments about those who govern have also sometimes been included in sedition. Indeed, any unfavorable comments about a government might *tend* to undermine government and thus be described as seditious. The Federalist inspired Sedition Act of 1798 did make truth a defense, but the Republicans insisted that such a limitation on speech and the press is prohibited by the First Amendment.

Sovereignty—the notion of an ultimate earthly authority over a people. Kings were sovereign in Europe. The question arose, and has continued to arise, in America as to whether the Federal government or the state governments are sovereign. The constitutional answer, by inference, is that neither are; each has a jurisdiction distinct from and not under the control of the other. Sovereignty is not vested in any government in the United States but remains with the populace.

Specie—coined money. A requirement to pay *in specie* is to have to pay in actual coins. Specie is antecedent to and has historically been the foundation of paper money.

State—a territory under a single governmental authority usually. Thus, England is a state; France is a state. The situation is more complex in the United States, where originally independent states yielded up part of their governmental authority to the general government. The word "state" is usually used in a different sense in the United States than in Europe.

Strict Construction—usually used in connection with construing the Constitution. It means to stick to the actual provisions and grants of power as they are found in the Constitution in interpreting the document.

Tariff for Revenue—a tariff passed for the primary purpose of raising revenue rather than to prevent foreign goods from coming into the country. The dividing line between a tariff for revenue and one for protection occurs at the point where any further increase in the tariff brings in less revenue. Then, it is clearly a protective tariff.

Tender Laws—see Legal Tender.

Township—in surveys in the United States is 6 miles square or 36 sections. The Northwest Territory was surveyed into townships. In some parts of the country, townships have governments within the framework of county governments.

Tribute—a sum paid by one government to another as the price of peace, security, or being let alone. In effect, it is a bribe, and has overtones of submission by the country which pays the tribute.

Unalienable Rights—are rights that are inseparable from being a person. They are natural, God given rights; rights which no power can, by right, take away, though persons may forfeit them by their behavior.

Writ of Mandamus—a court order to a public official requiring him to do his duty.

Suggestions for
Additional Reading

In looking for additional readings for much of this period, it is especially important to consider original materials. All history has been winnowed through the mind of one or more persons, partakes of their outlook and interest, is apt to be more or less colored by their biases, and will almost certainly reflect in some measure the times in which it was written. One way to check on historical accounts is to go back to the documents and compare them with what is written about them. Students of American history are especially fortunate on this score. The United States was founded at a time when many men were literate and when prominent persons, and some not so prominent, left behind treasures of their writings: letters, diaries, journals, accounts, speeches, essays, and so on. Moreover, many of these have been collected and published. The founding of the United States is not shrouded by the mists of time, or simply contrived out of a few hints and artifacts, but is an occurrence which is described in numerous documents written at the time. Thus, we are not dependent solely upon the reconstructions of historians for our knowledge of them.

Some measure of what is available may be suggested by naming some of the collections that have been made. E.C. Burnett collected and edited 8 volumes of *Letters of Members of the Continental Congress;* The *Writings* of George Washington were collected by J.C. Fitzpatrick and published in 39 volumes; the *Papers* of Thomas Jefferson by P.L. Ford in 10 volumes; the *Works* of John Adams by Charles Francis Adams in 10 volumes; the *Works* of Alexander Hamilton by H.C. Lodge in 12 volumes; the *Writings* of Albert Gallatin by Henry Adams in 3 volumes; the *Writings* of John Quincy Adams covering the years 1779-1823 by W.C. Ford in 7 volumes. More to the point, there are many collections of documents and writings on particular subjects. On the making of the Constitution, Max Farrand has collected the important primary materials in 4 volumes under the title *The Records of the Federal Convention of 1787*, and Charles C. Tansill selected and arranged many of the same documents earlier in a single volume entitled *Documents Illustrative of the Formation of the Union of the American States*. James Madison's *Notes on the Federal Convention of 1787* is the single best source on what happened at the Constitutional Convention, and they have been often reprinted and are included in the above collections. The best contemporary commentary on the Constitution is contained in *The Federalist* by Alexander Hamilton, James Madison, and John Jay, and there have been many printings of these papers in a single volume.

James D. Richardson's *Messages and Papers of the Presidents* contains the public papers of Presidents down to 1897 in 10 volumes. Elliot's *Debates* contains the debates over ratification of the Constitution in the states. The *Debates and Proceedings in the Congress of the United States*, 1789-1824 contains this information in 42 volumes. Many basic documents for the period are contained in Henry S. Commager, *Documents of American History* in 2 volumes. Jack P. Greene, ed., *Colonies to Nation*: 1763-1789 contains much useful primary material for the founding of the United States. Many, many more could be listed, but perhaps this gives some idea of the great variety of primary sources in print.

Histories that deal with some period of American history rarely, if ever, cover the years 1775-1825 as a unit or whole. There are books, such as L.H. Gipson's *The Coming of the Revolution*, which cover the background to it; Merrill Jensen, *The Founding of a Nation*, which covers the years 1763-1776; Forrest McDonald's *The Formation of the American Republic*, dealing mainly with the years 1763-1790; and other volumes dealing with other years. But most who have written chronological histories have not covered the whole period treated in the present work. It is best, therefore, to treat the more specialized works within a narrower framework.

The broader aspects of independence have not occupied much of the attention of American historians. While it is clear on review of the evidence that national independence was uppermost in American foreign policy during the early years of the Republic, historians have not usually focused upon or written books about it. Thus, what we are left with on this theme is largely the Declaration of Independence and the events and developments surrounding it. Two important works which provide the background ideas for that are: Bernard Bailyn, *The Ideological Origins of American Independence* and Clinton Rossiter, *The Political Thought of the American Revolution*. On the Declaration itself, see: David Hawke, *A Transaction of Freemen*; Edward Dumbauld, *The Declaration of Independence and What It Means Today*; and Julian P. Boyd, *The Declaration of Independence*.

The various aspects of the War for Independence are thoroughly covered in John C. Miller, *Triumph of Freedom*, 1775-1783. John R. Alden provides a well balanced account in *The American Revolution*. Military history is sufficiently covered in Piers G. Mackesy, *The*

War for America and Christopher Ward, *The War of the Revolution.* The standard work on diplomacy is Samuel F. Bemis, *The Diplomacy of the American Revolution.* And for the activities of Congress, see Edmund C. Burnett, *The Continental Congress.*

The Confederation period has been much neglected by American historians. An older work on the period is John Fiske, *The Critical Period in American History.* A briefer account, written by a major constitutional historian is Andrew C. McLaughlin, *The Confederation and the Constitution.* Merrill Jensen has made the most extensive study of the Confederation period, especially in *The New Nation: A History of the United States During the Confederation.* However, it is important to be aware that Jensen was much influenced by Charles A. Beard, that his history is infused with class theories, and that he attempts to downgrade the necessity for the Constitution of 1787.

On the drawing of the Constitution, see Clinton Rossiter, *1787, The Grand Convention* and Max Farrand, *The Framing of the Constitution.* An important work somewhat broader in scale is Charles Warren, *The Making of the Constitution. The Birth of the Bill of Rights* is told in detail by Robert A. Rutland. Gottfried Dietze has made a careful exposition of *The Federalist: A Classic on Federalism and Free Government.* Charles A. Beard made a large impact in the early 20th century with *An Economic Interpretation of the Constitution.* A partial antidote, at least, for this is Robert E. Brown, *Charles Beard and the Constitution.*

Of the changes between 1776-1789, see J. Franklin Jameson, *The American Revolution Considered as a Social Movement.* See also the first six chapters of Clarence B. Carson, *The American Tradition.*

A very thorough account of the role of the Washington and Adams administration in establishing the federal government is L.D. White, *The Federalists.* Much more politically oriented is John C. Miller, *The Federalist Era.* For the role of George Washington, see Douglas S. Freeman, *George Washington*, vol. VI, *Patriot and President.* For Hamilton's role, see John C. Miller, *Alexander Hamilton and the Growth of the Nation.* For briefer accounts of the men who participated in these events, see Nathan Schachner, *The Founding Fathers* and John Dos Passos, *The Men Who Made the Nation.*

The rise of political parties and the struggle for political leadership comes out in the following works: Stephen G. Kurtz, *The Presidency of John Adams: The Collapse of Federalism*; Nathan Schachner, *Aaron Burr: A Biography*; Paul Goodman, ed., *The Federalists vs. Jeffersonian Republicans*; Dumas Malone, *Jefferson and the Ordeal of Liberty*; Russell Kirk, *The Conservative Mind.*

The Jeffersonians are variously treated in Dumas Malone, *Jeffer-*

son the President; Irving Brant's multi-volumed biography of *James Madison*; Allen Johnson, *Jefferson and His Colleagues*; L.D. White, *The Jeffersonians*; Henry Adams, *History of the United States During the Administrations of Jefferson and Madison*; George Dangerfield, *The Era of Good Feelings*. Other aspects of these years are treated in Edward S. Corwin, *John Marshall and the Constitution*; Adrienne Koch, *The Philosophy of Thomas Jefferson*; Murray Rothbard, *The Panic of 1819*. Foreign policy and war are dealt with in Reginald Horsman, *The Causes of the War of 1812*; Bradford Perkins, *Prologue to War: England and the United States, 1805-1812*; Marquis James, *Andrew Jackson: The Border Captain*; Samuel F. Bemis, *John Quincy Adams and the Foundations of American Foreign Policy*; Dexter Perkins, *A History of the Monroe Doctrine*.

APPENDIX 1.

Declaration of Independence

In Congress, July 4, 1776
The Unanimous Declaration of the
Thirteen United States of America

When in the Course of human events, it becomes necessary for one people to dissolve the political bands which have connected them with another, and to assume among the Powers of the earth, the separate and equal station to which the Laws of Nature and of Nature's God entitle them, a decent respect to the opinions of mankind requires that they should declare the causes which impel them to the separation.

We hold these truths to be self-evident, that all men are created equal, that they are endowed by their Creator with certain unalienable Rights, that among these are Life, Liberty and the pursuit of Happiness. That to secure these rights, Governments are instituted among Men, deriving their just powers from the consent of the governed, That whenever any Form of Government becomes destructive of these ends, it is the Right of the People to alter or to abolish it, and to institute new Government, laying its foundation on such principles and organizing its powers in such form, as to them shall seem most likely to effect their Safety and Happiness. Prudence, indeed, will dictate that Governments long established should not be changed for light and transient causes; and accordingly all experience hath shown, that mankind are more disposed to suffer, while evils are sufferable, than to right themselves by abolishing the forms to which they are accustomed. But when a long train of abuses and usurpations, pursuing invariably the same Object evinces a design to reduce them under absolute Despotism, it is their right, it is their duty, to throw off such Government, and to provide new Guards for their future security. Such has been the patient sufferance of these Colonies; and such is now the necessity which constrains them to alter their former Systems of Government. The history of the present King of Great Britain is a history of repeated injuries and usurpations, all having in direct object the establishment of an absolute Tyranny over these States. To prove this, lets Facts be submitted to a candid world.

He has refused his Assent to Laws, the most wholesome and necessary for the public good.

He has forbidden his Governors to pass laws of immediate and pressing importance, unless suspended in their operation till his Assent should be obtained; and when so suspended, he has utterly neglected to attend to them.

He has refused to pass other Laws for the accommodation of large districts of people, unless those people would relinquish the right of Representation in the Legislature, a right inestimable to them and formidable to tyrants only.

He has called together legislative bodies at places unusual, uncomfortable, and distant from the depository of their Public Records, for the sole purpose of fatiguing them into compliance with his measures.

He has dissolved Representative Houses repeatedly, for opposing with manly firmness his invasions on the rights of the people.

He has refused for a long time, after such dissolutions, to cause others to be elected, whereby the Legislative Powers, incapable of Annihilation, have returned to the People at large for their exercise; the State remaining in the mean time exposed to all the dangers of invasion from without, and convulsions within.

He has endeavoured to prevent the population of these States; for that purpose obstructing the Laws for Naturalization of Foreigners; refusing to pass others to encourage their migration hither, and raising the conditions of new Appropriations of Lands.

He has obstructed the Administration of Justice, by refusing his Assent to Laws for establishing Judiciary Powers.

He had made Judges dependent on his Will alone, for the tenure of their offices, and the amount and payment of their salaries.

He has erected a multitude of New Offices, and sent hither swarms of Officers to harrass our People, and eat out their substance.

He has kept among us, in times of peace, Standing Armies without the Consent of our legislature.

He has affected to render the Military independent of and superior to the Civil Power.

He has combined with others to subject us to a jurisdiction foreign to our constitution, and unacknowledged by our laws; giving his Assent to their Acts of pretended Legislation:

For quartering large bodies of armed troops among us:

For protecting them, by a mock Trial, from Punishment for any Murders which they should commit on the Inhabitants of these States:

For cutting off our Trade with all parts of the world:

For imposing Taxes on us without our Consent:

For depriving us in many cases, of the benefits of Trial by Jury:

For transporting us beyond Seas to be tried for pretended offences:

For abolishing the free System of English Laws in a neighbouring Province, establishing therein an Arbitrary government, and enlarging its Boundaries so as to render it at once an example and fit instrument for introducing the same absolute rule into these Colonies:

For taking away our Charters, abolishing our most valuable Laws, and altering fundamentally the Forms of our Governments:

For suspending our own Legislatures, and declaring themselves invested with Power to legislate for us in all cases whatsoever.

He has abdicated Government here, by declaring us out of his Protection and waging War against us.

He has plundered our seas, ravaged our Coasts, burnt our towns, and destroyed the Lives of our people.

He is at this time transporting large Armies of foreign Mercenaries to compleat the works of death, desolation and tyranny, already begun with circumstances of Cruelty & perfidy scarcely paralleled in the most barbarous ages, and totally unworthy the Head of a civilized nation.

He has constrained our fellow Citizens taken Captive on the high Seas to bear Arms against their Country, to become the executioners of their friends and Brethren, or to fall themselves by their Hands.

He has excited domestic insurrections amongst us, and has endeavoured to bring on the inhabitants of our frontiers, the merciless Indian Savages, whose known rule of warfare, is an undistinguished destruction of all ages, sexes and conditions.

In every stage of these Oppressions We have Petitioned for Redress in the most humble terms: Our repeated Petitions have been answered only by repeated injury. A Prince, whose character is thus marked by every act which may define a Tyrant, is unfit to be the ruler of a free People.

Nor have We been wanting in attention to our British brethren. We have warned them from time to time of attempts by their legislature to extend an unwarrantable jurisdiction over us. We have reminded them of the circumstances of our emigration and settlement here. We have appealed to their native justice and magnanimity, and we have conjured them by the ties of our common kindred to disavow these usurpations, which would inevitably interrupt our connections and correspondence. They too have been deaf to the voice of justice and consanguinity. We must, therefore, acquiesce in the necessity, which denounces our Separation, and hold them, as we hold the rest of mankind, Enemies in War, in Peace Friends.

We, therefore, the Representatives of the United States of America, in General Congress, Assembled, appealing to the Supreme Judge of the world for the rectitude of our intentions, do, in the Name, and by Authority of the good People of these Colonies, solemnly publish and declare, That these United Colonies are, and of Right out to be Free and Independent States; that they are Absolved from all Allegiance to the British Crown, and that all political connection between them and the State of Great Britain, is and ought to be totally dissolved; and that as Free and Independent States, they have full Power to levy War, conclude Peace, contract Alliances, establish Commerce, and to do all other Acts and Things which Independent States may of right do. And for the support of this Declaration, with a firm reliance on the Protection of Divine Providence, we mutually pledge to each other our Lives, our Fortunes and our sacred Honor.

(Signatories)

John Hancock

New Hampshire
Josiah Bartlett,
Wm. Whipple,
Matthew Thornton.

Massachusetts Bay
Saml. Adams,
John Adams,
Robt. Treat Paine,
Elbridge Gerry.

Rhode Island
Step. Hopkins,
William Ellery.

Connecticut
Roger Sherman,
Sam'el Huntington,
Wm. Williams,
Oliver Wolcott.

New York
Wm. Floyd,
Phil. Livingston,
Francis Lewis,
Lewis Morris.

New Jersey
Richd. Stockton,
Jno. Witherspoon,
Fras. Hopkinson,
John Hart,
Abra. Clark.

Pennsylvania
Robt. Morris,
Benjamin Rush,
Benja. Franklin
John Morton,   Geo. Taylor,
Geo. Clymer,   James Wilson,
Jas. Smith,   Geo. Ross.

Delaware
Caesar Rodney,
Geo. Read,
Tho. M'Kean.

Maryland
Samuel Chase,
Wm. Paca,
Thos. Stone,
Charles Carroll of Carrollton.

Virginia
George Wythe,
Richard Henry Lee,
Th. Jefferson,
Benja. Harrison,
Thos. Nelson, Jr.,
Francis Lightfoot Lee,
Carter Braxton.

North Carolina
Wm. Hooper,
Joseph Hewes,
John Penn.

South Carolina
Edward Rutledge,
Thos. Heyward, Junr.,
Thomas Lynch, Junr.,
Arthur Middleton.

Georgia
Button Gwinnett,
Lyman Hall,
Geo. Walton.

APPENDIX 2.

Constitution of the
United States of America

(The bracketed words are designations for your convenience; they are not part of the Constitution.)

THE *oldest federal constitution in existence was framed by a convention of delegates from twelve of the thirteen original states in Philadelphia in May, 1787, Rhode Island failing to send a delegate. George Washington presided over the session, which lasted until September 17, 1787. The draft (originally a preamble and seven Articles) was submitted to all thirteen states and was to become effective when ratified by nine states. It went into effect on the first Wednesday in March, 1789, having been ratified by New Hampshire, the ninth state to approve, on June 21, 1788. The states ratified the Constitution in the following order:*

Delaware	December 7, 1787	South Carolina	May 23, 1788
Pennsylvania	December 12, 1787	New Hampshire	June 21, 1788
New Jersey	December 18, 1787	Virginia	June 25, 1788
Georgia	January 2, 1788	New York	July 26, 1788
Connecticut	January 9, 1788	North Carolina	November 21, 1789
Massachusetts	February 6, 1788	Rhode Island	May 29, 1790
Maryland	April 28, 1788		

[PREAMBLE]. WE THE PEOPLE of the United States, in Order to form a more perfect Union, establish Justice, insure domestic Tranquility, provide for the common defence, promote the general Welfare, and secure the Blessings of Liberty to ourselves and our Posterity, do ordain and establish this Constitution for the United States of America.

ARTICLE I

Section 1

[Legislative powers vested in Congress.] All legislative Powers herein granted shall be vested in a Congress of the United States, which shall consist of a Senate and House of Representatives.

Section 2

[Composition of the House of Representatives.—1.] The House of Representatives shall be composed of Members chosen every second Year by the People of the several States, and the Electors in each State shall have the Qualifications requisite for Electors of the most numerous Branch of the State Legislature.

[Qualifications of Representatives.—2.] No Person shall be a Representative who shall not have attained to the Age of twenty-five Years, and been seven Years a Citizen of the United States, and who shall not, when elected, be an Inhabitant of that State in which he shall be chosen.

[Apportionment of Representatives and direct taxes—census.*—3.] (Representatives and direct Taxes shall be apportioned among the several States which may be included within this Union, according to their respective Numbers, which shall be determined by adding to the whole Number of free Persons, including those bound to Service for a Term of Years, and ex-

cluding Indians not taxed, three fifths of all other Persons.) The actual Enumeration shall be made within three Years after the first Meeting of the Congress of the United States, and within every subsequent Term of ten Years, in such Manner as they shall by Law direct. The Number of Representatives shall not exceed one for every thirty Thousand, but each State shall have at Least one Representative; and until such enumeration shall be made, the State of New Hampshire shall be entitled to chuse three, Massachusetts eight, Rhode-Island and Providence Plantations one, Connecticut five, New York six, New Jersey four, Pennsylvania eight, Delaware one, Maryland six, Virginia ten, North Carolina five, South Carolina five, and Georgia three.

[Filling of vacancies in representation.— 4.] When vacancies happen in the Representation from any State, the Executive Authority thereof shall issue Writs of Election to fill such Vacancies.

[Selection of officers; power of impeachment.—5.] The House of Representatives shall chuse their Speaker and other Officers; and shall have the sole Power of Impeachment.

Section 3 †

[The Senate.—1.] The Senate of the United States shall be composed of two Senators from each State, chosen by the Legislature thereof, for six Years; and each Senator shall have one Vote.

[Classification of Senators; filling of vacancies.—2.] Immediately after they shall be assembled in Consequence of the first Election, they shall be divided as equally as may be into three Classes. The Seats of the Senators of the first Class shall be vacated at the Expiration of the second Year,

---

* The clause included in parentheses is amended by the 14th Amendment, Section 2.
† The 1st paragraph of this section and the part of the 2nd paragraph included in parentheses are amended by the 17th Amendment.

of the second Class at the Expiration of the fourth Year, and of the third Class at the Expiration of the sixth Year, so that one-third may be chosen every second Year; and if Vacancies happen by Resignation, or otherwise, during the Recess of the Legislature of any State, the Executive thereof may make temporary Appointments (until the next Meeting of the Legislature, which shall then fill such Vacancies).

[Qualification of Senators.—3.] No Person shall be a Senator who shall not have attained to the Age of thirty Years, and been nine Years a Citizen of the United States, and who shall not, when elected, be an Inhabitant of that State for which he shall be chosen.

[Vice President to be President of Senate. —4.] The Vice President of the United States shall be President of the Senate, but shall have no Vote, unless they be equally divided.

[Selection of Senate officers; President pro tempore.—5.] The Senate shall chuse their other Officers, and also a President pro tempore, in the Absence of the Vice President, or when he shall exercise the Office of President of the United States.

[Senate to try impeachments.—6.] The Senate shall have the sole Power to try all Impeachments. When sitting for that Purpose, they shall be on Oath or Affirmation. When the President of the United States is tried, the Chief Justice shall preside: And no Person shall be convicted without the Concurrence of two thirds of the Members present.

[Judgment in cases of impeachment.—7.] Judgment in Cases of Impeachment shall not extend further than to removal from Office, and disqualification to hold and enjoy any Office of honor, Trust, or Profit under the United States: but the Party convicted shall nevertheless be liable and subject to Indictment. Trial, Judgment and Punishment, according to Law.

Section 4

[Control of congressional elections.—1.] The Times, Places and Manner of holding Elections for Senators and Representatives, shall be prescribed in each State by the Legislature thereof; but the Congress may at any time by Law make or alter such Regulations, except as to the Places of chusing Senators.

[Time for assembling of Congress.*—2.] The Congress shall assemble at least once in every Year, and such Meeting shall be on the first Monday in December, unless they shall by Law appoint a different Day.

Section 5

[Each house to be the judge of the elec-

tion and qualifications of its members; regulations as to quorum.—1.] Each House shall be the Judge of the Elections, Returns and Qualifications of its own Members, and a Majority of each shall constitute a Quorum to do Business; but a smaller Number may adjourn from day to day, and may be authorized to compel the Attendance of absent Members, in such Manner, and under such Penalties as each House may provide.

[Each house to determine its own rules. —2.] Each House may determine the Rules of its Proceedings, punish its Members for disorderly Behaviour, and, with the Concurrence of two thirds, expel a Member.

[Journals and yeas and nays.—3.] Each House shall keep a Journal of its Proceedings, and from time to time publish the same, excepting such Parts as may in their Judgment require Secrecy; and the Yeas and Nays of the Members of either House on any question shall, at the Desire of one fifth of those Present, be entered on the Journal.

[Adjournment.—4.] Neither House, during the Session of Congress, shall, without the Consent of the other, adjourn for more than three days, nor to any other Place than that in which the two Houses shall be sitting.

Section 6

[Compensation and privileges of members of Congress.—1.] The Senators and Representatives shall receive a Compensation for their Services, to be ascertained by Law, and paid out of the Treasury of the United States. They shall in all Cases, except Treason, Felony and Breach of the Peace, be privileged from Arrest during their Attendance at the Session of their respective Houses, and in going to and returning from the same; and for any Speech or Debate in either House, they shall not be questioned in any other Place.

[Incompatible offices; exclusions.—2.] No Senator or Representative shall, during the Time for which he was elected, be appointed to any civil Office under the Authority of the United States, which shall have been created, or the Emoluments whereof shall have been encreased during such time; and no Person holding any Office under the United States, shall be a Member of either House during his Continuance in Office.

Section 7

[Revenue bills to originate in House.—1.] All Bills for raising Revenue shall originate in the House of Representatives; but the Senate may propose or concur with Amendments as on other Bills.

[Manner of passing bills; veto power of President.—2.] Every Bill which shall have

---

* Amended by the 20th Amendment, Section 2.

passed the House of Representatives and the Senate, shall, before it becomes a Law, be presented to the President of the United States; If he approve he shall sign it, but if not he shall return it, with his Objections to that House in which it shall have originated, who shall enter the Objections at large on their Journal, and proceed to reconsider it. If after such Reconsideration two thirds of that House shall agree to pass the Bill, it shall be sent, together with the Objections, to the other House, by which it shall likewise be reconsidered, and if approved by two thirds of that House, it shall become a Law. But in all such Cases the Votes of both Houses shall be determined by Yeas and Nays, and the Names of the Persons voting for and against the Bill shall be entered on the Journal of each House respectively. If any Bill shall not be returned by the President within ten Days (Sundays excepted) after it shall have been presented to him, the Same shall be a Law, in like Manner as if he had signed it, unless the Congress by their Adjournment prevent its Return, in which Case it shall not be a Law.

[Concurrent orders or resolutions, to be passed by President.—3.] Every Order, Resolution, or Vote to which the Concurrence of the Senate and House of Representatives may be necessary (except on a question of adjournment) shall be presented to the President of the United States; and before the Same shall take Effect, shall be approved by him, or being disapproved by him, shall be repassed by two thirds of the Senate and House of Representatives, according to the Rules and Limitations prescribed in the Case of a Bill.

Section 8
[General powers of Congress.*]

[Taxes, duties, imposts, and excises.—1.] The Congress shall have Power To lay and collect Taxes, Duties, Imposts and Excises, to pay the Debts and provide for the common Defence and general Welfare of the United States; but all Duties, Imposts and Excises shall be uniform throughout the United States;

[Borrowing of money.—2.] To borrow Money on the credit of the United States;

[Regulation of commerce.—3.] To regulate Commerce with foreign Nations, and among the several States, and with the Indian Tribes;

[Naturalization and bankruptcy.—4.] To establish an uniform Rule of Naturalization, and uniform Laws on the subject of Bankruptcies throughout the United States;

[Money, weights and measures.—5.] To coin Money, regulate the Value thereof, and of foreign Coin, and fix the Standard of Weights and Measures;

[Counterfeiting.—6.] To provide for the Punishment of counterfeiting the Securities and current Coin of the United States;

[Post offices.—7.] To establish Post Offices and post Roads;

[Patents and copyrights.—8.] To promote the Progress of Science and useful Arts, by securing for limited Times to Authors and Inventors the exclusive Right to their respective Writings and Discoveries;

[Inferior courts.—9.] To constitute Tribunals inferior to the supreme Court;

[Piracies and felonies.—10.] To define and punish Piracies and Felonies committed on the high Seas, and Offences against the Law of Nations;

[War; marque and reprisal.—11.] To declare War, grant Letters of Marque and Reprisal, and make Rules concerning Captures on Land and Water;

[Armies.—12.] To raise and support Armies, but no Appropriation of Money to that Use shall be for a longer Term than two Years;

[Navy.—13.] To provide and maintain a Navy;

[Land and naval forces.—14.] To make Rules for the Government and Regulation of the land and naval Forces;

[Calling out militia.—15.] To provide for calling forth the Militia to execute the Laws of the Union, suppress Insurrections and repel Invasions;

[Organizing, arming and disciplining militia.—16.] To provide for organizing, arming, and disciplining, the Militia, and for governing such Part of them as may be employed in the Service of the United States, reserving to the States respectively, the Appointment of the Officers, and the Authority of training the Militia according to the discipline prescribed by Congress;

[Exclusive legislation over District of Columbia.—17.] To exercise exclusive Legislation in all Cases whatsoever, over such District (not exceeding ten Miles square) as may, by Cession of particular States, and the Acceptance of Congress, become the Seat of the Government of the United States, and to exercise like Authority over all Places purchased by the Consent of the Legislature of the State in which the Same shall be, for the Erection of Forts, Magazines, Arsenals, dock-Yards, and other needful Buildings;—And

[To enact laws necessary to enforce Constitution.—18.] To make all Laws which shall be necessary and proper for carrying into Execution the foregoing Powers, and all other Powers vested by this Constitu-

---

* By the 16th Amendment, Congress is given the power to lay and collect taxes on incomes.

tion in the Government of the United States, or in any Department or Officer thereof.

Section 9

[Migration or importation of certain persons not to be prohibited before 1808.—1.] The Migration or Importation of such Persons as any of the States now existing shall think proper to admit, shall not be prohibited by the Congress prior to the Year one thousand eight hundred and eight, but a Tax or duty may be imposed on such Importation, not exceeding ten dollars for each Person.

[Writ of habeas corpus not to be suspended; exception.—2.] The Privilege of the Writ of Habeas Corpus shall not be suspended, unless when in Cases of Rebellion or Invasion the public Safety may require it.

[Bills of attainder and ex post facto laws prohibited.—3.] No Bill of Attainder or ex post facto Law shall be passed.

[Capitation and other direct taxes.—4.] No Capitation, or other direct, Tax shall be laid, unless in Proportion to the Census or Enumeration herein before directed to be taken.*

[Exports not to be taxed.—5.] No Tax or Duty shall be laid on Articles exported from any State.

[No preference to be given to ports of any State; interstate shipping.—6.] No Preference shall be given by any Regulation of Commerce or Revenue to the Ports of one State over those of another: nor shall Vessels bound to, or from, one State, be obliged to enter, clear, or pay Duties in another.

[Money, how drawn from treasury; financial statements to be published.—7.] No Money shall be drawn from the Treasury, but in Consequence of Appropriations made by Law; and a regular Statement and Account of the Receipts and Expenditures of all public Money shall be published from time to time.

[Titles of nobility not to be granted; acceptance by government officers of favors from foreign powers.—8.] No Title of Nobility shall be granted by the United States: And no Person holding any Office of Profit or Trust under them, shall, without the Consent of the Congress, accept of any present, Emolument, Office, or Title, of any kind whatever, from any King, Prince, or foreign State.

Section 10

[Limitations of the powers of the several States.—1.] No State shall enter into any Treaty, Alliance, or Confederation; grant Letters of Marque and Reprisal; coin Money; emit Bills of Credit; make any Thing but gold and silver Coin a Tender in Payment of Debts; pass any Bill of Attainder, ex post facto Law, or Law impairing the Obligation of Contracts, or grant any Title of Nobility.

[State imposts and duties.—2.] No State shall, without the Consent of the Congress, lay any Imposts or Duties on Imports or Exports, except what may be absolutely necessary for executing its inspection Laws: and the net Produce of all Duties and Imposts, laid by any State on Imports or Exports, shall be for the Use of the Treasury of the United States; and all such Laws shall be subject to the Revision and Control of the Congress.

[Further restrictions on powers of States.—3.] No State shall, without the Consent of Congress, lay any Duty of Tonnage, keep Troops, or Ships of War in time of Peace, enter into any Agreement or Compact with another State, or with a foreign Power, or engage in War, unless actually invaded, or in such imminent Danger as will not admit of delay.

ARTICLE II

Section 1

[The President; the executive power.—1.] The executive Power shall be vested in a President of the United States of America. He shall hold his Office during the Term of four Years, and, together with the Vice President, chosen for the same Term, be elected, as follows

[Appointment and qualifications of presidential electors.—2.] Each State shall appoint, in such Manner as the Legislature thereof may direct, a Number of Electors, equal to the whole Number of Senators and Representatives to which the State may be entitled in the Congress: but no Senator or Representative, or Person holding an Office of Trust or Profit under the United States, shall be appointed an Elector.

[Original method of electing the President and Vice President.†] (The Electors shall meet in their respective States, and vote by Ballot for two Persons, of whom one at least shall not be an Inhabitant of the same State with themselves. And they shall make a List of all the Persons voted for, and of the Number of Votes for each; which List they shall sign and certify, and transmit sealed to the Seat of the Government of the United States, directed to the President of the Senate. The President of the Senate shall, in the Presence of the Senate and House of Representatives, open all the Certificates, and the Votes shall

---

* See the 16th Amendment.
† This clause has been superseded by the 12th Amendment.

then be counted. The Person having the greatest Number of Votes shall be the President, if such Number be a Majority of the whole Number of Electors appointed; and if there be more than one who have such Majority, and have an equal Number of Votes, then the House of Representatives shall immediately chuse by Ballot one of them for President; and if no person have a Majority, then from the five highest on the List the said House shall in like Manner chuse the President. But in chusing the President, the Votes shall be taken by States, the Representation from each State having one Vote; A quorum for this Purpose shall consist of a Member or Members from two thirds of the States, and a Majority of all the States shall be necessary to a Choice. In every Case, after the Choice of the President, the Person having the greatest Number of Votes of the Electors shall be the Vice President. But if there should remain two or more who have equal Votes, the Senate should chuse from them by Ballot the Vice President.)

[Congress may determine time of choosing electors and day for casting their votes.—3.] The Congress may determine the Time of chusing the Electors, and the Day on which they shall give their Votes; which Day shall be the same throughout the United States.

[Qualifications for the office of President.*—4.] No Person except a natural born Citizen, or a Citizen of the United States, at the time of the Adoption of this Constitution, shall be eligible to the Office of President; neither shall any Person be eligible to that Office who shall not have attained to the Age of thirty five Years, and been fourteen Years a Resident within the United States.

[Filling vacancy in the office of President.†—5.] In Case of the Removal of the President from Office, or of his Death, Resignation, or Inability to discharge the Powers and Duties of the said Office, the same shall devolve on the Vice President, and the Congress may by Law provide for the Case of Removal, Death, Resignation or Inability, both of the President and Vice President, declaring what Officer shall then act as President, and such Officer shall act accordingly, until the Disability be removed, or a President shall be elected.

[Compensation of the President.—6.] The President shall, at stated Times, receive for his Services, a Compensation, which shall neither be encreased nor diminished during the Period for which he shall have been elected, and he shall not receive within that Period any other Emolument from the United States, or any of them.

[Oath to be taken by the President.—7.] Before he enter on the Execution of his Office, he shall take the following Oath or Affirmation:—"I do solemnly swear (or affirm) that I will faithfully execute the Office of President of the United States, and will to the best of my Ability, preserve, protect and defend the Constitution of the United States."

Section 2

[The President to be commander in chief of army and navy and head of executive departments; may grant reprieves and pardons.—1.] The President shall be Commander in Chief of the Army and Navy of the United States, and of the Militia of the several States, when called into the actual Service of the United States; he may require the Opinion, in writing, of the principal Officer in each of the executive Departments, upon any subject relating to the Duties of their respective Offices, and he shall have Power to grant Reprieves and Pardons for Offences against the United States, except in Cases of Impeachment.

[President may, with concurrence of Senate, make treaties, appoint ambassadors, etc.; appointment of inferior officers, authority of Congress over.—2.] He shall have Power, by and with the Advice and Consent of the Senate, to make Treaties, provided two thirds of the Senators present concur; and he shall nominate, and by and with the Advice and Consent of the Senate, shall appoint Ambassadors, other public Ministers and Consuls, Judges of the supreme Court, and all other Officers of the United States, whose Appointments are not herein otherwise provided for, and which shall be established by Law: but the Congress may by Law vest the Appointment of such inferior Officers, as they think proper, in the President alone, in the Courts of Law, or in the Heads of Departments.

[President may fill vacancies in office during recess of Senate.—3.] The President shall have Power to fill up all Vacancies that may happen during the Recess of the Senate, by granting Commissions which shall expire at the End of their next Session.

Section 3

[President to give advice to Congress; may convene or adjourn it on certain occasions; to receive ambassadors, etc.; have laws executed and commission all officers.] He shall from time to time give to the Congress Information of the State of the Union, and recommend to their Consideration such Measures as he shall judge necessary and expedient; he may, on extraordinary Occasions, convene both

---

* For qualifications of the Vice President, see 12th Amendment.

† Amended by the 20th Amendment, Sections 3 and 4.

Houses, or either of them, and in Case of Disagreement between them, with Respect to the Time of Adjournment, he may adjourn them to such Time as he shall think proper; he shall receive Ambassadors and other public Ministers; he shall take Care that the Laws be faithfully executed, and shall Commission all the Officers of the United States.

Section 4

[All civil officers removable by impeachment.] The President, Vice President and all civil Officers of the United States, shall be removed from Office on Impeachment for, and Conviction of, Treason, Bribery, or other high Crimes and Misdemeanors.

ARTICLE III

Section 1

[Judicial powers; how vested; term of office and compensation of judges.] The judicial Power of the United States, shall be vested in one supreme Court, and in such inferior Courts as the Congress may from time to time ordain and establish. The Judges, both of the supreme and inferior Courts, shall hold their Offices during good Behaviour, and shall, at stated Times, receive for their Services, a Compensation, which shall not be diminished during their Continuance in Office.

Section 2

[Jurisdiction of Federal courts.*—1.] The judicial Power shall extend to all Cases, in Law and Equity, arising under this Constitution, the Laws of the United States, and Treaties made, or which shall be made, under their Authority;—to all Cases affecting Ambassadors, other public Ministers and Consuls;—to all Cases of Admiralty and maritime Jurisdiction;—to Controversies to which the United States, shall be a Party;—to Controversies between two or more States;—between a State and Citizens of another State,—between Citizens of different States,—between Citizens of the same State claiming Lands under Grants of different States, and between a State, or the Citizens thereof, and foreign States, Citizens or Subjects.

[Original and appellate jurisdiction of Supreme Court.—2.] In all Cases affecting Ambassadors, other public Ministers and Consuls, and those in which a State shall be Party, the supreme Court shall have original Jurisdiction. In all the other Cases before mentioned, the supreme Court shall have appellate Jurisdiction, both as to Law and Fact, with such Exceptions, and under such Regulations as the Congress shall make.

[Trial of all crimes, except impeachment, to be by jury.—3.] The Trial of all Crimes,

except in Cases of Impeachment, shall be by Jury; and such Trial shall be held in the State where the said Crimes shall have been committed; but when not committed within any State, the Trial shall be at such Place or Places as the Congress may by Law have directed.

Section 3

[Treason defined; conviction of.—1.] Treason against the United States, shall consist only in levying War against them, or, in adhering to their Enemies, giving them Aid and Comfort. No Person shall be convicted of Treason unless on the Testimony of two Witnesses to the same overt Act, or on Confession in open Court.

[Congress to declare punishment for treason; proviso.—2.] The Congress shall have power to declare the Punishment of Treason, but no Attainder of Treason shall work Corruption of Blood, or Forfeiture except during the Life of the Person attainted.

ARTICLE IV

Section 1

[Each State to give full faith and credit to the public acts and records of other States.] Full Faith and Credit shall be given in each State to the public Acts, Records, and judicial Proceedings of every other State. And the Congress may by general Laws prescribe the Manner in which such Acts, Records and Proceedings shall be proved, and the Effect thereof.

Section 2

[Privileges of citizens.—1.] The Citizens of each State shall be entitled to all Privileges and Immunities of Citizens in the several States.

[Extradition between the several States. —2.] A Person charged in any State with Treason, Felony, or other Crime, who shall flee from Justice, and be found in another State, shall on Demand of the executive Authority of the State from which he fled, be delivered up, to be removed to the State having Jurisdiction of the Crime.

[Persons held to labor or service in one State, fleeing to another, to be returned.† —3.] No Person held to Service or Labour in one State, under the Laws thereof, escaping into another, shall, in Consequence of any Law or Regulation therein, be discharged from such Service or Labour, but shall be delivered up on Claim of the Party to whom such Service or Labour may be due.

Section 3

[New States.—1.] New States may be admitted by the Congress into this Union;

* This section is abridged by the 11th Amendment.
† See the 13th Amendment.

but no new State shall be formed or erected within the Jurisdiction of any other State; nor any State be formed by the Junction of two or more States, or Parts of States, without the Consent of the Legislatures of the States concerned as well as of the Congress.

[Regulations concerning territory.—2.] The Congress shall have Power to dispose of and make all needful Rules and Regulations respecting the Territory or other Property belonging to the United States; and nothing in this Constitution shall be so construed as to Prejudice any Claims of the United States, or of any particular State.

Section 4

[Republican form of government and protection guaranteed the several States.] The United States shall guarantee to every State in this Union a Republican Form of Government, and shall protect each of them against Invasion; and on Application of the Legislature, or of the Executive (when the Legislature cannot be convened) against domestic Violence.

ARTICLE V

[Ways in which the Constitution can be amended.] The Congress, whenever two thirds of both Houses shall deem it necessary, shall propose Amendments to this Constitution, or, on the Application of the Legislatures of two thirds of the several States, shall call a Convention for proposing Amendments, which, in either Case, shall be valid to all Intents and Purposes, as Part of this Constitution, when ratified by the Legislatures of three fourths of the several States, or by Conventions in three fourths thereof, as the one or the other Mode of Ratification may be proposed by the Congress; Provided that no Amendment which may be made prior to the Year One thousand eight hundred and eight shall in any Manner affect the first and fourth Clauses in the Ninth Section of the first Article; and that no State, without its Consent, shall be deprived of its equal Suffrage in the Senate.

ARTICLE VI

[Debts contracted under the confederation secured.—1.] All Debts contracted and Engagements entered into, before the Adoption of this Constitution, shall be as valid against the United States under this Constitution, as under the Confederation.

[Constitution, laws and treaties of the United States to be supreme.—2.] This Constitution, and the Laws of the United States which shall be made in Pursuance thereof; and all Treaties made, or which shall be made, under the Authority of the United States, shall be the supreme Law of the Land; and the Judges in every State shall be bound thereby, any Thing in the Constitution or Laws of any State to the Contrary notwithstanding.

[Who shall take constitutional oath; no religious test as to official qualification.—3.] The Senators and Representatives before mentioned, and the Members of the several State Legislatures, and all executive and judicial Officers, both of the United States and of the several States, shall be bound by Oath or Affirmation, to support this Constitution; but no religious Test shall ever be required as a Qualification to any Office or public Trust under the United States.

ARTICLE VII

[Constitution to be considered adopted when ratified by nine States.] The Ratification of the Conventions of nine States shall be sufficient for the Establishment of this Constitution between the States so ratifying the Same.

Done in Convention by the Unanimous Consent of the States present the Seventeenth Day of September in the Year of our Lord one thousand seven hundred and Eighty seven and of the Independence of the United States of America the Twelfth. In witness whereof We have hereunto subscribed our Names.

Go. WASHINGTON
Presidt and Deputy from Virginia

NEW HAMPSHIRE
| John Langdon | Nicholas Gilman |

MASSACHUSETTS
| Nathaniel Gorham | Rufus King |

CONNECTICUT
| Wm Saml Johnson | Roger Sherman |

NEW YORK
Alexander Hamilton

NEW JERSEY
| Wil: Livingston | Wm Paterson |
| David Brearley | Jona: Dayton |

PENNSYLVANIA
B Franklin	Thomas Mifflin
Robt Morris	Geo. Clymer
Thos FitzSimons	Jared Ingersoll
James Wilson	Gouv Morris

DELAWARE
Geo: Read	Gunning Bedford Jun
John Dickinson	Richard Bassett
Jaco: Broom	

MARYLAND
| James McHenry | Dan of St Thos Jenifer |
| Danl Carroll | |

VIRGINIA
| John Blair — | James Madison Jr. |

NORTH CAROLINA
| Wm Blount | Richd Dobbs Spaight |
| Hu Williamson | |

SOUTH CAROLINA
| J. Rutledge | Charles Cotesworth Pinckney |
| Charles Pinckney | Pierce Butler |

GEORGIA
| William Few | Abr Baldwin |

Attest: William Jackson, Secretary.

AMENDMENTS TO THE CONSTITUTION OF THE UNITED STATES

(Amendments I to X inclusive, popularly known as the Bill of Rights, were proposed and sent to the states by the first session of the First Congress. They became effective Dec. 15, 1791.)

ARTICLE I

[Freedom of religion, speech, of the press, and right of petition.] Congress shall make no law respecting an establishment of religion, or prohibiting the free exercise thereof; or abridging the freedom of speech, or of the press; or the right of the people peaceably to assemble, and to petition the Government for a redress of grievances.

ARTICLE II

[Right of people to bear arms not to be infringed.] A well regulated Militia, being necessary to the security of a free State, the right of the people to keep and bear Arms, shall not be infringed.

ARTICLE III

[Quartering of troops.] No Soldier shall, in time of peace be quartered in any house, without the consent of the Owner, nor in time of war, but in a manner to be prescribed by law.

ARTICLE IV

[Persons and houses to be secure from unreasonable searches and seizures.] The right of the people to be secure in their persons, houses, papers, and effects, against unreasonable searches and seizures, shall not be violated, and no Warrants shall issue, but upon probable cause, supported by Oath or affirmation, and particularly describing the place to be searched, and the persons or things to be seized.

ARTICLE V

[Trials for crimes; just compensation for private property taken for public use.] No person shall be held to answer for a capital, or otherwise infamous crime, unless on a presentment or indictment of a Grand Jury, except in cases arising in the land or naval forces, or in the Militia, when in actual service in time of War or public danger; nor shall any person be subject for the same offence to be twice put in jeopardy of life or limb; nor shall be compelled in any criminal case to be a witness against himself, nor be deprived of life, liberty, or property, without due process of law; nor shall private property be taken for public use, without just compensation.

ARTICLE VI

[Civil rights in trials for crimes enumerated.] In all criminal prosecutions, the accused shall enjoy the right to a speedy and public trial, by an impartial jury of the State and district wherein the crime shall have been committed, which district shall have been previously ascertained by law, and to be informed of the nature and cause of the accusation; to be confronted with the witnesses against him; to have compulsory process for obtaining witnesses in his favor, and to have the Assistance of Counsel for his defence.

ARTICLE VII

[Civil rights in civil suits.] In Suits at common law, where the value in controversy shall exceed twenty dollars, the right of trial by jury shall be preserved, and no fact tried by a jury, shall be otherwise re-examined in any Court of the United States, than according to the rules of the common law.

ARTICLE VIII

[Excessive bail, fines and punishments prohibited.] Excessive bail shall not be required, nor excessive fines imposed, nor cruel and unusual punishments inflicted.

ARTICLE IX

[Reserved rights of people.] The enumeration in the Constitution, of certain rights, shall not be construed to deny or disparage others retained by the people.

ARTICLE X

[Powers not delegated, reserved to states and people respectively.] The powers not delegated to the United States by the Constitution, nor prohibited by it to the States, are reserved to the States respectively, or to the people.

ARTICLE XI

(The proposed amendment was sent to the states Mar. 5, 1794, by the Third Congress. It became effective Jan. 8, 1798.)

[Judicial power of United States not to extend to suits against a State.] The Judicial power of the United States shall not be construed to extend to any suit in law or equity, commenced or prosecuted against one of the United States by Citizens of another State, or by Citizens or Subjects of any Foreign State.

ARTICLE XII

(The proposed amendment was sent to the states Dec. 12, 1803, by the Eighth Congress. It became effective Sept. 25, 1804.)

[Present mode of electing President and Vice-President by electors.*] The Electors shall meet in their respective states, and vote by ballot for President and Vice-President, one of whom, at least, shall not be an inhabitant of the same state with themselves; they shall name in their ballots the person voted for as President, and in distinct ballots the person voted for as Vice-

---

* Amended by the 20th Amendment, Sections 3 and 4.

President, and they shall make distinct lists of all persons voted for as President, and of all persons voted for as Vice-President, and of the number of votes for each, which lists they shall sign and certify, and transmit sealed to the seat of the government of the United States, directed to the President of the Senate;—The President of the Senate shall, in the presence of the Senate and House of Representatives, open all the certificates and the votes shall then be counted;—The person having the greatest number of votes for President, shall be the President, if such number be a majority of the whole number of Electors appointed; and if no person have such majority, then from the persons having the highest numbers not exceeding three on the list of those voted for as President, the House of Representatives shall choose immediately, by ballot. the President. But in choosing the President, the votes shall be taken by states, the representation from each State having one vote; a quorum for this purpose shall consist of a member or members from two-thirds of the states, and a majority of all the states shall be necessary to a choice. And if the House of Representatives shall not choose a President whenever the right of choice shall devolve upon them, before the fourth day of March next following, then the Vice-President shall act as President, as in the case of the death or other constitutional disability of the President.—The person having the greatest number of votes as Vice-President, shall be the Vice-President, if such number be a majority of the whole number of Electors appointed, and if no person have a majority, then from the two highest numbers on the list, the Senate shall choose the Vice-President; a quorum for the purpose shall consist of two-thirds of the whole number of Senators, and a majority of the whole number shall be necessary to a choice. But no person constitutionally ineligible to the office of President shall be eligible to that of Vice-President of the United States.

ARTICLE XIII

(The proposed amendment was sent to the states Feb. 1, 1865, by the Thirty-eighth Congress. It became effective Dec. 18, 1865.)

Section 1

[Slavery prohibited.] Neither slavery nor involuntary servitude, except as a punishment for crime whereof the party shall have been duly convicted, shall exist within the United States, or any place subject to their jurisdiction.

Section 2

[Congress given power to enforce this article.] Congress shall have power to enforce this article by appropriate legislation.

ARTICLE XIV

(The proposed amendment was sent to the states June 16, 1866, by the Thirty-ninth Congress. It became effective July 28, 1868.)

Section 1

[Citizenship defined; privileges of citizens.] All persons born or naturalized in the United States, and subject to the jurisdiction thereof, are citizens of the United States and of the State wherein they reside. No State shall make or enforce any law which shall abridge the privileges or immunities of citizens of the United States; nor shall any State deprive any person of life, liberty, or property, without due process of law; nor deny to any person within its jurisdiction the equal protection of the laws.

Section 2

[Apportionment of Representatives.] Representatives shall be apportioned among the several States according to their respective numbers, counting the whole number of persons in each State, excluding Indians not taxed. But when the right to vote at any election for the choice of electors for President and Vice-President of the United States, Representatives in Congress, the Executive and Judicial officers of a State, or the members of the Legislature thereof, is denied to any of the male inhabitants of such State, being twenty-one years of age, and citizens of the United States, or in any way abridged, except for participation in rebellion, or other crime, the basis of representation therein shall be reduced in the proportion which the number of such male citizens shall bear to the whole number of male citizens twenty-one years of age in such State.

Section 3

[Disqualification for office; removal of disability.] No person shall be a Senator or Representative in Congress, or elector of President and Vice President, or hold any office, civil or military, under the United States, or under any State, who, having previously taken an oath, as a member of Congress, or as an officer of the United States, or as a member of any State legislature, or as an executive or judicial officer of any State, to support the Constitution of the United States, shall have engaged in insurrection or rebellion against the same, or given aid or comfort to the enemies thereof. But Congress may by a vote of two-thirds of each House, remove such disability.

Section 4

[Public debt not to be questioned; payment of debts and claims incurred in aid of rebellion forbidden.] The validity of the public debt of the United States, authorized by law, including debts incurred for payment of pensions and bounties for services in suppressing insurrection or rebellion, shall not be questioned. But neither the United States nor any State shall assume or pay any debt or obligation incurred in aid of insurrection or rebellion against the United States, or any claim for the loss or emancipation of any slave; but all such debts, obligations and claims shall be held illegal and void.

Section 5

[Congress given power to enforce this article.] The Congress shall have power to enforce, by appropriate legislation, the provisions of this article.

ARTICLE XV

(The proposed amendment was sent to the states Feb. 27, 1869, by the Fortieth Congress. It became effective Mar. 30, 1870.)

Section 1

[Right of certain citizens to vote established.] The right of citizens of the United States to vote shall not be denied or abridged by the United States or by any State on account of race, color, or previous condition of servitude.

Section 2

[Congress given power to enforce this article.] The Congress shall have power to enforce this article by appropriate legislation.

ARTICLE XVI

(The proposed amendment was sent to the states July 12, 1909, by the Sixty-first Congress. It became effective Feb. 25, 1913.)

[Taxes on income; Congress given power to lay and collect.] The Congress shall have power to lay and collect taxes on incomes, from whatever source derived, without apportionment among the several States, and without regard to any census or enumeration.

ARTICLE XVII

(The proposed amendment was sent to the states May 16, 1912, by the Sixty-second Congress. It became effective May 31, 1913.)

[Election of United States Senators; filling of vacancies; qualifications of electors.]

The Senate of the United States shall be composed of two Senators from each State, elected by the people thereof, for six years; and each Senator shall have one vote. The electors in each State shall have the qualifications requisite for electors of the most numerous branch of the State legislatures.

When vacancies happen in the representation of any State in the Senate, the executive authority of such State shall issue writs of election to fill such vacancies: *Provided,* That the legislature of any State may empower the executive thereof to make temporary appointment

until the people fill the vacancies by election as the legislature may direct.

This amendment shall not be so construed as to affect the election or term of any Senator chosen before it becomes valid as part of the Constitution.

ARTICLE XVIII *

(The proposed amendment was sent to the states Dec. 18, 1917, by the Sixty-fifth Congress. It was approved by three-quarters of the states by Jan. 16, 1919, and became effective Jan. 16, 1920.)

Section 1

[Manufacture, sale or transportation of intoxicating liquors, for beverage purposes, prohibited.] After one year from the ratification of this article the manufacture, sale, or transportation of intoxicating liquors within, the importation thereof into, or the exportation thereof from the United States and all territory subject to the jurisdiction thereof for beverage purposes is hereby prohibited.

Section 2

[Congress and the several States given concurrent power to pass appropriate legislation to enforce this article.] The Congress and the several States shall have concurrent power to enforce this article by appropriate legislation.

Section 3

[Provisions of article to become operative, when adopted by three-fourths of the States.] This article shall be inoperative unless it shall have been ratified as an amendment to the Constitution by the legislatures of the several States, as provided in the Constitution, within seven years from the date of the submission hereof to the States by Congress.

ARTICLE XIX

(The proposed amendment was sent to the states June 4, 1919, by the Sixty-sixth Congress. It became effective Aug. 26, 1920.)

[The right of citizens to vote shall not be denied because of sex.] The right of citizens of the United States to vote shall not be denied or abridged by the United States or by any State on account of sex.

[Congress given power to enforce this article.] Congress shall have power to enforce this article by appropriate legislation.

ARTICLE XX

(The proposed amendment, sometimes called the "Lame Duck Amendment," was sent to the states Mar. 3, 1932, by the Seventy-second Congress. It became effective Feb. 6, 1933; but, in accordance with Section 5, Sections 1 and 2 did not go into effect until Oct. 15, 1933.)

Section 1

[Terms of President, Vice-President, Senators and Representatives.] The terms of the President and Vice-President shall end at noon on the twentieth day of January, and the terms of Senators and Representa-

---

* Repealed by the 21st Amendment.

tives at noon on the third day of January, of the years in which such terms would have ended if this article had not been ratified; and the terms of their successors shall then begin.

Section 2

[Time of assembling Congress.] The Congress shall assemble at least once in every year, and such meeting shall begin at noon on the third day of January, unless they shall by law appoint a different day.

Section 3

[Filling vacancy in office of President.] If, at the time fixed for the beginning of the term of the President, the President-elect shall have died, the Vice-President-elect shall become President. If a President shall not have been chosen before the time fixed for the beginning of his term, or if the President-elect shall have failed to qualify, then the Vice-President-elect shall act as President until a President shall have qualified; and the Congress may by law provide for the case wherein neither a President-elect nor a Vice-President-elect shall have qualified, declaring who shall then act as President, or the manner in which one who is to act shall be selected, and such person shall act accordingly until a President or Vice-President shall have qualified.

Section 4

[Power of Congress in Presidential succession.] The Congress may by law provide for the case of the death of any of the persons from whom the House of Representatives may choose a President whenever the right of choice shall have devolved upon them, and for the case of the death of any of the persons from whom the Senate may choose a Vice-President whenever the right of choice shall have devolved upon them.

Section 5

[Time of taking effect.] Sections 1 and 2 shall take effect on the 15th day of October following the ratification of this article.

Section 6

[Ratification.] This article shall be inoperative unless it shall have been ratified as an amendment to the Constitution by the legislatures of three-fourths of the several States within seven years from the date of its submission.

ARTICLE XXI

(The proposed amendment was sent to the states Feb. 20, 1933, by the Seventy-second Congress. It became effective Dec. 5, 1933.)

Section 1

[Repeal of Prohibition Amendment.] The eighteenth article of amendment to the Constitution of the United States is hereby repealed.

Section 2

[Transportation of intoxicating liquors.] The transportation or importation into any State, Territory, or possession of the United States for delivery or use therein of intoxicating liquors, in violation of the laws thereof, is hereby prohibited.

Section 3

[Ratification.] This article shall be inoperative unless it shall have been ratified as an amendment to the Constitution by convention in the several States, as provided in the Constitution, within seven years from the date of the submission thereof to the States by the Congress.

ARTICLE XXII

(The proposed amendment was sent to the states Mar. 21, 1947, by the Eightieth Congress. It became effective Feb. 26, 1951.)

Section 1

[Limit to number of terms a President may serve.] No person shall be elected to the office of the President more than twice, and no person who has held the office of President, or acted as President, for more than two years of a term to which some other person was elected President shall be elected to the office of the President more than once. But this Article shall not apply to any person holding the office of President when this Article was proposed by the Congress, and shall not prevent any person who may be holding the office of President, or acting as President, during the term within which this Article becomes operative from holding the office of President or acting as President during the remainder of such term.

Section 2

[Ratification.] This article shall be inoperative unless it shall have been ratified as an amendment to the Constitution by the legislatures of three-fourths of the several States within seven years from the date of its submission to the States by the Congress.

ARTICLE XXIII

(The proposed amendment was sent to the states June 16, 1960, by the Eighty-sixth Congress. It became effective Mar. 29, 1961.)

Section 1

[Electors for the District of Columbia.] The District constituting the seat of Government of the United States shall appoint in such manner as the Congress may direct:

A number of electors of President and Vice President equal to the whole number of Senators and Representatives in Congress to which the District would be entitled if it were a State, but in no event more than the least populous State; they shall be in addition to those appointed by the States, but they shall be considered, for the purposes of the election of President and Vice President, to be electors appointed by a State; and they shall meet in the District and perform such duties as provided by the twelfth article of amendment.

Section 2

[Congress given power to enforce this article.] The Congress shall have the power to enforce this article by appropriate legislation.

ARTICLE XXIV

(The proposed amendment was sent to the states Aug. 27, 1962, by the Eighty-seventh Congress. It became effective Jan. 23, .964.)

Section 1

[Payment of poll tax or other taxes not to be prerequisite for voting in federal elections.] The right of citizens of the United States to vote in any primary or other election for President or Vice-President, for electors for President or Vice-President, or for Senator or Representative in Congress, shall not be denied or abridged by the United States or any State by reasons of failure to pay any poll tax or other tax.

Section 2

[Congress given power to enforce this article.] The Congress shall have the power to enforce this article by appropriate legislation.

ARTICLE XXV

(The proposed amendment was sent to the states July 6, 1965, by the Eighty-ninth Congress. It became effective Feb. 10, 1967.)

Section 1

[Succession of Vice President to Presidency.] In case of the removal of the President from office or of his death or resignation, the Vice President shall become President.

Section 2

[Vacancy in office of Vice President.] Whenever there is a vacancy in the office of the Vice President, the President shall nominate a Vice President who shall take office upon confirmation by a majority vote of both Houses of Congress.

Section 3

[Vice President as Acting President.] Whenever the President transmits to the President pro tempore of the Senate and the Speaker of the House of Representatives his written declaration that he is unable to discharge the powers and duties of his office, and until he transmits to them a written declaration to the contrary, such powers and duties shall be discharged by the Vice President as Acting President.

Section 4

[Vice President as Acting President.] Whenever the Vice President and a majority of either the principal officers of the executive departments or of such other body as Congress may by law provide, transmit to the President pro tempore of the Senate and the Speaker of the House of Representatives their written declaration that the President is unable to discharge the powers and duties of his office, the Vice President shall immediately assume the powers and duties of the office as Acting President.

Thereafter, when the President transmits to the President pro tempore of the Senate and the Speaker of the House of Representatives his written declaration that no inability exists, he shall resume the powers and duties of his office unless the Vice President and a majority of either the principal officers of the executive department or of such other body as Congress may by law provide, transmit within four days to the President pro tempore of the Senate and the Speaker of the House of Representatives their written declaration that the President is unable to discharge the powers and duties of his office. Thereupon Congress shall decide the issue, assembling within forty-eight hours for that purpose if not in session. If the Congress, within twenty-one days after receipt of the latter written declaration, or, if Congress is not in session, within twenty-one days after Congress is required to assemble, determines by two-thirds vote of both Houses that the President is unable to discharge the powers and duties of his office, the Vice President shall continue to discharge the same as Acting President; otherwise, the President shall resume the powers and duties of his office.

ARTICLE XXVI

(The proposed amendment was sent to the states Mar. 23, 1971, by the Ninety-second Congress. It became effective July 1, 1971.)

Section 1

[Voting for 18-year-olds.] The right of citizens of the United States, who are 18 years of age or older, to vote shall not be denied or abridged by the United States or by any state on account of age.

Section 2

[Congress given power to enforce this article.] The Congress shall have power to enforce this article by appropriate legislation.

APPENDIX 3

Washington's Farewell Address

Friends and Fellow-Citizens:

The period for a new election of a citizen to administer the Executive Government of the United States being not far distant, and the time actually arrived when your thoughts must be employed in designating the person who is to be clothed with that important trust, it appears to me proper, especially as it may conduce to a more distinct expression of the public voice, that I should now apprise you of the resolution I have formed to decline being considered among the number of those out of whom a choice is to be made.

I beg you at the same time to do me the justice to be assured that this resolution has not been taken without a strict regard to all the considerations appertaining to the relation which binds a dutiful citizen to his country; and that in withdrawing the tender of service, which silence in my situation might imply, I am influenced by no diminution of zeal for your future interest, no deficiency of grateful respect for your past kindness, but am supported by a full conviction that the step is compatible with both.

The acceptance of and continuance hitherto in the office to which your suffrages have twice called me have been a uniform sacrifice of inclination to the opinion of duty and to a deference for what appeared to be your desire. I constantly hoped that it would have been much earlier in my power, consistently with motives which I was not at liberty to disregard, to return to that retirement from which I had been reluctantly drawn. The strength of my inclination to do this previous to the last election had even led to the preparation of an address to declare it to you; but mature reflection on the then perplexed and critical posture of our affairs with foreign nations and the unanimous advice of persons entitled to my confidence impelled me to abandon the idea. I rejoice that the state of your concerns, external as well as internal, no longer renders the pursuit of inclination incompatible with the sentiment of duty or propriety, and am persuaded, whatever partiality may be retained for my services, that in the present circumstances of our country you will not disapprove my determination to retire.

The impressions with which I first undertook the arduous trust were explained on the proper occasion. In the discharge of this trust I will only say that I have, with good intentions, contributed toward the organization and administration of the Government the best exertions of which a very fallible judgment was capable. Not unconscious in the outset of the inferiority of my qualifications, experience in my own eyes, perhaps still more in the eyes of others, has strengthened the motives to diffidence of myself; and every day the increasing weight of years admonishes me more and more that the shade of retirement is as necessary to me as it will be welcome. Satisfied that if any circumstances have given peculiar value to my services they were temporary, I have the consolation to believe that, while choice and prudence invite me to quit the political scene, patriotism does not forbid it.

In looking forward to the moment which is intended to terminate the career of my political life my feelings do not permit me to suspend the deep acknowledgment of that debt of gratitude which I owe to my beloved country for the many honors it has conferred upon me; still more for the steadfast confidence with which it has supported me, and for the opportunities I have thence enjoyed of manifesting my inviolable attachment by services faithful and persevering, though in usefulness unequal to my zeal. If benefits have resulted to our country from these services, let it always be remembered to your praise and as an instructive example in our annals that under circumstances in which the passions, agitated in every direction, were liable to mislead; amidst appearances sometimes dubious; vicissitudes of fortune often discouraging; in situations in which not unfrequently want of success has countenanced the spirit of criticism, the constancy of your support was the essential prop of the efforts and a guaranty of the plans by which they were effected. Profoundly penetrated with this idea, I shall carry it with me to my grave as a strong incitement to unceasing vows that Heaven may continue to you the choicest tokens of its beneficence; that your union and brotherly affection may be perpetual; that the free Constitution which is the work of your hands may be sacredly maintained; that its administration in every department may be stamped with wisdom and virtue; that, in fine, the happiness of the people of these States, under the auspices of liberty, may be made complete by so careful a preservation and so prudent a use of this blessing as will acquire to them the glory of recommending it to the applause, the affection, and adoption of every nation which is yet a stranger to it.

Here, perhaps, I ought to stop. But a solicitude for your welfare which can not end but with my life, and the apprehension of danger natural to that solicitude, urge me on an occasion like the present to offer to your solemn contemplation and to recommend to your frequent review some sentiments which are the result of much reflection, of no inconsiderable observation, and which appear to me all important to the permanency of your felicity as a people. These will be offered to you with the more freedom as you can only see in them the disinterested warnings of a parting friend, who can possibly have no personal motive to bias his counsel. Nor can I forget as an encouragement to it your indulgent reception of my sentiments on a former and not dissimilar occasion.

Interwoven as is the love of liberty with every ligament of your hearts, no recommendation of mine is necessary to fortify or confirm the attachment.

The unity of government which constitutes you one people is also now dear to you. It is justly so, for it is a main pillar in the edifice of your real independence, the support of your tranquillity at home, your peace abroad, of your safety, of your prosperity, of that very liberty which you so highly prize. But as it is easy to foresee that from different causes and from different quarters much pains will be taken, many artifices employed, to weaken in your minds the conviction of this truth, as this is the point in your political fortress against which the batteries of internal and external enemies will be most constantly and actively (though often covertly and insidiously) directed, it is of infinite moment that you should properly estimate the immense value of your national union to your collective and individual happiness; that you should cherish a cordial, habitual, and immovable attachment to it; accustoming yourselves to think and speak of it as of the palladium of your political safety and prosperity; watching for its preservation with jealous anxiety; discountenancing whatever may suggest even a suspicion that it can in any event be abandoned, and indignantly frowning upon the first dawning of every attempt to alienate any portion of our country from the rest or to enfeeble the sacred ties which now link together the various parts.

For this you have every inducement of sympathy and interest. Citizens by birth or choice of a common country, that country has a right to concentrate your affections. The name of American, which belongs to you in your national capacity, must exalt the just pride of patriotism more than any appellation derived from local discriminations. With slight shades of difference, you have the same religion, manners, habits, and political principles. You have in a common cause fought and triumphed together. The independence and liberty you possess are the work of joint councils and joint efforts, of common dangers, sufferings and successes.

But these considerations, however powerfully they address themselves to your sensibility, are greatly outweighed by those which apply more immediately to your interest. Here every portion of our country finds the most commanding motives for carefully guarding and preserving the union of the whole.

The *North*, in an unrestrained intercourse with the *South*, protected by the equal laws of a common government, finds in the productions of the latter great additional resources of maritime and commercial enterprise and precious materials of manufacturing industry. The *South*, in the same intercourse, benefiting by the same agency of the *North*, sees its agriculture grow and its commerce expand. Turning partly into its own channels the seamen of the *North*, it finds its particular navigation invigorated; and while it contributes in different ways to nourish and increase the general mass of the national navigation, it looks forward to the protection of a maritime strength to which itself is unequally adapted. The *East*, in a like intercourse with the *West*, already finds, and in the progressive improvement of interior communications by land and water will more and more find, a valuable vent for the commodities which it brings from abroad or manufactures at home. The *West* derives from the *East* supplies requisite to its growth and comfort, and what is perhaps of still greater consequence, it must of necessity owe the secure enjoyment of indispensable *outlets* for its own productions to the weight, influence, and the future maritime strength of the Atlantic side of the Union, directed by an indissoluble community of interest as *one nation*. Any other tenure by which the *West* can hold this essential advantage, whether derived from its own separate strength or from an apostate and unnatural connection with any foreign power, must be intrinsically precarious.

While, then, every part of our country thus feels an immediate and particular interest in union, all the parts combined can not fail to find in the united mass of means and efforts greater strength, greater resource, proportionably greater security from external danger, a less frequent interruption of their peace by foreign nations, and what is of inestimable value, they must derive from union an exemption from those broils and wars between themselves which so frequently afflict neighboring countries not tied together by the same governments which their own rivalships alone would be sufficient to product, but which opposite foreign alliances, attachments, and intrigues would stimulate and imbitter. Hence, likewise, they will avoid the necessity of those overgrown military establishments which, under any form of government, are inauspicious to liberty, and which are to be regarded as particularly hostile to republican liberty. In this sense it is that your union ought to be considered as a main prop of your liberty, and that the love of the one ought to endear to you the preservation of the other.

These considerations speak a persuasive language to every reflecting and vertuous mind, and exhibit the continuance of the union as a primary object of patriotic desire. Is there a doubt whether a common government can embrace so large a sphere? Let experience solve it. To listen to mere speculation in such a case were criminal. We are authorized to hope that a proper organization of the whole, with the auxiliary agency of governments for the respective subdivisions, will afford a happy issue to the experiment. It is well worth a fair and full experiment. With such powerful and obvious motives to union affecting all parts of our country, while experience shall not have demonstrated its impracticability, there will always be reason to distrust the patriotism of those who in any quarter may endeavor to weaken its bands.

In contemplating the causes which may disturb our union it occurs as matter of serious concern that any ground should have been furnished for characterizing parties by *geographical* discriminations—*Northern* and *Southern, Atlantic* and *Western*—whence designing men may endeavor to excite a belief that there is a real difference of local interests and views. One of the expedients of party to acquire influence within particular districts is to misrepresent the opinions and aims of other districts. You can not shield yourselves too much against the jealousies and heartburnings which spring from these misrepresentations; they tend to render alien to each other those who ought to be bound together by fraternal affection. The inhabitants of our Western country have lately had a useful lesson on this head. They have seen in the negotiation by the Executive and in the unanimous ratification by the Senate of the treaty with Spain, and in the universal satisfaction at that event throughout the United States, a decisive proof how unfounded were the suspicions propagated among them of a policy in the General Government and in the Atlantic States unfriendly to their interests in regard to the Mississippi. They have been witnesses to the formation of two treaties—that with Great Britain and that with Spain—which secure to them everything they could desire in respect to our foreign relations toward confirming their prosperity. Will it not be their wisdom to rely for the preservation of these advantages on the union by which they were procured? Will they not henceforth be deaf to those advisers, if such there are, who would sever them from their brethren and connect them with aliens?

To the efficacy and permanency of your union a government for the whole is indispensable. No Alliances, however strict, between the parts can be an adequate substitute. They must inevitably experience the infractions and interruptions which all alliances in all times have experienced. Sensible of this momentous truth, you have improved upon your first essay by the adoption of a Constitution of Government better calculated than your former for an intimate union and for the efficacious management of your common concerns. This Government, the off-spring of our own choice, uninfluenced and un-awed, adopted upon full investigation and mature deliberation, completely free in its principles, in the distribution of its powers, uniting security with energy, and containing within itself a provision for its own amendment, has a just claim to your confidence and your support. Respect for its authority, compliance with its laws, acquiescence in its measures, are duties enjoined by the fundamental maxims of true liberty. The basis of our political systems is the right of the people to make and to alter their constitutions of government. But the constitution which at any time exists till changed by an explicit and authentic act of the whole people is sacredly obligatory upon all. The very idea of the power and the right of the people to establish government presupposes the duty of every individual to obey the established government.

All obstructions to the execution of the laws, all combinations and associations, under whatever plausible character, with the real design to direct, control, counteract, or awe the regular deliberation and action of the constituted authorities, are destructive of this fundamental principle and of fatal tendency. They serve to organize faction; to give it an artificial and extraordinary force; to put in the place of the delegated will of the nation the will of a party, often a small but artful and enterprising minority of the community, and, according to the alternate triumphs of different parties, to make the public administration the mirror of the ill-concerted and incongruous projects of faction rather than the organ of consistent and wholesome plans, digested by common counsels and modified by mutual interests.

However combinations or associations of the above description may now and then answer popular ends, they are likely in the course of time and things to become potent engines by which cunning, ambitious, and unprincipled men will be enabled to subvert the power of the people, and to usurp for themselves the reins of government, destroying afterwards the very engines which have lifted them to unjust dominion.

Toward the preservation of your Government and the permanency of your present happy state, it is requisite not only that you steadily discountenance irregular opposition to its acknowledged authority, but also that you resist with care the spirit of innovation upon its principles, however specious the pretexts. One method of assault may be to effect in the forms of the Constitution alterations which will impair the energy of the system, and thus to undermine what can not be directly overthrown. In all the changes to which you may be invited remember that time and habit are at least as necessary to fix the true character of governments as of other human institutions; that experience is the surest standard by which to test the real tendency of the existing constitution of a country; that facility in changes upon the credit of mere hypothesis and opinion exposes to perpetual change, from the endless variety of hypothesis and opinion; and remember especially that for the efficient management of your common interests in a country so extensive as ours a government of as much vigor as is consistent with the perfect security of liberty is indispensable. Liberty itself will find in such a government, with powers properly distributed and adjusted, its surest guardian. It is, indeed, little else than a name where the government is too feeble to withstand the enterprises of faction, to confine each member of the society within the limits prescribed by the laws, and to maintain all in the secure and tranquil enjoyment of the rights of person and property.

I have already intimated to you the danger of parties in the State, with particular reference to the founding of them on geographical discriminations. Let me now take a more comprehensive view, and warn you in the most solemn manner against the baneful effects of the spirit of party generally.

This spirit, unfortunately, is inseparable from our nature, having its root in the strongest passions of the human mind. It exists under different shapes in all governments, more or less stifled, controlled, or repressed; but in those of the popular form it is seen in its greatest rankness and is truly their worst enemy.

The alternate domination of one faction over another, sharpened by the spirit of revenge natural to party dissension, which in different ages and countries has perpetrated the most horrid enormities, is itself a frightful despotism. But this leads at length to a more formal and permanent despotism. The disorders and miseries which result gradually incline the minds of men to seek security and repose in the absolute power of an individual, and sooner or later the chief of some prevailing faction, more able or more fortunate than his competitors, turns this disposition to the purposes of his own elevation on the ruins of public liberty.

Without looking forward to an extremity of this kind (which nevertheless ought not to be entirely out of sight), the common and continual mischiefs of the spirit of party are sufficient to make it the interest and duty of a wise people to discourage and restrain it.

It serves always to distract the public councils and enfeeble the public administration. It agitates the community with ill-founded jealousies and false alarms; kindles the animosity of one part against another; foments occasionally riot and insurrection. It opens the door to foreign influence and corruption, which find a facilitated access to the government itself through the channels of party passion. Thus the policy and the will of one country are subjected to the policy and will of another.

There is an opinion that parties in free countries are useful checks upon the administration of the government, and serve to keep alive the spirit of liberty. This within certain limits is probably true; and in governments of a monarchical cast patriotism may look with indulgence, if not with favor, upon the spirit of party. But in those of the popular character, in governments purely elective, it is a spirit not to be encouraged. From their natural tendency it is certain there will always be enough of that spirit for every salutary purpose; and there being constant danger of excess, the effort ought to be by force of public opinion to mitigate and assuage it. A fire not to be quenched, it demands a uniform vigilance to prevent its bursting into a flame, lest, instead of warming, it should consume.

It is important, likewise, that the habits of thinking in a free country should inspire caution in those intrusted with its administration to confine themselves within their respective constitutional spheres, avoiding in the exercise of the powers of one department to encroach upon another. The spirit of encroachment tends to consolidate the powers of all the departments in one, and thus to create, whatever the form of government, a real despotism. A just estimate of that love of power and proneness to abuse it which predominates in the human heart is sufficient to satisfy us of the truth of this position. The necessity of reciprocal checks in the exercise of political power, by dividing and distributing it into different depositories, and constituting each the guardian of the public weal against invasions by the others, has been evinced by experiments ancient and modern, some of them in our country and under our own eyes. To preserve them must be as necessary as to institute them. If in the opinion of the people the distribution or modification of the constitutional powers be in any particular wrong, let it be corrected by an amendment in the way which the Constitution designates. But let there be no change by usurpation; for though this in one instance may be the instrument of good, it is the customary weapon by which free governments are destroyed. The precedent must always greatly overbalance in permanent evil any partial or transient benefit which the use can at any time yield.

Of all the dispositions and habits which lead to political prosperity, religion and morality are indispensable supports. In vain would that man claim the tribute of patriotism who should labor to subvert these great pillars of human happiness—these firmest props of the duties of men and citizens. The mere politician, equally with the pious man, ought to respect and to cherish them. A volume could not trace all their connections with private and public felicity. Let it simply be asked, Where is the security for property, for reputation, for life, if the sense of religious obligation *desert* the oaths which are the instruments of investigation in courts of justice? And let us with caution indulge the supposition that morality can be maintained without religion. Whatever may be conceded to the influence of refined education on minds of peculiar structure, reason and experience both forbid us to expect that national morality can prevail in exclusion of religious principle.

It is substantially true that virtue or morality is a necessary spring of popular government. The rule indeed extends with more or less force to every species of free government. Who that is a sincere friend to it can look with indifference upon attempts to shake the foundation of the fabric? Promote, then, as an object of primary importance, institutions for the general diffusion of knowledge. In proportion as the structure of a government gives force to public opinion, it is essential that public opinion should be enlightened.

As a very important source of strength and security, cherish public credit. One method of preserving it is to use it as sparingly as possible, avoiding occasions of expense by cultivating peace, but remembering also that timely disbursements to prepare for danger frequently prevent much greater disbursements to repel it; avoiding likewise the accumulation of debt, not only by shunning occasions of expense, but by vigorous exertions in time of peace to discharge the debts which unavoidable wars have occasioned, not ungenerously throwing upon posterity the burthen which we ourselves ought to bear. The execution of these maxims belongs to your representatives; but it is necessary that public opinion should cooperate. To facilitate to them the performance of their duty it is essential that you should practically bear in mind that toward the payment of debts there must be revenue; that to have revenue there must be taxes; that no taxes can be devised which are not more or less inconvenient and unpleasant; that the intrinsic embarrassment inseparable from the selection of the proper objects (which is always a choice of difficulties), ought to be a decisive motive for a candid construction of the conduct of the Government in making it, and for a spirit of acquiescence in the measures for obtaining revenue which the public exigencies may at any time dictate.

Observe good faith and justice toward all nations. Cultivate peace and harmony with all. Religion and morality enjoin this conduct. And can it be that good policy does not equally enjoin it? It will be worthy of a free, enlightened, and at no distant period a great nation to give to mankind the magnanimous and too novel example of a people always guided by an exalted justice and benevolence. Who can doubt that in the course of time and things the fruits of such a plan would richly repay any temporary advantages which might be lost by a steady adherence to it? Can it be that Providence has not connected the permanent felicity of a nation with its virtue? The experiment, at least, is recommended by every sentiment which ennobles human nature. Alas! is it rendered impossible by its vices?

In the execution of such a plan nothing is more essential than that permanent, inveterate antipathies against particular nations and passionate attachments for others should be excluded, and that in place of them just and amicable feelings toward all should be cultivated. The nation which indulges toward another an habitual hatred or an habitual fondness is in some degree a slave. It is a slave to its animosity or to its affection, either of which is sufficient to lead it astray from its duty and its interest. Antipathy in one nation against another disposes each more readily to offer insult and injury, to lay hold of slight causes of umbrage, and to be haughty and intractable when accidental or trifling occasions of dispute occur.

Hence frequent collisions, obstinate, envenomed, and bloody contests. The nation prompted by ill will and resentment sometimes impels to war the government contrary to the best calculations of policy. The government sometimes participates in the national propensity, and adopts through passion what reason would reject. At other times it makes the animosity of the nation subservient to projects of hostility, instigated by pride, ambition, and other sinister and pernicious motives. The peace often, sometimes perhaps the liberty, of nations has been the victim.

So, likewise, a passionate attachment of one nation for another produces a variety of evils. Sympathy for the favorite nation, facilitating the illusion of an imaginary common interest in cases where no real common interest exists, and infusing into one the enmities of the other, betrays the former into a participation in the quarrels and wars of the latter without adequate inducement or justification. It leads also to concessions to the favorite nation of privileges denied to others, which is apt doubly to injure the nation making the concessions by unnecessarily parting with what ought to have been retained, and by exciting jealousy, ill will, and a disposition to retaliate in the parties from whom equal privileges are withheld; and it gives to ambitious, corrupted, or deluded citizens (who devote themselves to the favorite nation) facility to betray or sacrifice the interests of their own country without odium, sometimes even with popularity, gilding with the appearances of a virtuous sense of obligation, a commendable deference for public opinion, or a laudable zeal for public good the base or foolish compliances of ambition, corruption, or infatuation.

As avenues to foreign influence in innumerable ways, such attachments are particularly alarming to the truly enlightened and independent patriot. How many opportunities do they afford to tamper with domestic factions, to practice the arts of seduction, to mislead public opinion, to influence or awe the public councils! Such an attachment of a small or weak toward a great and powerful nation dooms the former to be the satellite of the latter. Against the insidious wiles of foreign influence (I conjure you to believe me, fellow-citizens) the jealousy of a free people ought to be *constantly* awake, since history and experience prove that foreign influence is one of the most baneful foes of republican government. But that jealousy, to be useful, must be impartial, else it becomes the instrument of the very influence to be avoided, instead of a defense against it. Excessive partiality for one foreign nation and excessive dislike of another cause those whom they actuate to see danger only on one side, and serve to veil and even second the arts of influence on the other. Real patriots who may resist the intrigues of the favorite are liable to become suspected and odious, while its tools and dupes usurp the applause and confidence of the people to surrender their interests.

The great rule of conduct for us in regard to foreign nations, is in extending our commercial relations to have with them as little *political* connection as possible. So far as we have already formed engagements let them be fulfilled with perfect good faith. Here let us stop.

Europe has a set of primary interests which to us have none or a very remote relation. Hence she must be engaged in frequent controversies, the causes of which are essentially foreign to our concerns. Hence, therefore, it must be unwise in us to implicate ourselves by artificial ties in the ordinary vicissitudes of her politics or the ordinary combinations and collisions of her friendships or enmities.

Our detached and distant situation invites and enables us to pursue a different course. If we remain one people, under an efficient government, the period is not far off when we may defy material injury from external annoyance; when we may take such an attitude as will cause the neutrality we may at any time resolve upon to be scrupulously respected; when belligerent nations, under the impossibility of making acquisitions upon us, will not lightly hazard the giving us provocation; when we may choose peace or war, as our interest, guided by justice, shall counsel.

Why forego the advantages of so peculiar a situation? Why quit our own to stand upon foreign ground? Why, by interweaving our destiny with that of any part of Europe, entangle our peace and prosperity in the toils of European ambition, rivalship, interest, humor, or caprice?

It is our true policy to steer clear of permanent alliances with any portion of the foreign world, so far, I mean, as we are now at liberty to do it; for let me not be understood as capable of patronizing infidelity to existing engagements. I hold the maxim no less applicable to public than to private affairs that honesty is always the best policy. I repeat, therefore, let those engagements be observed in their genuine sense. But in my opinion it is unnecessary and would be unwise to extend them.

Taking care always to keep ourselves by suitable establishments on a respectable defensive posture, we may safely trust to temporary alliances for extraordinary emergencies.

Harmony, liberal intercourse with all nations are recommended by policy, humanity, and interest. But even our commercial policy should hold an equal and impartial hand, neither seeking nor granting exclusive favors or preferences; consulting the natural course of things; diffusing and diversifying by gentle means the streams of commerce, but forcing nothing; establishing with powers so disposed, in order to give trade a stable course, to define the rights of our merchants, and to enable the Government to support them, conventional rules of intercourse, the best that present circumstances and mutual opinion will permit, but temporary and liable to be from time to time abandoned or varied as experience and circumstances shall dictate; constantly keeping in view that it is folly in one nation to look for disinterested favors from another; that it must pay with a portion of its independence for whatever it may accept under that character; that by such acceptance it may place itself in the condition of having given equivalents for nominal favors, and yet of being reproached with ingratitude for not giving more. There can be no greater error than to expect or calculate upon real favors from nation to nation. It is an illusion which experience must cure, which a just pride ought to discard.

In offering to you, my countrymen, these counsels of an old and affectionate friend I dare not hope they will make the strong and lasting impression I could wish—that they will control the usual current of the passions or prevent our nation from running the course which has hitherto marked the destiny of nations. But if I may even flatter myself that they may be productive of some partial benefit, some occasional good—that they may now and then recur to moderate the fury of party spirit, to warn against the mischiefs of foreign intrigue, to guard against the impostures of pretended patriotism—this hope will be a full recompense for the solicitude for your welfare by which they have been dictated.

How far in the discharge of my official duties I have been guided by the principles which have been delineated the public records and other evidences of my conduct must witness to you and to the world. To myself, the assurance of my own conscience is that I have at least believed myself to be guided by them.

In relation to the still subsisting war in Europe my proclamation of the 22nd of April, 1793, is the index to my plan. Sanctioned by your approving voice and by that of your representatives in both Houses of Congress, the spirit of that measure has continually governed me, uninfluenced by any attempts to deter or divert me from it.

After deliberate examination, with the aid of the best lights I could obtain, I was well satisfied that our country, under all the circumstances of the case, had a right to take, and was bound in duty and interest to take, a neutral position. Having taken it, I determined as far as should depend upon me to maintain it with moderation, perseverance, and firmness.

The considerations which respect the right to hold this conduct it is not necessary on this occasion to detail. I will only observe that, according to my understanding of the matter, that right, so far from being denied by any of the belligerent powers, has been virtually admitted by all.

The duty of holding a neutral conduct may be inferred, without anything more, from the obligation which justice and humanity impose on every nation, in cases in which it is free to act, to maintain inviolate the relations of peace and amity toward other nations.

The inducements of interest for observing that conduct will best be referred to your own reflections and experience. With me a predominant motive has been to endeavor to gain time to our country to settle and mature its yet recent institutions, and to progress without interruption to that degree of strength and consistency which is necessary to give it, humanly speaking, the command of its own fortunes.

Though in reviewing the incidents of my Administration I am unconscious of intentional error, I am nevertheless too sensible of my defects not to think it probable that I may have committed many errors. Whatever they may be, I fervently beseech the Almighty to avert or mitigate the evils to which they may tend. I shall also carry with me the hope that my country will never cease to view them with indulgence, and that, after forty-five years of my life dedicated to its service with an upright zeal, the faults of incompetent abilities will be consigned to oblivion, as myself must soon to to the mansions of rest.

Relying on its kindness in this as in other things, and actuated by that fervent love toward it which is so natural to a man who views in it the native soil of himself and his progenitors for several generations, I anticipate with pleasing expectation that retreat in which I promise myself to realize without alloy the sweet enjoyment of partaking in the midst of my fellow-citizens the benign influence of good laws under a free government—the ever-favorite object of my heart, and the happy reward, as I trust, of our mutual cares, labors, and dangers.

APPENDIX 4.

Jefferson's First
Inaugural Address

Friends and Fellow-Citizens.

Called upon to undertake the duties of the first executive office of our country, I avail myself of the presence of that portion of my fellow-citizens which is here assembled to express my grateful thanks for the favor with which they have been pleased to look toward me, to declare a sincere consciousness that the task is above my talents, and that I approach it with those anxious and awful presentiments which the greatness of the charge and the weakness of my powers so justly inspire. A rising nation, spread over a wide and fruitful land, traversing all the seas with the rich productions of their industry, engaged in commerce with nations who feel power and forget right, advancing rapidly to destinies beyond the reach of mortal eye—when I contemplate these transcendent objects, and see the honor, the happiness, and the hopes of this beloved country committed to the issue and the auspices of this day, I shrink from the contemplation, and humble myself before the magnitude of the undertaking. Utterly, indeed, should I despair did not the presence of many whom I here see remind me that in the other high authorities provided by our Constitution I shall find resources of wisdom, of virtue, and of zeal on which to rely under all difficulties. To you, then, gentlemen, who are charged with the sovereign functions of legislation, and to those associated with you, I look with encouragement for that guidance and support which may enable us to steer with safety the vessel in which we are all embarked amidst the conflicting elements of a troubled world.

During the contest of opinion through which we have passed the animation of discussions and of exertions has sometimes worn an aspect which might impose on strangers unused to think freely and to speak and to write what they think; but this being now decided by the voice of the nation, announced according to the rules of the Constitution, all will, of course, arrange themselves under the will of the law, and unite in common efforts for the common good. All, too, will bear in mind this sacred principle, that though the will of the majority is in all cases to prevail, that will to be rightful must be reasonable; that the minority possess their equal rights, which equal law must protect, and to violate would be oppression. Let us, then, fellow-citizens, unite with one heart and one mind. Let us restore to social intercourse that harmony and affection without which liberty and even life itself are but dreary things. And let us reflect that, having banished from our land that religious intolerance under which mankind so long bled and suffered, we have yet gained little if we countenance a political intolerance as despotic, as wicked, and capable of as bitter and bloody persecutions. During the throes and convulsions of the ancient world, during the agonizing spasms of infuriated man, seeking through blood and slaughter his long-lost liberty, it was not wonderful that the agitation of the billows should reach even this distant and peaceful shore;

that this should be more felt and feared by some and less by others, and should divide opinions as to measures of safety. But every difference of opinion is not a difference of principle. We have called by different names brethren of the same principle. We are all Republicans, we are all Federalists. If there be any among us who would wish to dissolve this Union or to change its republican form, let them stand undisturbed as monuments of the safety to combat it. I know, indeed, that some honest men fear that a republican government can not be strong, that this Government is not strong enough; but would the honest patriot, in the full tide of successful experiment, abandon a government which has so far kept us free and firm on the theoretic and visionary fear that this Government, the world's best hope, may by possibility want energy to preserve itself, I trust not. I believe this, on the contrary, the strongest Government on earth. I believe it the only one where every man, at the call of the law, would fly to the standard of the law, and would meet invasions of the public order as his own personal concern. Sometimes it is said that man cannot be trusted with the government of himself. Can he, then, be trusted with the government of others? Or have we found angels in the forms of kings to govern him? Let history answer this question.

Let us, then, with courage and confidence pursue our own Federal and Republican principles, our attachment to union and representative government. Kindly separated by nature and a wide ocean from the exterminating havoc of one quarter of the globe; too high-minded to endure the degradations of the others; possessing a chosen country, with room enough for our descendants to the thousandth and thousandth generation; entertaining a due sense of our equal right to the use of our own faculties, to the acquisitions of our own industry, to honor and confidence from our fellow-citizens, resulting not from birth, but from our actions and their sense of them; enlightened by a benign religion, professed, indeed, and practiced in various forms, yet all of them inculcating honesty, truth, temperance, gratitude, and the love of men; acknowledging and adoring an overruling Providence, which by all its dispensations proves that it delights in the happiness of man here and his greater happiness hereafter—with all these blessings, what more is necessary to make us a happy and a prosperous people? Still one thing more fellow-citizens—a wise and frugal Government, which shall restrain men from injuring one another, shall leave them otherwise free to regulate their own pursuits of industry and improvement, and shall not take from the mouth of labor the bread it has earned. This is the sum of good government, and this is necessary to close the circle of our felicities.

About to enter, fellow-citizens, on the exercises of duties which comprehend everything dear and valuable to you, it is proper you should understand what I deem the essential principles of our Government, and consequently those which ought to shape its Administration. I will compress them within the narrowest compass they will bear, stating the general principle, but not all its limitations. Equal and exact justice to all men, of whatever state or persuasion, religious or political; peace, commerce, and honest friendship with all nations, entangling alliances with none; the support of the State governments in all their rights; as the most competent administrations for our domestic concerns and the surest bulwarks against antirepublican tendencies; the preservation of the General Government in its whole constitutional vigor, as the sheet anchor of our peace at home and safety abroad; a jealous care of the right of election by the people—a mild and safe corrective of abuses which are lopped by the sword of revolution where peaceable remedies are unprovided; absolute acquiescence in the decisions of the majority, the vital principle of republics, from which is no appeal but to force, the vital principle and immediate parent of despotism; a well-disciplined militia, our best reliance in peace and for the first moments of war, till regulars may relieve them; the supremacy of the civil over the military authority; economy in the public expense, that labor may be lightly burdened; the honest payment of our debts and sacred preservation of the public faith; encouragement of agriculture, and of commerce as its handmaid; the diffusion of information and arraignment of all abuses at the bar of the public reason; freedom of religion; freedom of the press, and freedom of persons under the protection of the habeas corpus, and trial by juries impartially selected. These principles form the bright constellation which has gone before us and guided our steps through an age of revolution and reformation. The wisdom of our sages and blood of our heroes have been devoted to their attainment. They should be the creed of our political faith, the text of civic instruction, the touchstone by which to try the services of those we trust; and should we wander from them in moments of error or of alarm, let us hasten to retrace our steps and to regain the road which alone leads to peace, liberty, and safety.

I repair, then, fellow-citizens, to the post you have assigned me. With experience enough in subordinate offices to have seen the difficulties of this the greatest of all, I have learnt to expect that it will rarely fall to the lot of imperfect man to retire from this station with the reputation and the favor which bring him into it. Without pretensions to the high confidence you reposed in our first and greatest revolutionary character, whose preeminent services had entitled him to the first place in his country's love and destined for him the fairest page in the volume of faithful history, I ask so much confidence only as may give firmness and effect to the legal administration of your affairs. I shall often go wrong through defect of judgment. When right, I shall often be thought wrong by those whose positions will not command a view of the whole ground. I ask your indulgence for my own errors, which will never be intentional, and your support against the errors of others, who may condemn what they would not if seen in all its parts. The approbation implied by your suffrage is a great consolation to me for the past, and my future solicitude will be to retain the good opinion of those who have bestowed it in advance, to conciliate that of others by doing them all the good in my power, and to be instrumental to the happiness and freedom of all.

Relying, then, on the patronage of your good will, I advance with obedience to the work, ready to retire from it whenever you become sensible how much better choice it is in your power to make. And may that Infinite Power which rules the destinies of the universe lead our councils to what is best, and give them a favorable issue for your peace and prosperity.

APPENDIX 5.

The Monroe Doctrine

In the discussions to which this interest [claim of Russia on the northwest coast] has given rise, and in the arrangements by which they may terminate, the occasion has been judged proper for asserting, as a principle in which the rights and interests of the United States are involved, that the American continents, by the free and independent condition which they have assumed and maintain, are henceforth not to be considered as subjects for future colonization by any European powers....

It was stated at the commencement of the last session, that a great effort was then making in Spain and Portugal, to improve the condition of the people of those countries, and that it appeared to be conducted with extraordinary moderation. It need scarcely be remarked, that the result has been, so far, very different from what was then anticipated. Of events in that quarter of the globe, with which we have so much intercourse, and from which we derive our origin, we have always been anxious and interested spectators. The citizens of the United States cherish sentiments the most friendly, in favor of the liberty and happiness of their fellow men on that side of the Atlantic. In the wars of the European powers, in matters relating to themselves, we have never taken any part, nor does it comport with our policy so to do. It is only when our rights are invaded, or seriously menaced, that we resent injuries, or make preparation for our defence. With the movements in this hemisphere, we are, of necessity, more immediately connected, and by causes which must be obvious to all enlightened and impartial observers. The political system of the allied powers is essentially different, in this respect, from that of America. This difference proceeds from that which exists in their respective governments. And to the defence of our own, which has been achieved by the loss of so much blood and treasure, and matured by the wisdom of their most enlightened citizens, and under which we have enjoyed unexampled felicity, this whole nation is devoted. We owe it, therefore, to candor, and to the amicable relations existing between the United States and those powers, to declare, that we should consider any attempt on their part to extend their system to any portion of this hemisphere, as dangerous to our peace and safety. With the existing colonies or dependencies of any European power, we have not interfered, and shall not interfere. But with the governments who have declared their independence, and maintained it, and whose independence we have, on great consideration, and on just principles, acknowledged, we could not view any interposition for the purpose of oppressing them, or controlling, in any other manner, their destiny, by any European power, in any other light than as the manifestation of an unfriendly disposition towards the United States. In the war between those new governments and Spain, we declared our neutrality at the time of their recognition, and to this we have adhered, and shall continue to adhere, provided no change shall occur, which, in the judgment of the competent authorities of this government, shall make a corresponding change, on the part of the United States, indispensable to their security.

The late events in Spain and Portugal, show that Europe is still unsettled. Of this important fact, no stronger proof can be adduced than that the allied powers should have thought it proper, on any principle satisfactory to themselves, to have interposed, by force, in the internal concerns of Spain. To what extent such interposition may be carried, on the same principle, is a question, in which all independent powers, whose governments differ from theirs, are interested; even those most remote, and surely none more so than the United States. Our policy, in regard to Europe, which was adopted at an early stage of the wars which have so long agitated that quarter of the globe, nevertheless remains the same, which is, not to interfere in the internal concerns of any of its powers; to consider the government *de facto* as the legitimate government for us; to cultivate friendly relations with it, and to preserve those relations by a frank, firm, and manly policy; meeting, in all instances, the just claims of every power; submitting to injuries from none. But, in regard to those continents, circumstances are eminently and conspicuously different. It is impossible that the allied powers should extend their political system to any portion of either continent, without endangering our peace and happiness; nor can any one believe that our southern brethren, if left to themselves, would adopt it of their own accord. It is equally impossible, therefore, that we should behold such interposition, in any form, with indifference. If we look to the comparative strength and resources of Spain and those new governments, and their distance from each other, it must be obvious that she can never subdue them. It is still the true policy of the United States to leave the parties to themselves, in the hope that other powers will pursue the same course.

INDEX